Coaching Culture

Susanne Knowles

Coaching Culture

Strategies for CEOs, Organisational Leaders, and HR Professionals

Springer

Susanne Knowles
Department of Business, Economics and Law
University of Queensland
St Lucia, QLD, Australia

ISBN 978-3-031-09049-3 ISBN 978-3-031-09050-9 (eBook)
https://doi.org/10.1007/978-3-031-09050-9

This Springer imprint is published by the registered company Springer Nature Switzerland AG
The registered company address is: Gewerbestrasse 11, 6330 Cham, Switzerland

Acknowledgements

I would like to thank my supervisors at the University of Queensland, Australia, for their tremendous support during the completion of my PhD research. Their immense knowledge of the topic and methodological approaches to qualitative research significantly assisted me progress the research and achieve the outcomes explained in this book which hopefully will benefit many organisational leaders.

Professor Polly Parker, Associate Dean (Academic), Faculty of Business, Economics and Law, University of Queensland.

Associate Professor April Wright, Faculty of Business, Economics and Law, University of Queensland.

Also, special thanks to Glenda Waring, National Education Manager, Australian Institute of Professional Coaches, for your astute guidance in the editing and development of this text as the narrative unfolded. I greatly appreciate your dedication to the message and the coaching profession.

About the Book

Coaching of organisational leaders, managers and employees has grown in popularity over several decades. During this time, researchers have demonstrated the effectiveness of coaching as a valid organisational practice to improve performance, foster employee engagement, and promote well-being. Subsequently, leaders and practitioners proposed that the benefits of individual coaching could be more widely applied to developing a coaching culture within an organisation to increase team effectiveness and productivity, and contribute to competitive advantage and sustainability. With extensive practitioner interest yet little empirical evidence of how to achieve cultural change through coaching, my research study investigated the question: *How do organisations develop a coaching culture?* The extant individual and organisational approaches to developing a coaching culture are first outlined in this book and arguments made for why these approaches are insufficient to guide organisational leaders and practitioners in implementing transformational cultural change through coaching. Then, from my research findings, a dynamic, theoretical process model of coaching culture development over four stages is presented as the major finding of the study. The model identifies the strategies and mechanisms which promote transitions between stages as well as those that may hinder or regress that progression. It contributes to the growth of coaching as a profession and the emergence of coaching as a discipline in its own right. A blueprint to guide CEOs and senior executives, organisational leaders, and HR professionals in developing a coaching culture concludes this exposition.

Contents

List of Figures

List of Tables

About the Author

Susanne Knowles is an educational, coaching, organisational and counselling psychologist and the chair and founder of the Australian Institute of Professional Coaches. With a PhD in management and three master's degrees in education, psychology and business administration, she is focused on assisting individuals achieve their personal and professional goals, motivating teams to peak performance, and supporting organisations to increase employee engagement, retain talent and improve profitability. Susanne has held teaching positions at the University of Queensland Business School, the Queensland University of Technology Business School, and Griffith University School of Applied Psychology. In addition, she has held senior executive positions in government and private sector organisations and served as a board member on several government, not-for-profit and professional services firms. Her executive coaching experience has been gained from 20 years as a consultant to national and international organisations, focused on facilitating the strategic direction of these firms. Susanne's PhD thesis, which she completed at the University of Queensland, investigated how organisations develop and embed a coaching culture for competitive advantage and cultural change.

Susanne can be contacted at susanne.knowles@uq.net.au or chair@professional-coachtraining.com.au

About the Authors

Chapter 1
Introduction

Organisations continue to look for ways to increase the profitability of the business and gain competitive advantage in the marketplace. Having downsized, rightsized and exploited the organisation's physical assets, CEOs and senior executives seek to identify ways to maximise the returns from their human resources. The focus is on finding ways to increase the capability of organisational leaders, improve staff performance and retain valuable talent. A particularly effective developmental tool to bring about these outcomes is *coaching*. Research has proven that there are considerable personal and professional benefits when individuals and teams are coached, including increased employee engagement, motivation and performance. This chapter introduces coaching as a valuable developmental process to promote and support cultural change in organisations. It identifies coaching as a dynamic, relational, and social process[1] by which organisational leaders develop increased self-awareness and insight, learn and grow, and change their behaviour. When everyone in the organisation coaches and enacts the philosophy of coaching, the organisation also benefits financially and achieves a higher reputational standing in the external environment.

The term *coach* originated in Hungary in the 1800s. At that time, a coach was a horse-drawn carriage that took very important people from their present location to where they wanted to go. Over the years, the service expanded throughout Europe and the Hungarian word *kocs* was translated into the French word *coach*. From there, the term spread across the channel to England where, in the early 1900s, its meaning changed from a vehicle for physical transportation to a means of transporting mental capability to a higher level. In the early 1920s, a *coach* was reported to be a tutor of scholars in Oxford and Cambridge. The term *coach* migrated further in the early 1950s to become entrenched in the sporting arena where it remains today as a way of improving physical capability. From the late 1990s, the term *coaching*

[1]The evidence for coaching as a dynamic, relational and social process is presented in "Positive Psychology Coaching" by the same author, also available from Springer.

S. Knowles, *Coaching Culture*, https://doi.org/10.1007/978-3-031-09050-9_1

entered the organisational lexicon as a way of improving executive capability. Over the past two decades, as a result of initially practitioner and subsequently academic interest, coaching has become recognised as a valuable process to support the personal and professional development of all organisational members.

Initially, coaching was not viewed favourably by organisational leaders as it had no reputable evidence-based foundation even though professional associations such as the European Mentoring and Coaching Council (EMCC), the Chartered Institute of Personnel and Development (CIPD) and the International Coaching Federation (ICF) were established in the northern hemisphere in the 1990s. These professional organisations set the standards for ethical, legal and competent coaching practice worldwide. They began to initiate their own research into the concept of coaching and how it can benefit individuals and organisations. This push by professional associations and practitioners resulted in increasing interest in coaching from academics and growth in empirical evidence for coaching from the early 2000s onwards.

What Is Coaching?

Coaching is a particularly effective way of helping individuals solve their own problems and achieve their goals more quickly than they would have if they were to attempt to achieve these alone. It is a dynamic process of interaction between coach and coachee, led by the coachee's agenda. The coaching relationship supports the coachee's attempts to change. Reflection on their situation prompts coachees to acknowledge the part they have played in creating it and consider the part they will play in resolving it. The coach's skilful questioning surfaces tacit understandings to a level of conscious awareness which allows the coachee to recognise who they really are as opposed to who they want to be. The coach does not provide answers or solutions to issues raised by the coachee but instead assists them gain the necessary insights to solve their own problems. The coaching that occurs is a facilitative and supportive process focused on achieving present and future goals which contribute to the coachee's wellbeing and happiness. The coachee is responsible for taking action; however, there is joint accountability for achieving results. If discrepancies or uncertainties emerge during the coaching, the coach may revisit the desired goals to confirm their priority for coaching. But before coachees can change their behaviour, they often need to change their *mental model* and *mindset* so they can achieve a different outcome.[2]

The definition of coaching proposed by the International Coaching Federation (ICF) highlights the quintessential nature of coaching. Coaching is:

> *Partnering with clients in a thought-provoking and creative process that inspires them to maximize their personal and professional potential, which is particularly important in*

[2] Detailed information on coaching, the coaching process and coaching practice, is available in "Positive Psychology Coaching" by the same author, also available from Springer.

today's uncertain and complex environment. Coaches honour the client as the expert in their life and work and believe every client is creative.
(www.coachfederation.org)

This definition characterises what I call *pure coaching*, that is, coaching which is content-free, coachee-led, with no predetermined outcomes. In contrast, coaching by leaders of their direct reports usually has an agenda which is leader-led, with predetermined business outcomes for how an employee should behave or what they need to do differently to improve their performance – what I call *performance coaching*. Because coaching in organisations can be a combination of both *pure* and *performance* coaching, the definition that acknowledges the dual nature of coaching for life and work purposes is that which guides the delivery of all coach-training programmes delivered by the Australian Institute of Professional Coaches:

Australian Institute
OF PROFESSIONAL COACHES

Coaching is the process of working with individuals to help them achieve their life goals and create a more positive future. This involves facilitating self-awareness of issues and problems concerning them in their work and/or personal life, or goals to be achieved. It is a supportive and encouraging process that utilises clients' existing knowledge and strengths to help them understand their current situation, broaden their horizon, be open to other possibilities and lead them towards effective, often creative, solutions to their problems.
(www.professionalcoachtraining.com.au)

Misconceptions of Coaching

Common misconceptions of organisational coaching as it has emerged from community-based, life coaching beginnings are that coaching is "weird" and "fluffy" with no solid underpinnings for professional practice. However, if one extrapolates from a sports-coaching perspective, coaching is definitely not "weird" or "fluffy". It is calculated, measured and controlled. It is a team-oriented strategy to achieve a targeted, performance-based outcome. Sports coaches are on the field with their team every day, motivating their players to succeed. The notion of leaders in the workplace using coaching to motivate their employees towards improved performance was initially foreign to organisations. However over time, many organisational leaders who are also sports coaches have begun using the sporting analogy within their business teams to motivate employees to succeed. This has, in part, caused the benefits of coaching to migrate into the organisational arena.

Coaching was also once viewed as a "fringe" activity conducted by those without formal qualifications in human behaviour or psychology. Coaches were considered to be practising in areas beyond their expertise. This perception was, and still is, accurate to some extent because coaching is an unregulated industry in which anyone can participate. However, as international coaching associations were formed and developed coaching standards, private coach-training companies were also established to train individuals as coaches to these standards. Most of the private coach-training companies and organisations (including some universities) adhere to the self-regulated industry standards that have been developed to guide practitioner coaching. Self-regulation of coaching to professional standards results in greater rigour being applied to coaching practice and increases confidence in its veracity and effectiveness as a valid developmental tool. Research into individual differences, motivation and organisational behaviour over the past 70 years has informed the evolving coach-training and coaching practice. In recent years, the benefits of coaching have been verified by extensive research including how coaching may benefit leadership practice in organisations.

Those who view coaching as a "waste of time" have typically had negative experiences of coaching in the past and do not regard coaching highly. They may have been misled or misinformed as to what coaching is and how it could help them and, consequently, may have found that coaching didn't meet their expectations or needs. The disappointed individual may not have been coached by a professional coach and, as a result, found the experience less than fulfilling. As a result, they may have become suspicious of coaching and sceptical of any value that coaching can offer. Unfortunately, individuals whose needs have not been met do what any customer does. They tell their friends about the bad experience and, as we know, word of mouth spreads, and negative publicity has a way of being transmitted quickly through the peer group and colleagues.

Contemporary Views of Coaching

Coaching was initially introduced into the general organisational arena as a remedial exercise – a "last resort" effort to reorient employees who were underperforming. Underperformers thought that being sent to coaching was shameful, and it was particularly stressful since the individual knew that if they didn't improve their performance, they would be fired. Managers under the old-school *command-and-control* style of management considered employees who were sent to coaching to be weak, a view which is still firmly entrenched in some organisations today. An executive coach who has been coaching since the early 1990s tells the story of how this view has started to change:

> *When I first started coaching, I was working with a coaching guru on developing the Australian coaching standards and we had to make a point of differentiation between* remedial *coaching and* development *coaching, and you wouldn't even hear that kind of language any more today –* remedial *coaching. And yet it was the dominant form of coaching in 2008–2009.* He went on to note that nobody gets badged *remedial* anymore.

These days, employees are more discerning about the organisation they work for. Hence, when there is a misalignment between personal and organisational values, purpose and direction, an individual being coached for remedial purposes may choose to leave the organisation voluntarily rather than be exited involuntarily from their position. An executive coach estimates that about 30% of coaching engagements result in the coachee leaving the organisation not because they've been "given the push" but because, through coaching, they have recognised a mismatch of their personal values with the organisation's values and hence, they self-select out of the organisation. The benefits to both are that the organisation replaces the disaffected employee with an enthusiastic new recruit, and the individual experiences increased happiness in a new position.

Some sceptics of coaching view coaching as a fad, something that won't stand the test of time and will soon be replaced by the "next best thing". One reason for this view may be lack of knowledge about coaching. Another reason may be that most individuals don't like change and, as managers, they may be asked to do things differently. Some Human Resource (HR) professionals may be scared of losing their job or, at least, their skills base if coaching moves into the leadership arena. What HR activities will leaders take over next? However, in those organisations that really believe in the benefits of coaching, have embraced coaching and are establishing the beginnings of a coaching culture, coaching is definitely not a fad as one organisational leader explains:

> *If it's a fad, then we're goners. No one responds to the old* command-and-control – *if they ever did. The bureaucratic nature of government hierarchies is disheartening and disempowering. And this coaching is a glimmer of light.*

As coaching becomes more accepted within organisations, it is conducted as an effective intervention for *developmental* purposes. Line managers may recommend that certain talented individuals who are included in the organisation's succession plan be coached. Thereafter, as the benefits of coaching spread, employees who aren't being coached may express discontent at what they see as an unfair situation, expecting to be coached as well. An executive coach tells the story of working with an individual for 4 months and then one of her peers said: *"If she is entitled to a coach, surely I can have one too?"*

From an organisational perspective, as HR professionals become better acquainted with coaching either from knowing someone who has been coached or being coached themselves, or undertaking formal coach-training from an external accredited provider, they may feel compelled to check out coaching as possibly a highly valuable addition to their organisation's suite of development tools for leaders. An organisational leader explains this "copy-cat" syndrome thus:

> *I think somebody may have been exposed to coaching and then thought:* 'Hey, we probably need some of that here. We need to get some coaching.' *And then they just push for a token representation in that arena so they can say:* 'Oh yeah, we've hired a coach for these two people. We do coaching here.

On the contrary, organisational leaders and HR professionals who are better informed about coaching may be concerned that their organisation is missing out on one of the latest, evidence-based, effective development tools available to leaders. From this valued perspective, as coaching enters their organisation, it takes on a completely different conception – as an intervention that is considered *prestigious* and sought after by discerning individuals who want to benefit from the insights and developmental opportunities that the coaching process enables. An organisational leader notes that 10 years ago, individuals were adamant that they didn't need a coach and, consequently, coaching was often sugar-coated as *mentoring* to get individuals involved in personal conversations in a way that they understood. Nowadays, however, that view has changed:

> *In the private sector, it's becoming* prestigious *to have a coach. It used to be a stigma. People used to think:* 'I don't need a coach. I don't need help.' *A coach was seen as a psychologist. These days, it's my observation that they see it as:* 'Oh I'm having a coach. I must be on a fast-track for promotion.' *So it's seen as a prestige status thing rather than an* 'I need help' *thing.*

In summary, these early conceptions of coaching have changed over the past decade as the coaching profession has matured and as individuals and organisations have gained more knowledge and understanding of what coaching is and how it can benefit individuals, teams and organisations. Coaching has shaken off the *stigma* that it once had. Individuals who are coached now consider coaching to be a *prestigious* activity in which they are fortunate to engage. As the demand for coaching grows, organisations proudly display the fact that they coach as a *badge of honour*. Many executives expect that once they get to a certain level within the organisation, they'll be entitled to a coach even though they may not actually know what a coach can do for them or what they want out of the coaching experience. The coaching process identifies their individual coaching needs and assists them reach their goals much sooner than expected, overcoming any barriers along the way.

Research Study

The research study that I conducted set out to identify the extent to which coaching is prevalent in Australian organisations and how these organisations are attempting to develop a coaching culture. Why is coaching being introduced? Is it a fad? Is it the "next big, shiny thing"? Or is there some real purpose for introducing coaching as an organisational initiative? Semi-structured interviews were conducted with leaders whose titles included positions such as: Manager, People & Culture; Organisation Capability Manager; Human Resource Manager; Executive Sales Coach; General Manager, Sales Operations; Executive General Manager, People Services; Manager, Organisational Capability and Talent Management; Organisational Development Manager; Learning and Development Consultant. In addition, a number of executive coaches in private practice were interviewed to obtain a broader industry perspective from their knowledge of what's happening in the organisations to which they consult and coach. The interviews were conducted to discover what *coaching* and a *coaching culture* mean to participants in the study and ascertain how they believe a coaching culture can be developed to embed transformational cultural change into an organisation.

A qualitative, inductive research design was used to generate as wide a range of views as possible from the interviewees. Data analysis revealed findings in four key areas: (1) conceptions of coaching and how this understanding affects learning and growth in organisations; (2) the motivations and expectations that drive leaders to introduce coaching into their organisation; (3) the people who are the key drivers of coaching throughout the organisation; and (4) the various ways that coaching is delivered within organisations. Themes were combined into a dynamic, theoretical, process model of coaching culture development over four stages, and illustrative organisational examples revealed the strategies and mechanisms essential for organisations to learn, grow, and lead differently in order to transition between stages to achieve transformational cultural change.

The views of research participants provided a window into the workings and aspirations of organisations as leaders attempt to influence those in senior decision-making positions to adopt what research has shown to be one of the most powerful ways of developing employees, growing an organisation's productivity and competitive advantage, and achieving transformational cultural change – establishing a coaching culture. Interviewees provided powerful stories of how individuals are coached in their organisation, how they respond to being coached, and how leaders attempt to spread the word about how coaching can assist individuals and teams improve their performance and reach their potential.

Summary of Findings

Significant to the academic literature, the research study resulted in the formulation of an empirically based, theoretical model of coaching culture development over four stages. This is the first model of coaching culture development that goes beyond the listing of stages and strategies in the academic literature based on pracademic experience. Findings from the research study revealed that, conceptually, leaders view coaching in four distinct ways as: (1) an intervention to fix a problem in individuals; (2) a learning experience as HR professionals train leaders in coaching skills; (3) an essential capability of organisational leaders as they progress in their career; and (4) a vehicle that CEOs and senior executives can use to bring about transformational cultural change. These four stages have been labelled as Stage 1, *Coaching-as-Intervention*; Stage 2, *Coaching-as-HR-Function*; Stage 3, *Coaching-as-Leader-Capability*; and Stage 4, *Coaching-as-Culture*. They explain organisational leaders' *understanding* of what *coaching* and a *coaching culture* mean to them and their organisations, their *motivation* for engaging in coaching, the *key drivers* of coaching in their organisations and the *delivery mechanisms* that are used by organisations to achieve transformational cultural change.

As a dynamic process, coaching culture development may progress or wane depending on emerging circumstances and the theoretical, process model developed from my study accounts for possible changes in the organisational environment. In addition, the study identified the strategies that facilitate progression across the four stages and those which constitute barriers to hinder progress or cause regression as the organisation changes in response to external forces that influence its direction, priorities and initiatives. The findings also revealed illustrative examples of how the strategies can be implemented by line managers, HR professionals, CEOs and senior executives, to assist the organisation transition between the stages. This information is presented in the dynamic model and later in tabular form and then summarised as a blueprint to guide practitioners who are tasked with implementing a coaching culture across their entire organisation.

My research study was based on the evidence for coaching and coaching culture development from the disciplines of psychology and education and management research. The strategies presented in this book show how organisational leaders *learn* as a result of participating in coaching skills training programmes and being coached, *grow* and develop as a result of their increased self-awareness and insight, and *lead* differently according to a coaching philosophy and *coaching leadership style* to achieve improved performance from individuals and teams and increased productivity at the organisational level. Significantly, the empirically based, theoretical model of coaching culture development contributes to the academic literature and the growing calls for coaching to become a discipline in its own right, inviting researchers to validate the findings.

From a practitioner perspective, findings indicate that, in a coaching culture, coaching is delivered at all levels of the organisation to individuals and teams. A leader passionate about coaching may emerge at any level of the organisation. However, it is not until a *coaching champion* is nominated at the senior executive level, and sufficient funds allocated to support the coaching initiative and build the coaching infrastructure that the organisation commits to a journey to develop a coaching culture. Often, an external executive coach is engaged to assist the coaching champion design the transformational cultural change programme. A Coaching Culture Development Team may be established to support the implementation of the cultural change blueprint.

As the blueprint is enacted and coaching cascades down and across organisational levels, additional external coaches may be engaged to work with business unit leaders to customise the coaching skills training for their leadership team. As an important component of the training, and to ensure that the learnings are transferred back into the workplace, the experience of being coached is integrated into the programme. Thereafter, coaching becomes the predominant way of interacting with, and relating to, individuals within and without each business unit. The coaching philosophy and practices are applied to everyday relationships and business transactions. Leaders formally coach their direct reports and others including managers and team leaders who go on to coach their front-line staff. Peer coaching is introduced to ensure that all employees have access to informal coaching when needed. The coaching approach is extended to others external to the organisation resulting in improved customer engagement, longer-term customer loyalty and retention, and increased revenue in long-term, secure pipelines.

A coordinated approach to training in coaching skills and the delivery of coaching to individuals and teams is necessary to ensure "blanket" coverage across the organisation. A fragmented approach has no long-term benefits. The coaching commences. The individual or team improves. The coaching concludes. Some change occurs. However, if the coaching is not sustained or internalised, individuals often return to previous habits, drawn back into expected behaviours by colleagues and/or the contextual environment or both. The benefits of coaching are lost. This type of coaching has typically been arranged by an organisational leader with little or no knowledge of, or skills in, coaching – someone who just wants a "problem" to go away or a team to "work better together". However, when there is an organisational leader with a passion for coaching who knows or has personally experienced the benefits of coaching, the outcome is different. The piecemeal approach to coaching is replaced by a whole-of-organisation focus which starts to develop a coaching culture in *pockets* of the organisation. These *pockets* of coaching occur in areas of the business where there is a committed leader with the authority to make decisions and allocate resources, often within revenue-generating sales and services functions. As *pockets* develop in all business units, a coaching culture starts to form. But organisational culture is not "something that grows in the corner of an office" as one of the study participants flippantly suggested. Rather, it's "the way we do things around here" [1] and is represented by the signs, symbols, artefacts, stories and toolkits [2] that develop over the life of an organisation as it grows and evolves.

The main conclusions I drew from my research study, which may guide organisations wanting to develop a coaching culture, are the following:

1. A coaching culture is more effectively developed from the top-down by the CEO and senior executives of the organisation, although it can develop in *pockets* within the organisation where the business unit leader is passionate and committed and has the authority to expend to gain productivity improvements, increase staff engagement and retain talent.
2. Cultural change takes investment. The organisation needs to be prepared to make a considerable financial investment and measure the return on investment (ROI) from the coaching programmes that will operate until a coaching culture is developed and embedded. By this time all employees will be taking a coaching approach to internal and external relationships and business transactions on a daily basis. The return will be able to be measured in real dollar value, for example, by profitability, share price and/or market share increases.
3. Cultural change takes time. To introduce and embed a coaching culture takes 18 months minimum. To sustain it takes a coaching champion, ongoing training and development, and mindsets that believe in the potential of all employees to grow and reach their performance.
4. The journey to develop a coaching culture is best guided by an external executive coach who has a broader industry perspective beyond that of the organisation's boundaries – someone who can expand and challenge organisational leaders' current thinking, mindset and outlook.

5. The organisation should be prepared to be disturbed by "out-of-the-box" disrupters in terms of different processes, systems and procedures – different "ways we do things around here". Leaders need to be prepared to examine every aspect of the business to identify where coaching can deliver maximum benefit. As coaching practice spreads throughout the organisation, it may create a tsunami of possibilities requiring small and, at times, large changes, all creating maybe unexpected or unintended yet positive outcomes for individuals, teams and the organisation.

Structure of the Chapters

Chapter 1 has introduced coaching as a valuable developmental process to promote and support cultural change in organisations. It identifies coaching as a dynamic, relational and social process by which organisational leaders develop self-awareness and insight, learn and grow, and change their behaviour.

Chapter 2 provides the evidence for the development of a coaching culture in organisations. Research findings in relation to *coaching culture* build on those for *coaching*[3] as a developmental process resulting in increased self-awareness and insight, learnings, and behavioural change. An integrated model of the evidence for a coaching culture is derived from combined educational, psychological and management research underpinnings. Coaching is proposed as a subculture of organisational culture, consistent with the dominant models of culture identified in the extant literature: culture as *values*, *stories*, *frames*, *categories* and *toolkits*.

Chapter 3 explains that, with extensive practitioner interest yet little empirical evidence of how to achieve cultural change through coaching, my research study investigated the question: *How do organisations develop a coaching culture?* The chapter begins with a review of the extant individual and organisational approaches to developing a coaching culture and provides arguments for the reasons why these approaches are insufficient to guide practitioners on the journey of cultural change in their organisation. A dynamic, theoretical, process model of coaching culture development over four stages was developed from the research findings and the strategies that promote and hinder progression across stages identified. The model not only guides successful implementation of a coaching culture but also contributes to the emergence of coaching as a discipline in its own right.

Chapter 4 addresses the first of four stages in the development of a coaching culture. During this stage, line managers arrange for individuals who are behaving inappropriately or not performing to role expectations to be coached. This first stage is characterised by a *utilitarian conceptualisation* of coaching as a skill set or tool, an *instrumental motivation* for coaching to remediate an underperformer and an

[3] The evidence for coaching is presented in "Positive Psychology Coaching", also available from Springer.

intervention driven by *line managers* within a line management structure but delivered by an *outsourced* external coach.

Chapter 5 addresses the second of four stages in the development of a coaching culture. During this stage, coaching resides within the HR function which is responsible for the training of managers in coaching skills and the delivery of coaching to employees in the organisation. In this stage, coaching is characterised by a *pedagogical conceptualisation* as a training and learning experience. The motivation for coaching is *developmental*, designed to change managers' mindset and behaviour, improve individual performance and support career progression. The *functional drivers* for coaching are positioned within the HR function which builds the infrastructure and support for coaching skills training to begin and coaching to be conducted throughout the organisation. HR professionals arrange for the *targeted delivery* of coaching to leaders and talented individuals within the organisation.

Chapter 6 addresses the third of four stages in the development of a coaching culture. During this stage, coaching is an expected capability of leaders which is embedded within a leadership development framework. Coaching is conceptualised as a *practice* and an understood requirement of leaders who have a *performance* motivation to uplift team and business results. *Business units* are responsible for driving coaching throughout the organisation, and coaching is *internally delivered* by leaders to their teams and team members.

Chapter 7 addresses the last of four stages in the development of a coaching culture. During this stage, coaching is an essential component of the cultural change process which aims to develop all employees in the organisation to reach their potential. This final stage is characterised by an *organic conceptualisation* of coaching as naturally occurring and a *transformational motivation* to achieve personal, business and organisational change. The CEO and senior executives are responsible for driving coaching *top-down* throughout the organisation via the *integrated* delivery of coaching into everything everybody does as they communicate and relate in daily business transactions.

Chapter 8 addresses the strategies by which organisations transition between stages as they develop a coaching culture. From academic research and practitioner experience, lists of strategies have been proposed as contributing to its development. In contrast, the strategies reported in this book are based on empirically validated, theoretically informed, academic underpinnings from my research. These strategies relate to actions that line managers, HR professionals and organisational leaders can take as they learn and grow from being coached and trained in coaching skills, enact policy and procedural changes to support coaching in the workplace, and make coaching a strategic priority by which to effect transformational cultural change.

Chapter 9 details the strategies and mechanisms by which organisations transition from Stage 1 *Coaching-as-Intervention*, to Stage 2, *Coaching-as-HR-Function*. The strategies start with HR professionals providing the opportunity for line managers to learn more about coaching *(Learn)* and how psychological mechanisms can change their mental perspective (*Grow*). Thereafter, they utilise strategies from management research to prepare the infrastructure for coaching and for coaching skills training to be delivered into the wider organisation, overcoming any barriers and enabling the transition from Stage 1 to Stage 2 (*Lead*). The chapter also outlines the mechanisms that may hinder an organisation from progressing to the next stage.

Chapter 10 details the strategies and mechanisms by which HR professionals and organisational leaders assist the transition from Stage 2, *Coaching-as-HR-Function*, to Stage 3, *Coaching-as-Leader-Capability*. It explains the educational processes by which line managers receive training to gain knowledge and skills relating to coaching *(Learn)* and the psychological mechanisms by which they experience a mindset shift from a *command-and-control* management style to a *coaching leadership style* (*Grow*). Thereafter, organisational leaders enact strategies from management research which assist them conduct coaching practice within their business units, overcoming any barriers and enabling the transition from Stage 2 to Stage 3 (*Lead*). The chapter also outlines the mechanisms that may hinder an organisation from progressing to the next stage.

Chapter 11 details the strategies and mechanisms by which organisational leaders assist the transition from Stage 3, *Coaching-as-Leader-Capability*, to Stage 4, *Coaching-as-Culture.* It explains the educational processes by which CEOs and senior leaders learn more about coaching and experience being coached *(Learn)* and the psychological mechanisms that support their mental transformation from thinking about ways to develop individual human capital into identifying strategies to unleash the potential of all employees (*Grow*). They enact findings from management research to lead the transition from Stage 3 to Stage 4 in the development of a coaching culture (*Lead*). The chapter also outlines the mechanisms that may hinder an organisation from progressing to the final stage.

Chapter 12 introduces a blueprint to guide practitioner implementation in the workplace. It addresses the implications for CEOs and senior executives, organisational leaders and HR professionals who wish to introduce a coaching culture into their organisation using the model of coaching culture development derived from my research study. This final chapter summarises the strategies that CEOs and senior executives, organisational leaders and HR professionals need to take to progress the organisation's journey towards a coaching culture. It also signals a number of areas that may present potential pitfalls that must be overcome along the way.

***

This first chapter has introduced the rationale for developing a coaching culture in organisations. The following chapters detail the findings from educational and psychological studies and management research that underpin the development of a *coaching culture*. Whilst strategies have been proposed in the practitioner literature, there is clearly a need to develop an empirically validated, theoretical model of coaching culture development to guide leaders and practitioners in their attempts to develop a coaching culture in organisations.

References

1. Schein, E. (1985). *Organizational culture and leadership: A dynamic view*. Jossey-Bass.
2. Giorgi, S., Lockwood, C., & Glynn, M. (2015). The many faces of culture: Making sense of 30 years of research on culture in organization studies. *The Academy of Management Annals, 9*(1), 1–54.

Chapter 2
Research on Coaching and Coaching Culture

This chapter provides the evidence for the development of a coaching culture in organisations. Research findings in relation to *coaching culture* build on those for *coaching* as a dynamic, relational and social process[1] resulting in increased self-awareness and insight, learning and growth, and behavioural change. In this chapter, definitions of a coaching culture are presented, types of organisational coaching discussed, and the coaching practice intervention outlined. How coaching supports leadership capability, performance and talent management is explained as well as the benefits associated with these purposes for introducing a coaching culture into an organisation. An integrated model of the evidence for a coaching culture is derived from educational, psychological and management research findings. Finally, coaching is proposed as a subculture of organisational culture, consistent with the dominant models of culture identified in the extant literature: culture as *values*, *stories*, *frames*, *categories* and *toolkits*.

There is broad agreement within the research literature that coaching can help people improve their performance and achieve their goals. Coaching is a well-accepted business practice in Europe and the USA and an emerging growth industry elsewhere in the world. The incidence of coaching within organisations is expanding rapidly, becoming an extensive new field of practice and one of the fastest-growing interventions in the professional development of managers especially those in large organisations. Throughout Europe and the UK, several coaching associations have been established, the leading ones being the International Coaching Federation (ICF) and the European Mentoring and Coaching Council (EMCC). Both the ICF and the EMCC share interests and concerns related to the state of coaching, specifically regarding the credentialing of coaches, quality assessment, continuing professional education, governance and regulatory affairs.

---

[1] The evidence for coaching is presented in "Positive Psychology Coaching", also available from Springer.

S. Knowles, *Coaching Culture*, https://doi.org/10.1007/978-3-031-09050-9_2

In the UK, the Chartered Institute of Personnel and Development [1] reported that 32% of organisations responding to their survey use coaching by line managers or peers and 12% engage external coaches; hence, over a third of organisations in the UK sample used coaching in some way at that time. Furthermore, 46,800 people worldwide called themselves *executive coaches*, an increase of 75% from 10 years before. More recently, the ICF reported that there are an estimated 71,000 coaching practitioners worldwide including 15,900 line managers and leaders who use coaching skills, an increase of 33% on their 2015 survey results [2]. Furthermore, they estimated worldwide *revenue from coaching* at US$2.849 billion, a 21% increase over the 2015 estimate [2]. However, whilst this evidence clearly demonstrates the growth of coaching within UK, Europe and US business communities over the past 10 years, coaching is still not well-known or accepted as a valid organisational practice in many organisations.

Historically, although performance concepts from sports coaching were starting to be incorporated into what was then called Human Resource Development (HRD) in the 1970s, interest in *coaching* did not gain traction until *executive coaching* was introduced as an organisational practice in the 1990s. Validation for this practice was achieved when the American Society for Training and Development (ASTD) included *coaching* in their 2004 Competency Framework as an area of expertise among workplace learning and performance specialists, a view that was reinforced in their 2013 revised version of the *ASTD Competency Model*. Coaching subsequently migrated into the organisational development (OD) arena as a special form of intervention to help organisational members clarify their goals, remove roadblocks and obstacles, and improve performance effectiveness. From there, the responsibility for coaching migrated into the Human Resource (HR) function as an important developmental activity although, in some organisations, coaching still sits within the HRD, OD, Workforce Development or People and Culture functions.

Definitions

No single definition of coaching exists or of when, how and by whom it can be delivered to benefit individuals, teams and organisations. A review of the academic literature reveals the confusion for organisations wishing to offer coaching and for coaching recipients, with 37 definitions of coaching proposed based on the audience and purpose for coaching including what and for whom it is delivered, what it involves and the context in which it is applied [3]. These definitions highlight the essential ingredients of coaching and the coaching relationship as personal responsibility, dyadic relationship, achieving individual personal and professional goals, reflection and self-development, and behavioural change. A composite definition of coaching as it was enacted within the HRD environment at that time was proposed as follows:

> [Coaching] is designed to improve existing skills, competence and performance, and to enhance … personal effectiveness … development or … growth. [4]

Within organisations, a plethora of approaches claim to stimulate individual development and growth including coaching, mentoring, training, supervision and counselling. In many organisations and to many people's minds, the terms *coaching* and *mentoring* are interchangeable. However, these two activities are not the same, nor are they related to other organisational activities such as training, supervision and counselling. Whilst coaching and mentoring both promote personal and professional growth, mentoring usually involves an ongoing professional relationship between a junior and a more senior person within the same or possibly a different organisation in which the mentor imparts wisdom and knowledge to the mentee. Mentors are role models and the mentoring relationship is based on the sharing of professional experience to improve the mentee's personal and professional effectiveness as well as deepen understanding of their career prospects. The relationship is hierarchical and sometimes paternalistic. The mentor has extensive skills and experience to share with the mentee in what is typically a *telling* rather than an *asking* relationship.

Conversely, coaching is a partnership between two people of equal status in the coaching room who, together, surface a solution to resolve a problem or achieve a specific goal. The coaching is conducted in a supportive and non-judgemental way, allowing a trusting relationship to form. Coaches bring essential skills of rapport building, active listening and powerful questioning, to the process. The coachee brings knowledge of their situation and needs. Coach and coachee work together to achieve an outcome that promotes the coachee's wellbeing and productivity. The coaching conversation is focused on expanding the coachee's awareness of self and others, encouraging insight and discovery, and taking action. Coaches assist coachees discover what they really want and need in life and work. Together, they explore the unexplored – the world of possibilities – during which process coachees discover their true self, what motivates them, and what causes them conflict and concern. Coaches work with coachees to help them envision their best possible future and then goal set and action plan with them so they achieve their desired outcomes, revisiting the goals as necessary throughout the process.

Like *coaching*, there is no shared understanding or definition of, or theoretical basis in the academic literature for, what constitutes a *coaching culture* [5]. Instead, there are eight definitions which highlight the different components of a coaching culture as experienced by individuals in organisations. A *coaching culture* has been described as one in which "people coach each other all the time as a natural part of meetings, reviews, and one-to-one discussions of all kinds" [6], suggesting that frequent coaching can strengthen collaborative, supportive relationships and the sharing of constructive feedback. A coaching culture has also been described as existing when "coaching behaviour motivates people, increases job satisfaction and morale, and strengthens bonds between individuals" [7] suggesting a *developmental* component to a coaching culture. There is "a commitment to grow the organisation …[together with] a parallel commitment to grow the people in the organisation"

[8], suggesting a *business* component to a coaching culture. Coaching has also been described as "a key aspect of how the leaders, managers and staff engage and develop all their people and engage their stakeholders in ways that create increased individual, team and organisational performance and shared value for all stakeholders" [9], suggesting a *leadership* component and key *purposes* for conducting coaching in the workplace. A composite definition of a coaching culture derived from a review of the extant literature at that time is that "a coaching culture exists within an organisation when it has embedded a coaching approach as part of its strategic plans in a transparent way. Coaching cultures should motivate individuals and facilitate cooperation, collaboration and connection within the organisation and with its external stakeholders" [5]. These researchers propose that a coaching culture exists when "groups of people embrace coaching as a way of making *holistic improvements* to individuals within their organisations through formal and informal coaching interactions" [5]. Table 2.1 captures these definitions of a coaching culture and their key features.

These definitions of a coaching culture differ on four key dimensions: *what* coaching is; *why* coaching is conducted in organisations; *who* delivers the coaching and its recipients; and *how* coaching is delivered within organisations (Table 2.2). The gaps in these definition dimensions were addressed in my research study.

With no definitive agreement on what a coaching culture *is*, what is known from the academic literature is that it is driven by the "principles, beliefs, and mindsets" [11] of individuals in the organisation. Employees who adopt a coaching approach share a common philosophy and performance objectives characterised by high overall levels of involvement, consistency, adaptability and dedication from leaders [12, 13]. A coaching culture in which everybody coaches everybody else aligns with what has been called a *deliberately developmental organisation* (DDO) [14]. In a DDO, employees receive continuous development in the course of a day's work by virtue of the coaching conversations they have with others to accelerate their growth. As a result, "an organisational culture which supports people's ongoing development is woven into the daily fabric of working life, visible in the company's regular operations, day-to-day routines, and conversations" [14].

Types of Coaching

The expansion of academic literature and research into workplace coaching in the last two decades has led to a diversification in the types of coaching offered by external, executive coaches and internal line managers who coach [15]. The types of coaching offered within organisations, whilst often used interchangeably [16], have specific characteristics that best serve the groups who are the target of the coaching. For example, in an organisational setting, individual coaching typically focuses on behavioural or performance issues which are causing concern for the manager or employee such as communication and relationship difficulties, stress-related anxiety, or role clarity. At the team level, coaching often addresses issues relating to

Table 2.1 Definitions of a coaching culture

Authors	Definition of a coaching culture	Key feature
Hardingham et al. [6, p. 184]	"people coach each other all the time as a natural part of meetings, reviews and one-to-one discussions of all kinds"	Natural occurrence in organisational events
Clutterbuck and Megginson [10, p. 19]	"the predominant style of managing and working together, and where a commitment to grow the organization is embedded in a parallel commitment to grow the people in the organization"	Commitment to people and the organisation
Clutterbuck et al. [11, p. 22]	"A coaching culture is one where the principles, beliefs, and mindsets driving people's behavior in the workplace are deeply rooted in the discipline of coaching".	Mindsets drive behaviour
Hart [7, p. 7]	"Coaching behaviour motivates people, increases job satisfaction and morale, and strengthens bonds between individuals".	Motivational and relational
Lindbom [12, p. 102]	"…culture of coaching requires commitment, consistency, and dedication from leadership"	Emphasises leadership
Passmore and Jastrzebska [219, p. 5]	"A coaching culture is one where coaching, the use of reflective and provocative questions, is used consistently by all employees and by key partners, to help develop understanding, insight and personal responsibility for those responsible in delivering the organizational outcomes. While it is not the only way which the organization leads and manages its employees or works with its partners, it is the primary leadership, development and learning style used in the organization".	Insight, personal responsibility, primary leadership style
Hawkins [9, p. 21]	"A coaching culture exists in an organisation when a coaching approach is a key aspect of how the leaders, managers, and staff engage and develop all their people and engage their stakeholders, in ways that create increased individual, team and organisational performance and shared value for all stakeholders".	Leaders engage and develop all employees and stakeholders
Gormley and van Nieuwerburgh [5, p. 99]	"A coaching culture exists within an organisation when it has embedded a coaching approach as part of its strategic plans in a transparent way. Coaching cultures should motivate individuals and facilitate cooperation, collaboration and connection within the organisation and with its external stakeholders".	Strategic agenda to engender cooperation and collaboration

collaboration, cooperation and conflict, which may be causing job dissatisfaction and low team morale. At the organisational level, coaches are typically engaged to extend executives' leadership capability, improve their role performance, and identify opportunities for career progression.

Executive coaching was the first type of coaching to be recognised within an organisational setting. Other types of coaching that emerged from these origins include managerial, leadership, team, and peer coaching [17–19], as discussed below.

Executive coaching is a developmental process which is both personal and performance-related, delivered by an external executive coach who is engaged on an

Table 2.2 Differing dimensions among coaching culture definitions

Authors	*What* they say a coaching culture is	*Why* a coaching culture is developed	*Who* is involved in developing and delivering a coaching culture	*How* a coaching culture is delivered
Hardingham et al. [6, p. 184]	What people do and observers see		Receiving: Organisational members	
Clutterbuck and Megginson [10, p. 19]		Grow people and the organisation		Coaching is the primary leadership behaviour
Clutterbuck et al. [11, p. 22]	A discipline			Transparent use of coaching principles, beliefs and mindsets which drive coaching behaviour
Hart [7, p. 7]		Motivate, increase job satisfaction and morale, strengthen relationships		Transparent use of coaching which drives coaching behaviour
Lindbom [12, p. 102]			Enacting: Organisational leaders	
Passmore and Jastrzebska [219, p. 5]		Develop personal insight and responsibility, promote collaborative learning and development, and achieve organisational outcomes	Enacting: Organisational leaders Receiving: Organisational members	Coaching is the predominant leadership style/ behaviour
Hawkins [9, p. 21]		Increase individual, team and organisational performance and shareholder value	Enacting: Organisational leaders Receiving: Organisational members and external stakeholders	Coaching is the predominant leadership style/ behaviour
Gormley and van Nieuwerburgh [5, p. 99]		Facilitate cooperation, collaboration and connection	Receiving: Organisational members and external stakeholders	Coaching is included in the strategic plan

outsourced contract. It is a developmental process based on mutual trust and respect within a partnership relationship between coach and executive [20, 21]. The success of the process lies in the quality of the relationship. Executive coaching improves the executive's ability to relate and communicate more effectively with colleagues, customers and direct reports, perform as a strategic leader and transform into peak performance. The coaching positively affects the executive's judgement, improves critical thinking and decision-making skills, increases their social influence and promotes a transformational leadership style. Transforming executives from good to peak performers [17, 22, 23] relies on one-on-one interactions about work-related issues [24–26]. Multi-source feedback on strengths and weaknesses provides baseline data against which to measure improvements in personal effectiveness, leadership competency, organisational performance and change management [25, 27]. Executive coaching positively affects the executive's self-awareness, transformational leadership behaviour, social capital, and career planning [16, 25, 28–31]. As the coaching proceeds, the executive develops strategic leadership competencies, plans for the future growth of the business and identifies ways to manage and lead transformational cultural change programmes.

Managerial coaching is conducted with middle managers so they can improve the performance of direct reports by facilitating their learning of work-related skills and abilities [32]. It focuses on the planning, organising, staffing and controlling functions managers need to effectively perform their line management responsibilities [33–37] and the competencies they need to succeed in their role [38–41]. Managers are coached to develop their knowledge of alternate ways, or more appropriate behaviours, to improve their team's performance. The coaching provides timely feedback to them so they can better navigate workplace challenges, formulate work goals, clarify team performance targets and expectations, improve employee job performance and adjust job/role functions [42, 43]. Managers learn how to provide frequent performance feedback to their team members, promote employee engagement and reduce turnover intention [44, 45]. Prominent in this type of coaching is finding ways to improve the manager's ability to achieve organisational objectives [33–37]. Managerial coaching is reported to be a more effective process for performance improvement than training programmes alone because the integration of coaching into training programmes significantly improves transfer of learning rates [46, 47]. The mediating mechanisms between managerial coaching and work-related outcomes have been identified as *role clarity* and *satisfaction with work* [48, 49]. The benefit of managerial coaching is that it impacts on the coachee's ability to self-regulate their behaviour and performance, particularly their persistence to cope with and overcome challenging problems.

Leadership coaching is the most common form of coaching in organisations today [32, 50]. It is focused on supporting leaders who inspire and motivate their direct reports to increase employee engagement and assist them cope with change [51–53]. Leadership coaching impacts the leader's behaviour and cognitive functioning, and their ability to translate individual learnings into team learnings. Shared group-level beliefs support the implementation of change efforts [54]. Sustained change is achieved when leadership coaching satisfies the leader's needs for autonomy, relatedness and competence [55]. Two styles of leadership coaching – guidance and facilitation – have been reported in the literature [56]. The guidance style combines clear expectations of performance requirements with observational learning, behavioural re-alignment and role modelling, to achieve performance mastery. The facilitation style enables adaptive learning from the environment, one-on-one feedback and the adoption of a transformational leadership style. A focus on coaching new leaders to integrate multiple identities as they settle into their role highlights the latest development in the field [57]. Leadership coaching may be conducted by external leadership coaches who are engaged by the organisation to perform a specific task within a work group or by internal, qualified leadership coaches.

Team coaching is an emerging organisational practice that focuses on both results and relationships [58, 59], facilitating problem-solving and conflict management, and coordinating the task-appropriate use of collective resources to achieve team targets. It confirms common goals, identifies issues challenging the team or team members, assists them reflect on their performance and review progress, and coordinates collective resources to accomplish the work of the team [60–62]. Team coaching improves communication and decision-making [63], facilitates problem solving and conflict management [64] and enables teams to learn how to improve their performance through "assisted reflection, analysis and motivation for change" [65]. As team members reflect on their performance, they identify opportunities for systemic change and innovation [66, 67].

Peer coaching supplements other forms of organisational coaching as an effective, informal, relational practice that promotes and supports the achievement of performance, leadership and career aspirations [68]. It is delivered one-on-one by employees informally as opportunities arise to innovate or improve performance, systems and processes [69]. As "a helping relationship that facilitates mutual learning and development to accomplish specific tasks or goals" [70], peer coaching provides mutual support to achieve individual, immediate and short-term goals and build leadership capacity [71]. It has been described as an overlooked resource in the development of an employee's critical thinking, reasoning skills and effective judgement [72]. "Peer coaching is a low-cost resource. It has high impact. It can be just-in-time. It is easily learned. And it is self-renewing, sustainable" [73]. Peer coaching has been used effectively in educational settings to support learning and growth [71, 74].

Fundamental to all types of coaching is the desire to achieve behavioural and performance changes to support productivity improvements [75, 76]. Workplace coaching methodologies and systems support a type of learning that, over time, becomes implicit, tacit and assumed [77]. The next section addresses how these types of coaching are conducted in the workplace.

Coaching Culture Practice

Coaching practice has been described as a "goal-directed interaction between the coach and the coachee which reflects what leaders do when engaging with their direct reports to improve their performance" [78]. Although coaching has traditionally been delivered in organisations by external coaches engaged to coach an executive, the considerable growth of coaching over the past decade and the identified benefits for individuals, teams and organisations have legitimised coaching as a function of line managers as well as HR professionals to stimulate employee growth and performance improvements [79]. As coaching-based initiatives influence, leverage and change company cultures, organisational leaders are increasingly encouraged to enable enhanced work engagement of all employees, facilitate organisational learning, and manage strategic change agendas through coaching [80, 81].

Conceptual papers relating to the development of a coaching culture discuss issues relating to the managers' motivation to coach, willingness to be coached and openness to discovery, commitment and team learning, as well as their ability to build a shared vision and develop personal mastery of coaching [82–84]. More recently, the focus of coaching is on developmental and empowerment perspectives so that employees can improve their own performance. Hence, from vague conceptions of coaching as "an activity, a function with specific outcomes" [85], coaching is now seen as a "facilitative process designed to improve existing skills, competence and performance and embrace personal effectiveness, personal development or personal growth" [4].

Coaching involves the use of a variety of techniques which enable coachees to learn new behaviours and improve their communication and relationship skills through intensive feedback and role modelling. Using these techniques, coaches help coachees increase their self-awareness and insight, change their behaviour, and improve their performance. The value of coaching is that it can be customised to meet both an individual's specific learning needs as well as organisational expectations. Hence, it develops individual and team capabilities, leading to simultaneous improvements in the individual's work performance and team productivity.

The push to deliver coaching within organisations has been largely practitioner-led, strongly supported by the establishment of coaching practice standards by professional associations such as the ICF and the American Psychological Association which have developed their own rules, rituals and competencies based on ethical and legal standards of professionalism [86, 87]. Hence, coaching as a professional practice and field of expertise expanded from early conceptions as an intervention to develop individual leaders, into opportunities for "in-the-moment team coaching, group coaching, coach mentoring … and other coaching-based approaches … [to effect] comprehensive change initiatives" [88].

A recent, qualitative, inductive and deductive study of subject matter experts has uncovered six main themes relating to organisational factors that support the development of a coaching culture (organisational factors that support coaching; reflective practice; whole-self focused; values driven; actively using coaching skills; and respect) and four subthemes (coaching broadly used; coaching strategy; decision-making; and people matter) [77]. The study also identified five key themes related to implementing a coaching culture including leaders' demonstration of coaching behaviours, coaching conversations prioritised in the organisation, coaching behaviours embedded into everyday interactions, coaching skills training used as a developmental tool, and coaching utilised as a strategic tool [77]. Ways that middle managers can evaluate the coaching ability of front-line supervisors, and strategies to address issues relating to their coaching ability, have also been qualitatively investigated. Five key findings which have a direct effect on the success of implementing a coaching culture were identified as: leaders are completely aligned on organisational coaching expectations, behaviours and definitions; a robust coaching supervision programme is in place to evaluate current front-line supervisors; a comprehensive interviewing process ascertains the coaching ability of potential candidates for the front-line supervisor role; leaders mitigate factors that inhibit coaching activity particularly emphasising the importance of the coaching dyad; and the organisation ensures the quality and consistency of the coaching conducted throughout the organisation [89].

Why Develop a Coaching Culture?

The need for organisations to be flexible in a global environment has highlighted the importance of two key factors: adaptive leadership strategies and organisational culture [90]. Leadership is an important element in developing a coaching culture although an understanding of the dynamics and nuances of how leaders and leadership shape coaching culture is not well-known [91–93]. Hence, before committing resources to develop a coaching culture, the CEO and senior executives need to determine the purpose for introducing coaching into the organisation as a systemic change initiative [5]. Is it to develop the capacity of leaders? Is it to improve employee performance? Is it to retain talent? Research has linked the development of a coaching culture with all these outcomes [93]. These three main purposes for developing a coaching culture are addressed in the next few sections.

First, as understandings of coaching spread, coaching is becoming an accepted practice to develop leadership capability. In particular, the need to build the internal coaching capability of front-line supervisors and managers has been recognised, as these are the leaders who are increasingly being charged with additional responsibility for a range of HR and development functions including the coaching of their employees. Hence, HR is increasingly responsible for developing coaching skills training programmes for managers so they can learn how to coach their employees. In a coaching culture, the HR function is particularly effective in aligning employee behaviour with organisational priorities, cascading coaching skills training programmes down the organisation and following up with coaching support. They may even be charged with appointing an internal coaching team [94]. Such strategies are adopted when coaching behaviour is included as a job performance competency and linked to systems for advancement, rewards and incentives. Establishing the infrastructure for coaching has been empirically validated as a positive and supportive approach to coaching culture development [9, 95].

Second, coaching has been recognised as an effective intervention to improve employee performance. Dyadic coaching helps employees grow personally and professionally and progress in their career. Employees gain greater clarity on what is expected of them in their role and receive immediate feedback to improve their performance, communication and relationships, and better manage differences and conflict in the workplace. In a coaching culture, coaching is an important vehicle to enhance the performance of all team members to produce peak performance. When employees are coached, feedback on work performance is given in a timely and supportive rather than punitive manner, the underlying belief being that all employees are capable of additional growth and development when they are provided with personalised, constructive feedback on their performance. The assumption of leaders is that employees want to utilise their strengths and initiative in a way that is meaningful and purposive and which supports the strategic direction of the organisation.

Third, research has shown that the coaching of talented individuals is an essential component of the succession planning process [96]. Adopting a coaching philosophy and supportive approach towards work and co-workers is central to employee growth and development and the retention of talent [58]. Talent management has been identified as one of the main strategies used by organisations to grow the human capital of the business, thereby securing competitive advantage for the firm. As an integral component of a talent management strategy, coaching assists the identification of high-potential individuals whose strengths and abilities contribute to the achievement of both short- and long-term benefits for the organisation as they progress into other positions or accept other developmental opportunities within the organisation. Global talent management has been increasingly explored in the cross-cultural literature, especially in relation to the management of expatriates, the search for global leadership talent, organisational success and organisational reputation [97].

Benefits of Coaching and a Coaching Culture

Once the purpose for introducing a coaching culture into the organisation has been identified, the benefits that the organisation desires as a result need to be determined. Research is clear on the individual benefits from coaching. Coachees gain in self-awareness and insight, learn how to change their behaviour so that it is consistent with organisational values and expectations, improve in the performance of their role, and communicate better with others to form strong relationships within their team. In addition, leaders develop their leadership capability and ability to influence key stakeholders to meet business needs. Leaders who learn how to team coach improve team cohesion, increase cooperation and collaboration, reduce conflict and raise team morale. Issues are addressed as they occur, negating the need to take the matter further which may cause a decrease in staff motivation and engagement. The organisation benefits from increased productivity as the team forges to higher performance levels resulting in an improved market position and competitive advantage. Coaching has been described as "more than a set of skills; it is a rich, holistic approach for releasing the potential in people and in organisations" [98].

The academic literature has identified the major benefits of a coaching culture for organisations as greater employee engagement [99–101], retention of talent [102–105], increased productivity and competitive advantage [106, 107], significant return on investment [75, 108–111] and cultural change [112, 113]. As coaching is conducted, teams and team members reflect on their performance to identify opportunities for systemic change and innovation [66, 67]. Coaching all employees encourages independence and self-reliance which enables them to strengthen relationships and contribute to the long-term benefits for the organisation [114].

Three main benefits have been identified in the practitioner literature: higher employee engagement (60% of employees rated as highly engaged compared with 48% of all other organisations); higher revenue growth (63% of organisations report being above their industry peer group revenue compared with 45% of all other organisations); and higher engagement levels for high potentials with access to external coaches or leaders as coaches (as reported by 60% of organisations) [115]. Employees who are coached tend to stay longer in the organisation because of their belief that they are valued and that the organisation wants to support their development and career progression.

Organisations which embrace a coaching culture capture all these benefits for all their employees. In addition, they accrue major benefits for the organisation as a whole. Coaching cultures promote organisational learning and adaptability to change, and encourage collaborative learning. Developing the coaching competencies of organisational leaders results in increased motivation, happiness and job satisfaction for employees; improved team communication, cooperation, knowledge sharing and performance; reduced staff turnover; and increased organisational profitability.

Theoretical Basis for Coaching and a Coaching Culture

The historical evidence for coaching as an effective intervention to promote personal insight, behavioural change and performance improvement lies within two well-established disciplines – education and psychology – and management research, as explained below.[2]

---

[2] For a more detailed discussion, see "Positive Psychology Coaching" by the same author, also available from Springer.

Educational Underpinnings to Coaching

The evidence for coaching from education and adult learning theories positions it as a pluralist process that surfaces self-awareness, insight, learnings and behavioural change. Specifically, education provides the evidence for coaching as grounded in the learning process, personal mindsets, motivation and self-efficacy. In particular, implicit person theory [116, 117] proposes that coachees who believe in their ability to learn, perform or change as a result of effort, persistence and, at times, assistance are malleable [118, 119]. Mindset theory [116], applied to an individual's ability to change and grow [78, 120, 121], integrates principles of self-efficacy, social learning theory and work motivation theory, to effect change [122, 123]. Educators and practitioners have been urged to develop a "more integrated, systemic, global approach to coaching to accommodate the challenges posed by a new global paradigm" [124]. Combined with principles of adult learning [125–128], these frameworks provide the basis for the development of adult learning strategies in the workplace.

Psychological Underpinnings to Coaching

Coaching practice is informed by an understanding of human behaviour from psychological approaches which are based on well-researched methods of modifying behaviour and motivating individuals to better meet their needs. Within psychology, coaching research has focused on the psychodynamics of the individual [129]. The primary influences on personal effectiveness began from observations of human behaviour and behavioural manipulation to condition new responses [130]. Cognitive therapeutic approaches then proposed that difficulties are caused by habits and associated thought patterns which can be rectified by focusing on goal-oriented behaviours [131] so that coachees find their own solutions rather than blame external forces [132]. Subsequently, solution-focused coaching was found to reduce negative affect, increase positive affect and support goal attainment [133–135], helping coachees build a greater depth of understanding and self-efficacy [136–138]. Coaching has been found to be most effective when solution-focused coaching is combined with cognitive and rational–emotive behavioural approaches [139, 140].

Motivational and developmental psychology address issues that promote mental and emotional wellbeing, growth and development [141–143]. The coach uses humanistic psychology to identify the coachee's needs, drives and expectations and ensure that they are realistic and attainable [144–146]. Positive psychology seeks ways in which the coachee can become authentically happy and achieve "flow" in their life [147, 148]. Social psychology recognises the importance of the social environment as coachees attempt to conform with, and make sense of, their environment and adjust their behaviour to meet their needs [149, 150]. Social psychologists

Table 2.3 The psychological evidence for coaching

Theoretical area	Key areas of research
Behavioural psychology	Classical versus operant conditioning, observation of human behaviour
Cognitive psychology	Cognitive-based therapy, rational–emotive behaviour therapy, goal setting, solution-focused coaching
Motivational psychology	Needs, drives, motivations, expectations, satisfaction
Developmental psychology	Experiential learning, prosocial development, brain malleability, growth and persistence
Personality psychology	Attitudes, preferences, traits
Humanistic psychology	Self-psychology, individuation, unconscious competence, person-centred therapy
Social psychology	Social learning, social conformity, cognitive dissonance, self-efficacy
Positive psychology	Authentic happiness, "flow", learned helplessness, mindset

encourage individuals to adopt new ways of relating to others and the external world to develop self-regulation and goal attainment, motivation and personality, and emotional competence [151–156]. These different streams of research provide the theoretical underpinnings for coaching practice from a psychological perspective (see Table 2.3).

Management Underpinnings to Coaching

In addition to the findings from psychological and educational research, coaching practice has been informed by management literature based on workplace research. Theoretical approaches have focused on the acquisition of competencies to enhance leadership development [157, 158], job satisfaction [159–161], motivation and work performance [48, 123, 162–164] and interpersonal and team relationships [165–167]. Empirical research has also investigated ways to stimulate employee growth and development based on measurable outcomes [15].

Integrated Model of the Evidence for a Coaching Culture

In summary, the educational foundations for coaching lie in concepts related to mindset, malleability, and learning and development. In a coaching culture, leaders adopt a *growth mindset* to assist employees develop and reach their full potential. This mindset is applied in interactions with all employees, not just employees who are regarded as talent. With this mindset, leaders believe that all employees can, and will be willing to, change their behaviour to become more adaptable and embrace new experiences which enhance their development.

The psychological foundations for coaching are based on the individual's ability to restructure their thinking and change their behaviour given feedback from their social environment, leading to self-regulation and emotional competence. When coaching is viewed from this perspective, managers replace their *command-and-control* mindset with a *coaching leadership style* to empower and encourage all employees to excel. This shift creates a safe working environment for coaching to occur and shows due care and concern for direct reports as people. Cognitive reframing allows leaders and employees to restructure their social relationships with others, including customers and suppliers, so that they become more interpersonally effective. As employees are coached, they develop greater self-awareness and the ability to self-regulate their emotions, leading to more productive interactions with others in and out of the organisation.

The management foundations of coaching focus on the acquisition of leader competencies to enhance employee motivation and performance, resulting in improved business relationships and increased productivity. In a coaching culture, everybody is able to coach and be coached and have informal coaching conversations with peers. Equipping leaders with coaching skills and using the coaching language and philosophy throughout the organisation facilitates the development of a platform for cultural change to occur. Coaching motivates individuals to engage in more open and honest conversations that are based on trust and a genuine desire for leaders and employees to succeed.

These underpinnings of coaching from educational, psychological and management perspectives together form an integrated model of the evidence for a coaching culture, as represented in Fig. 2.1.

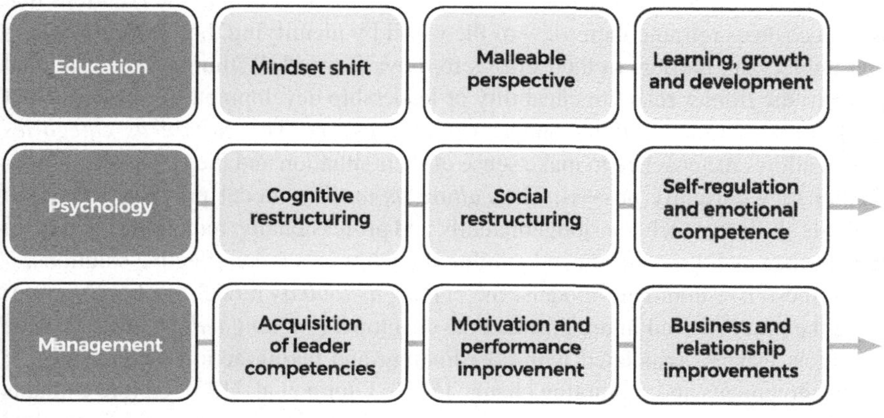

Fig. 2.1 Integrated model of the evidence for a coaching culture

Organisational Culture

Research into the development of a coaching culture has also been informed by findings from the academic literature in relation to *organisational culture* – what it is and how it develops. Schein [168] described culture as "what a group learns over a period of time as that group solves its problems of survival in an external environment and its problems of internal integration". He believed that such learning is simultaneously a behavioural, cognitive and emotional process. Subsequently, the term *culture* has been used to indicate how *values* guide and constrain people in organisations [169], how individuals weave stories to obtain resources [170] or how individuals discriminately use tools to meet personal needs and interests [171, 172].

Schein identified three fundamental levels at which culture manifests: observable artefacts, values, and basic underlying assumptions. *Artefacts* are the external representations of what an organisation holds dear. *Values* are represented by the behavioural norms that develop within an organisation. Underlying *assumptions* are uncovered by a process of enquiry that brings them to the surface to create mutual understanding. The process of questioning and reflective listening is the basis for the development of cultural norms within an organisation in relation to values and appropriate behaviours. Creating a common language and shared understandings enables the space for trust, friendship and inclusion to evolve and grow. Questioning, reflective listening and developing a common language and shared understandings are some of the basic processes that coaches use in their coaching practice.

Giorgi et al. [173] reviewed the organisational culture research over the past 30 years. They identified five dominant models of culture: culture as *values*, *stories*, *frames*, *categories* and *toolkits*. When related to coaching, the *culture as values* model represents the shared understandings of what coaching is and the philosophy that underpins the coaching process. The *culture as stories* model represents the narratives and conversations that transact between coach and coachee as the coaching unfolds. The *culture as frames* model represents the coaching interventions that assist coachees reframe their view of the world by identifying their limiting beliefs and unblocking barriers to their efforts to move forward. Within an organisational context, the *frames* relate to capability or leadership development frameworks that guide organisational activity and career progression. The *culture as categories* model allows the coachee to make sense of their situation and the skills and competencies they currently possess. The *culture as toolkits* model provides the coach with the skills to coach non-judgementally and professionally, remaining centred on the coachee and their agenda and guiding them towards more effective solutions.

Of these five dominant models, the *culture as toolkits* model most aptly represents the practice used in organisations to develop a *coaching culture* since it is the one most usually associated with coordinating and taking action, helping people reach agreements and promoting change [5]. To Giorgi et al. [173], culture explains the differences in outcomes that result not only from differences in individual behaviours and organisational practices but also from the culture of the organisation. They propose that "culture should remain a code of many colors that envelops different theoretical perspectives" [173].

Repertoires of actions [174] are the resources that actors use to make meaning of their work. The *coaching as toolkits* model of organisational culture explains how actors use cultural repertoires in practice, i.e. the various skills, knowledge and resources that employees can draw upon to solve everyday problems [175]. Repertoires of action bring together habits, styles, skills and symbols [173] and operationalise the mental models, strategies and actions that organisational members work from (e.g. how to manage their workload, how to be a good leader, how to coach). These repertoires are backed up by skills, habits and styles that are translatable into practice [176]. Repertoires of action have been related to constructs such as cultural repertoires [175, 177], cultural capital [178] and theories of practice [179]. Developing *coaching competencies* in order to coach others to peak performance is an essential component of a leader's behavioural repertoire [5, 180]. However it cannot be assumed that leaders know how to coach; rather they may need to be trained in coaching skills to guide and facilitate self-reflection and learning.

The use of cultural toolkits has been empirically verified in studies including justification for different life events [181]; conferring worth to social standing [182]; and drawing social boundaries and establishing identities [177]. Employees use personal cultural resources [183] and socio-cultural values [184] within their toolkit to make sense of specific work situations and events. Shared toolkits have been empirically associated with the coordination of team efforts in product innovation [185], evaluating products at the field level [186] and work practices in organisations [187–192]. Thus, the *culture as toolkits* model of organisational culture suggests that introducing a coaching culture into an organisation consists of sharing the values associated with coaching together with the cultural norms associated with coaching (e.g. philosophy, mindset, behaviours), as well as the skills and knowledge required to enable managers and leaders to coach confidently and consistently (i.e. training them in how to coach and providing them with a coaching toolkit).

Organisations with a coaching culture fit the description of a *deliberately developmental organisation* [14] which is one in which coaching skills are deliberately applied to all conversations, meetings, training programmes, transactions, interactions and relationships throughout and external to the organisation. The culture is open and supportive of the growth that employees experience when they are developmentally coached. Employees who do not feel comfortable with this level of "exposure" may not remain long in the organisation. Those who do remain experience a rate of personal and professional growth that is intense and potentially life-changing.

The concept of organisational culture has been extended over the years to include understandings of more nuanced subcultures, for example, safety culture, service culture and sales culture. This research provides the historical rationale for the development of a coaching culture as a subset of organisational culture, as explained below.

Coaching Culture as a Subculture

From a historical perspective, reference to a coaching culture was made in 1989 when a "culture of coaching" was proposed as the new paradigm for management [193]. However, researchers at that time were preoccupied with exploring the newly formed construct of "executive coaching" and failed to pay attention to the concept of a coaching culture [20, 25, 194–196]. The focus was on evaluating the effectiveness of executive coaching [17, 22, 25, 27, 197–201] and establishing its return on investment [75, 108, 110, 111, 202, 203]. Hence, it was not until 2005 that interest in identifying and understanding more about how coaching could be utilised within the organisational/management arena that the concept of developing a coaching culture surfaced into academic awareness [10].

Early subculture research had identified a number of relatively cohesive social systems of "shared, learned behaviors which are common to a specific group or category" [204]. A subculture was thought to exist when culture is idiosyncratic to a particular group that explains differences across or within an organisation [205]. It was defined as consisting of "the norms, life ways and values of members of some groups at a systems level" [206]. Moreover, research determined that multiple climates (or cultures) can exist simultaneously [207]. Specific research into organisational culture identified a number of subcultures either nested within the overarching organisational culture or existing beside it. These narrower, more nuanced aspects of culture such as safety, service and sales cultures demonstrated "the multiplicity of climate facets that exist" [208]. The definitions in Table 2.4 indicate their similarities as subcultures and highlight their differences in terms of the populations that each of these subcultures represent.

By investigating the structural elements of these multiple cultures such as efficiency and effectiveness, researchers adopted the view that a subculture is a part of organisational culture which influences and impacts on outcomes relating to that particular field of study [213, 214]. According to Antonsen [215], the development of separate cultures has to do with creating the principles and processes necessary for that particular aspect of organisational culture to thrive, suggesting that separate

Table 2.4 Definitions of subcultures

Organisational culture	
Subculture	"a distinctive subgroup of society that self-selects on the basis of a shared commitment to a particular product class, brand, or … activity" [209].
Safety	"the product of individual and group values, attitudes, perceptions, competencies, and patterns of behaviour that determine the commitment to, and the style and proficiency of, an organisation's health and safety management" [210].
Services	"a customer-centric culture aimed at exceeding customer expectations and creating superior customer value through the development of service and related performance competencies" [211].
Sales	"a growth oriented facet of the market orientation in which all employees are expected to contribute to the creation of value for customers by actively participating in the selling process" [212].

cultures are a subset of the overarching organisational culture. When attention is paid to the particular principles and processes associated with that aspect of organisational culture in a coordinated fashion, that particular subset of the culture grows. Antonsen's model [215] highlights the interplay between structural aspects of the organisation and the interactions between individuals who have a significant effect on the growth and development of shared language and cultural norms in relation to that aspect of culture. Hence, a safety culture has emerged as a discrete concept separate from, but related to, organisational culture with its own particular set of rules and regulations regarding how employees keep themselves and fellow workers safe in a workplace. The majority of research into a safety culture has been based on a functionalist approach into how people think – their attitudes, beliefs and perceptions – based on a belief that culture can be managed and changed [216]. Caldwell [216] constructed an implementation *toolkit* that provides a practical guide for assessing, monitoring and improving the leadership aspects of organisational culture in relation to safety.

Studies from *safety culture* research demonstrate that a particular approach can be taken to investigating a nuanced aspect of an organisation's culture. The research study that I conducted adopted the lens of *coaching* and a *coaching culture* rather than *safety* to investigate organisational activities. It investigated how coaching is defined, how cultural norms for coaching are developed and how a coaching culture is operationalised within organisations. This research is important because as Smircich [217] noted in Alvesson [218], organisations are composed of various systems of shared meanings which allow employees to readily interact in a continuous, organised way without the confusion of having to reinterpret meaning. Just as the documented subcultures have their own set of rules and rituals, conceptualisations of coaching as a subculture of organisational culture indicate that it, too, has its own set of principles and practices to which organisational members subscribe.

***

This chapter has explicated the educational, psychological and management evidence that constitutes the basis for the concept of a coaching culture. The next chapter contains details of my research study and reveals the model of coaching culture development which resulted from interrogation of the findings.

References

1. CIPD. (2014). *Learning and development survey*. Chartered Institute of Personnel and Development.
2. ICF. (2020). *Global coaching study: Executive summary*. PricewaterhouseCoopers LLP.
3. Bachkirova, T., & Kauffman, C. (2009). The blind men and the elephant: Using criteria of universality and uniqueness in evaluating our attempts to define coaching. *Coaching: An International Journal of Theory, Research and Practice, 2*(2), 95–105.

4. Hamlin, R., Ellinger, A. D., & Beattie, R. (2008). The emergent 'coaching industry': A wake-up call for HRD professionals. *Human Resource Development International, 11*(3), 287–305.
5. Gormley, H., & Van Nieuwerburgh, C. (2014). Developing coaching cultures: A review of the literature. *Coaching: An International Journal of Theory, Research and Practice, 7*(2), 90–101.
6. Hardingham, A., et al. (2004). *The coach's coach: Personal development for personal developers* (Vol. 37). Emerald Group Publishing Limited.
7. Hart, W. (2005). Getting culture: Imbuing your organization with coaching behavior. *Leadership in Action, 25*(4), 7–10.
8. Megginson, D., & Clutterbuck, D. (2006). Creating a coaching culture. *Industrial and Commercial Training, 38*(5), 232–237.
9. Hawkins, P. (2012). Creating a coaching culture. *Strategic HR Review, 11*(6), 364.
10. Clutterbuck, D., & Megginson, D. (2005). *Making coaching work: Creating a coaching culture*. Chartered Institute of Personnel and Development.
11. Clutterbuck, D., Megginson, D., & Bajer, A. (2016). *Building and sustaining a coaching culture*. Chartered Institute of Personnel and Development.
12. Lindbom, D. (2007). A culture of coaching: The challenge of managing performance for long-term results. *Organisation Development Journal, 25*(2), 101.
13. Boyce, A., et al. (2015). Which comes first, organizational culture or performance? A longitudinal study of causal priority with automobile dealerships. *Journal of Organizational Behavior, 36*(3), 339–359.
14. Kegan, R., et al. (2014). *The deliberately developmental organisation*. Extended Whitepaper. Way to Grow Inc, LLC.
15. Ellinger, A. D., & Kim, S. (2014). Coaching and Human Resource Development: Examining relevant theories, coaching genres, and scales to advance research and practice. *Advances in Developing Human Resources, 16*(2), 127–138.
16. Theeboom, T., Beersma, B., & van Vianen, A. (2014). Does coaching work? A meta-analysis on the effects of coaching on individual level outcomes in an organizational context. *The Journal of Positive Psychology, 9*(1), 1–18.
17. Athanasopoulou, A., & Dopson, S. (2018). A systematic review of executive coaching outcomes: Is it the journey or the destination that matters the most? *The Leadership Quarterly, 29*(1), 70–88.
18. Klopper, S., & van Coller-Peter, S. (2018). Business coaching processes that facilitate the successful implementation of business improvement projects. *International Journal of Evidence Based Coaching and Mentoring, 16*(2), 20–31.
19. Parker, P., Hall, D., & Kram, K. (2008). Peer coaching: A relational process for accelerating career learning. *Academy of Management Learning & Education, 7*(4), 487–503.
20. Stern, L. (2004). Executive coaching: A working definition. *Consulting Psychology Journal: Practice and Research, 56*(3), 154–162.
21. Hannafey, F., & Vitulano, L. (2013). Ethics and executive coaching: An agency theory approach. *Journal of Business Ethics, 115*(3), 599–603.
22. Baron, L., Morin, L., & Morin, D. (2011). Executive coaching: The effect of working alliance discrepancy on the development of coachees' self-efficacy. *Journal of Management Development, 30*(9), 847–864.
23. Kets de Vries, M. (2014). Dream journeys: A new territory for executive coaching. *Consulting Psychology Journal: Practice and Research, 66*(2), 77–92.
24. Joo, B.-K., Sushko, J., & McLean, G. (2012). Multiple faces of coaching: Manager-as-coach, executive coaching, and formal mentoring. *Organization Development Journal, 30*(1), 19.
25. Feldman, D., & Lankau, M. (2005). Executive coaching: A review and agenda for future research. *Journal of Management, 31*(6), 829–848.
26. Luthans, F., & Peterson, S. (2003). 360-degree feedback with systematic coaching: Empirical analysis suggests a winning combination. *Human Resource Management, 42*(3), 243–256.

27. Bickerich, K., Michel, A., & O'Shea, D. (2018). Executive coaching during organisational change: A qualitative study of executives and coaches perspectives. *Coaching: An International Journal of Theory, Research and Practice, 11*(2), 117–143.
28. Roberts, C. (2013). Building social capital through leadership development. *Journal of Leadership Education, 12*(1), 54–73.
29. MacKie, D. (2014). The effectiveness of strength-based executive coaching in enhancing full range leadership development: A controlled study. *Consulting Psychology Journal: Practice and Research, 66*(2), 118.
30. Moen, F., & Federici, R. (2012). The effect of external executive coaching and coaching-based leadership on need satisfaction. *Organisation Development Journal, 30*(3), 63–74.
31. Jha, S. (2014). Transformational leadership and psychological empowerment. *South Asian Journal of Global Business Research, 3*(1), 18–35.
32. Beattie, R., et al. (2014). Managerial coaching: A review of the empirical literature and development of a model to guide future practice. *Advances in Developing Human Resources, 16*(2), 184–201.
33. Boyatzis, R. (2011). Managerial and leadership competencies: A behavioral approach to emotional, social and cognitive intelligence. *Vision, 15*(2), 91–100.
34. Gunawan, J., & Aungsuroch, Y. (2017). Managerial competence of first-line nurse managers: A concept analysis. *International Journal of Nursing Practice, 23*(1), e12502.
35. Zacca, R., & Dayan, M. (2018). Linking managerial competence to small enterprise performance within the dynamic capability logic. *Journal of Small Business and Enterprise Development, 25*(2), 256–276.
36. Gilley, A., et al. (2010). The competencies used by effective managers to build teams: An empirical study. *Advances in Developing Human Resources, 12*(1), 29–45.
37. Cascio, W., & Boudreau, J. (2016). The search for global competence: From international HR to talent management. *Journal of World Business, 51*(1), 103–114.
38. Gilley, A., Gilley, J., & Kouider, E. (2010). Characteristics of managerial coaching. *Performance Improvement Quarterly, 23*(1), 53–70.
39. Bommelje, R. (2015). Managerial coaching. *New Directions for Adult and Continuing Education, 2015*(148), 69–77.
40. Matsuo, M. (2018). How does managerial coaching affect individual learning? The mediating roles of team and individual reflexivity. *Personnel Review, 47*(1), 118–132.
41. Ellinger, A. D., et al. (2011). Organizational investments in social capital, managerial coaching, and employee work-related performance. *Management Learning, 42*(1), 67–85.
42. Kunst, E., et al. (2018). Stability and change in teachers' goal orientation profiles over time: Managerial coaching behavior as a predictor of profile change. *Journal of Vocational Behavior, 104*, 115–127.
43. Batson, V., & Yoder, L. (2012). Managerial coaching: A concept analysis. *Journal of Advanced Nursing, 68*(7), 1658–1669.
44. Lee, M., Idris, M., & Tuckey, M. (2019). Supervisory coaching and performance feedback as mediators of the relationships between leadership styles, work engagement, and turnover intention. *Human Resource Development International, 22*(3), 257–282.
45. Park, S., Yang, B., & McLean, G. (2008). *An examination of relationships between managerial coaching and employee development*. In Academy of human resource development conference. ERIC Document Reproduction Service No. ED 501 641, Panama City, FL.
46. Chatterjee, A., Pereira, A., & Bates, R. (2018). Impact of individual perception of organizational culture on the learning transfer environment. *International Journal of Training & Development, 22*(1), 15–33.
47. Nicolaidou, M., Karagiorgi, Y., & Petridou, A. (2018). Professional learning through reflection promoted by feedback and coaching (PROFLEC) in Cyprus. *International Journal of Leadership in Education, 21*(4), 412–426.

48. Jayaweera, T. (2015). Impact of work environmental factors on job performance, mediating role of work motivation: A study of hotel sector in England. *International Journal of Business and Management, 10*(3), 271–278.
49. Kurland, H., & Hasson-Gilad, D. (2015). Organizational learning and extra effort: The mediating effect of job satisfaction. *Teaching and Teacher Education, 49*, 56–67.
50. Wise, D., & Cavazos, B. (2017). Leadership coaching for principals: A national study. *Mentoring & Tutoring: Partnership in Learning, 25*(2), 223–245.
51. Kotter, J. (2001). What leaders really do. *Harvard Business Review, 79*(11), 85.
52. Solaimani, S., Haghighi Talab, A., & van der Rhee, B. (2019). An integrative view on lean innovation management. *Journal of Business Research, 105*, 109–120.
53. Boyatzis, R. (1982). *The competent manager: A model for effective performance*. Wiley.
54. Higgins, M., Weiner, J., & Young, L. (2012). Implementation teams: A new lever for organizational change. *Journal of Organizational Behavior, 33*, 366–388.
55. Taylor, S., Passarelli, A., & Van Oosten, E. (2019). Leadership coach effectiveness as fostering self-determined, sustained change. *The Leadership Quarterly, 30*, 1013.
56. Hui, R., & Sue-Chan, C. (2018). Variations in coaching style and their impact on subordinates' work outcomes. *Journal of Organizational Behavior, 39*(5), 663–679.
57. Yip, J., et al. (2020). Coaching new leaders: A relational process of integrating multiple identities. *Academy of Management Learning & Education, 19*(4), 503–520.
58. Britton, J. (2015). Expanding the coaching conversation: Group and team coaching. *Industrial and Commercial Training, 47*(3), 116–120.
59. Wotruba, S. (2016). Leadership team coaching; A trust-based coaching relationship. *International Journal of Evidence Based Coaching and Mentoring, 10*, 98–109.
60. Shuffler, M., et al. (2018). Developing, sustaining, and maximizing team effectiveness: An integrative, dynamic perspective of team development interventions. *Academy of Management Annals, 12*(2), 688–724.
61. Thornton, C. (2010). *Group and team coaching*. Routledge.
62. Hackman, J., & Wageman, R. (2005). A theory of team coaching. *The Academy of Management Review, 30*(2), 269–287.
63. Peters, J., & Carr, C. (2013). Team effectiveness and team coaching literature review. *Coaching: An International Journal of Theory, Research and Practice, 6*(2), 116–136.
64. Zeus, P., & Skiffington, S. (2002). *The coaching at work toolkit: A complete guide to techniques and practices*. McGraw-Hill.
65. Clutterbuck, D. (2007). *Coaching the team at work*. Nicholas Brealey Publishing.
66. Akella, D. (2010). Learning together: Kolb's experiential theory and its application. *Journal of Management and Organization, 16*(1), 100–112.
67. Batista-Foguet, J., et al. (2015). An alternative approach to analyze ipsative data: Revisiting experiential learning theory. *Frontiers in Psychology, 6*, 1742.
68. Johnson, S., et al. (2017). Promoting student–teacher interactions: Exploring a peer coaching model for teachers in a preschool setting. *Early Childhood Education Journal, 45*(4), 461–470.
69. Hagen, M., Bialek, T., & Peterson, S. (2017). The nature of peer coaching: Definitions, goals, processes and outcomes. *European Journal of Training and Development, 41*(6), 540–558.
70. Parker, P., et al. (2015). A relational communication approach to peer coaching. *The Journal of Applied Behavioral Science, 51*(2), 231–252.
71. Charteris, J., & Smardon, D. (2014). Dialogic peer coaching as teacher leadership for professional inquiry. *International Journal of Mentoring and Coaching in Education, 3*(2), 108.
72. McQuiston, L., & Hanna, K. (2015). Peer coaching. *Nurse Educator, 40*(2), 105–108.
73. Parker, P., Kram, K., & Hall, D. (2014). Peer coaching: An untapped resource for development. *Organizational Dynamics, 43*(2), 122–129.
74. Murray, S., Ma, X., & Mazur, J. (2009). Effects of peer coaching on teachers' collaborative interactions and students' mathematics achievement. *The Journal of Educational Research, 102*(3), 203–212.

75. Lawrence, P., & Whyte, A. (2014). Return on investment in executive coaching: A practical model for measuring ROI in organisations. *Coaching: An International Journal of Theory, Research and Practice, 7*(1), 4–17.
76. Phillips, J. (2007). Measuring the ROI of a coaching intervention, Part 2. *Performance Improvement, 46*(10), 10–23.
77. Jenkins, J. (2018). *Developing a coaching culture pilot measure* (p. 145). Adler School of Professional Psychology.
78. Sue-Chan, C., Wood, R., & Latham, G. (2012). Effect of a coach's regulatory focus and an individual's implicit person theory on individual performance. *Journal of Management, 38*(3), 809–835.
79. Ellinger, A. D. (2013). Supportive supervisors and managerial coaching: Exploring their intersections. *Journal of Occupational & Organizational Psychology, 86*(3), 310–316.
80. Holten, A., Bøllingtoft, A., & Wilms, I. (2015). Leadership in a changing world: Developing managers through a teaching and learning programme. *Management Decision, 53*(5), 1107–1124.
81. Ladyshewsky, R., & Taplin, R. (2018). The interplay between organisational learning culture, the manager as coach, self-efficacy and workload on employee work engagement. *International Journal of Evidence Based Coaching & Mentoring, 16*, 3–19.
82. McComb, C. (2012). Developing coaching culture: Are your coaching relationships healthy? *Industrial and Commercial Training, 44*(4), 232–235.
83. McComb, C. (2012). Developing coaching culture: Are your managers good coachees? *Industrial and Commercial Training, 44*(6), 345–348.
84. McComb, C. (2012). Developing coaching culture: Are your managers motivated coaches? (Part 1). *Industrial and Commercial Training, 44*(2), 90–93.
85. Grant, A. (2004). Executive, workplace and life coaching: Findings from a large-scale survey of International Coach Federation members. *International Journal of Evidence Based Coaching and Mentoring, 2*(2), 1–5.
86. Grant, A. (2017). Reflections on quagmires for clinicians and coaches: Comment on Gebhardt (2016). *American Psychologist, 72*(2), 180–181.
87. Whyte, A. (2010). *Standards Australia guidelines for coaching in organizations*. Standards Australia.
88. Anderson, M., Frankovelgia, C., & Hernez-Broome, G. (2009). Business leaders reflect on coaching cultures. *Leadership in Action, 28*(6), 20–22.
89. Jamison, J. (2018). The importance of front-line supervisor coaching ability and performance to employment decisions and coaching culture success. In *School of business and technology* (p. 172). Capella University.
90. Seah, M., Hsieh, M.-H., & Huang, H.-Y. (2014). Leader driven organizational adaptation. *Management Decision, 52*(8), 1410–1432.
91. O'Broin, A., & McDowall, A. (2014). Coaching – psychological concepts and coaching cultures. *Coaching: An International Journal of Theory, Research and Practice, 7*(2), 87–89.
92. Rahim, N., Mansor, N., & Anvari, R. (2014). Driving the Involvement of line managers' role in creating coaching culture in Malaysia. *Procedia – Social and Behavioral Sciences, 129*, 221–226.
93. Abington, A. (2013). Croydon health services NHS Trust creates an internal-coaching culture: New skills promote organizational change and performance. *Human Resource Management International Digest, 21*(4), 6–11.
94. Castillo-Ramsey, C. (2011). *Coaching from the inside out: Exploring internal coaching practices in organizations* (p. 153). Alliant International University.
95. Cox, E., Bachkirova, T., & Clutterbuck, D. (2014). *The complete handbook of coaching* (2nd ed.). SAGE.
96. Brant, J., Dooley, R., & Iman, S. (2008). Leadership succession: An approach to filling the pipeline. *Strategic HR Review, 7*(4), 17–24.

97. Kim, S., & McLean, G. (2012). Global talent management: Necessity, challenges, and the roles of HRD. *Advances in Developing Human Resources, 14*(4), 566–585.
98. Anderson, D., & Anderson, M. (2005). *Coaching that counts: Harnessing the power of leadership coaching to deliver strategic value*. Elsevier/Butterworth-Heinemann.
99. Carasco-Saul, M., Kim, W., & Kim, T. (2015). Leadership and employee engagement: Proposing research agendas through a review of literature. *Human Resource Development Review, 14*(1), 38–63.
100. Crabb, S. (2011). The use of coaching principles to foster employee engagement. *The Coaching Psychologist, 7*(1), 27.
101. Sparrow, P., et al. (2013). Employee engagement in theory and practice. *The International Journal of Human Resource Management, 24*(9), 1777–1798.
102. Lopes, S., et al. (2015). A new approach to talent management in law firms: Integrating performance appraisal and assessment center data. *International Journal of Productivity and Performance Management, 64*(4), 523–543.
103. Mensah, J. (2015). A "coalesced framework" of talent management and employee performance: For further research and practice. *International Journal of Productivity and Performance Management, 64*(4), 544–566.
104. Sparrow, P., & Makram, H. (2015). What is the value of talent management? Building value-driven processes within a talent management architecture. *Human Resource Management Review, 25*(3), 249–263.
105. Meyers, M., van Woerkom, M., & Dries, N. (2013). Talent – Innate or acquired? Theoretical considerations and their implications for talent management. *Human Resource Management Review, 23*(4), 305–321.
106. Gillen, J. (2018). How to attract and retain talent. *Northeast Pennsylvania Business Journal, 33*(10), 23.
107. Bolli, T., & Somogyi, F. (2011). Do competitively acquired funds induce universities to increase productivity? *Research Policy, 40*(1), 136–147.
108. Anderson, M. (2002). *Executive briefing: Case study on the return on investment of executive coaching*. MetrixGlobal LLC.
109. Walker-Fraser, A. (2011). Coaching and the link to organizational performance: An HR perspective on how to demonstrate return on investment. *Development and Learning in Organizations: An International Journal, 25*(4), 8–10.
110. McGovern, J., et al. (2001). Maximizing the impact of executive coaching: Behavioral change, organizational outcomes, and return on investment. *Manchester Review, 6*(1), 3–11.
111. Atkinson, P. (2012). Return on investment in executive coaching: Effective organisational change. *Management Services, 56*(1), 20–23.
112. Anderson, M., Anderson, D., & Mayo, W. (2008). Team coaching helps a leadership team drive cultural change at Caterpillar. *Global Business and Organizational Excellence, 27*(4), 40–50.
113. Lawrence, P. (2015). Building a coaching culture in a small Australian multinational organisation. *Coaching: An International Journal of Theory, Research and Practice, 8*(1), 53–60.
114. Rogers, S., & Hargadon, J. (2018). Coaching for performance: The art of coaching distant professionals. *Journal of Practical Consulting, 6*(1), 108–114.
115. ICF. (2015). *Building a coaching culture for increased employee engagement*. In Report of the survey conducted on behalf of the International Coach Federation.
116. Dweck, C. (2012). Mindsets and human nature: Promoting change in the Middle East, the schoolyard, the racial divide, and willpower. *American Psychologist, 67*(8), 614–622.
117. Dweck, C. (2014). Teachers' mindsets: "Every student has something to teach me". *Educational Horizons, 93*(2), 10–15.
118. Dweck, C., Chiu, C., & Hong, Y. (1995). Implicit theories: Elaboration and extension of the model. *Psychological Inquiry, 6*(4), 322–333.

119. Molden, D., & Dweck, C. (2006). Finding "meaning" in psychology: A lay theories approach to self-regulation, social perception, and social development. *American Psychologist, 61*(3), 192–203.
120. Kam, C., et al. (2014). Do subordinates formulate an impression of their manager's implicit person theory? *Applied Psychology, 63*(2), 267–299.
121. Heslin, P., & VandeWalle, D. (2011). Performance appraisal procedural justice: The role of a manager's implicit person theory. *Journal of Management, 37*(6), 1694–1718.
122. Bandura, A. (1977). Self-efficacy: Toward a unifying theory of behavioral change. *Psychological Review, 84*, 191–215.
123. Latham, G., & Pinder, C. (2005). Work motivation theory and research at the dawn of the twenty-first century. *Annual Review of Psychology, 56*, 485–516.
124. Wilson, W. (2013). Coaching with a global mindset. *International Journal of Evidence Based Coaching & Mentoring, 11*(2), 33–52.
125. Kolb, D. (1984). *Experiential learning experience as a source of learning and development*. Prentice Hall.
126. Kolb, A., et al. (2014). On becoming an experiential educator: The educator role profile. *Simulation & Gaming, 45*(2), 204–234.
127. Knowles, M. (1980). *The modern practice of adult education: From pedagogy to andragogy* (2nd ed.). Cambride Books.
128. Knowles, M. (Ed.). (2004). *The adult learner: A neglected species* (3rd ed.). Gulf.
129. Grant, A., et al. (2013). *Handbook of the psychology of coaching and mentoring*. Wiley.
130. Skinner, B. (1938). *The behaviour of organisms: An experimental analysis*. Appleton-Century.
131. Locke, E., & Latham, G. (2002). Building a practically useful theory of goal setting and task motivation: A 35-year odyssey. *American Psychologist, 57*(9), 705–717.
132. Neenan, M. (2008). From cognitive behaviour therapy (CBT) to cognitive behaviour coaching (CBC). *Journal of Rational-Emotive & Cognitive-Behavior Therapy, 26*(1), 3–15.
133. Grant, A., et al. (2012). Development and validation of the solution-focused inventory. *The Journal of Positive Psychology, 7*(4), 334–348.
134. Nagel, R. (2008). Coaching with a solutions focus – focusing on the solution not the problem. *Development and Learning in Organizations: An International Journal, 22*(4), 11–14.
135. Wakefield, M. (2006). New views on leadership coaching. *The Journal for Quality and Participation, 29*(2), 9–12.
136. Ives, Y., & Cox, E. (2012). *Goal-focused Coaching: Theory and practice*. Routledge.
137. O'Connell, B., Palmer, S., & Williams, H. (2013). *Solution-focused Coaching in Practice*. Taylor and Francis.
138. Roeden, J., Maaskant, M., & Curfs, L. (2012). The Nominal Group Technique as an evaluation tool for solution-focused coaching. *Journal of Applied Research in Intellectual Disabilities, 25*(6), 588–593.
139. Beck, A. (1975). *Cognitive therapy and the emotional disorders*. International Universities Press.
140. Ellis, A. (1962). *Reason and emotion in psychotherapy*. L. Stuart.
141. Maslow, A. (1943). A theory of human motivation. *Psychological Review, 50*(4), 370–396.
142. Maslow, A. (1954). *Motivation and personality*. Harper and Row.
143. McClelland, D. (1951). The effects of motivation on behavior. In *Personality* (pp. 478–525). William Sloane Assoc.
144. Adler, A., Ansbacher, H., & Ansbacher, R. (1956). *The individual psychology of alfred adler: A systematic presentation in selections from his writings*. Basic Books.
145. Jung, C. (1921). *Personality theory*. Zurich.
146. Rogers, C. (1951). *Client-centred therapy: Its current practice, implications and theory*. Houghton Mifflin.
147 Csikszentmihalyi, M. (1990). *Flow: The psychology of optimal experience*. Harper & Row.
148 Seligman, M. (2011). *Authentic Happiness: Using the new positive psychology to realise your potential for lasting fulfilment*. Nicholas Brealey Publishing.

149. Bandura, A., Davidson, H., & Davidson, J. (2003). *Bandura's social cognitive theory: An introduction*. Davidson Films, Inc.
150. Bandura, A. (1977). *Social learning theory*. Prentice Hall.
151. Bandura, A. (2006). Toward a psychology of human agency. *Perspectives on Psychological Science, 1*, 164–180.
152. Bandura, A., & Locke, E. (2003). Negative self-efficacy and goal effects revisited. *Journal of Applied Psychology, 88*(1), 87–99.
153. Allard-Poesi, F. (1998). Representations and influence processes in groups: Towards a socio-cognitive perspective on cognition in organisation. *Scandinavian Journal of Management, 14*(4), 395–420.
154. Dweck, C., & Leggett, E. (1988). A social-cognitive approach to motivation and personality. *Psychological Review, 95*(2), 256–273.
155. Johan, S. (1997). How institutions learn: A socio-cognitive perspective. *Journal of Economic Issues, 31*(3), 729–740.
156. Mizokawa, A., & Koyasu, M. (2015). Digging deeper into the link between socio-cognitive ability and social relationships. *British Journal of Developmental Psychology, 33*(1), 21–23.
157. Goleman, D. (1995). *Emotional Intelligence: Why it can matter more than IQ*. Bantam Books.
158. Goleman, D., & Cherniss, C. (2001). *The Emotionally Intelligent Workplace: How to select for, measure, and improve emotional intelligence in individuals, groups, and organizations*. Jossey-Bass.
159. Bright, D., & Crockett, A. (2012). Training combined with coaching can make a significant difference in job performance and satisfaction. *Coaching: An International Journal of Theory, Research and Practice, 5*(1), 4–21.
160. Britton, J. (2008). Increasing job satisfaction: Coaching with evidence-based interventions. *Coaching: An International Journal of Theory, Research and Practice, 1*(2), 176–185.
161. Kim, S. (2014). Assessing the influence of managerial coaching on employee outcomes. *Human Resource Development Quarterly, 25*(1), 59–85.
162. Latham, G. (2007). Theory and research on coaching practices. *Australian Psychologist, 42*(4), 268–270.
163. Kim, S., et al. (2013). The impact of managerial coaching behavior on employee work-related reactions. *Journal of Business and Psychology, 28*(3), 315–330.
164. Ryan, J. (2014). The work motivation of research scientists and its effect on research performance. *R&D Management, 44*(4), 355–369.
165. Tse, H., & Dasborough, M. (2008). A study of exchange and emotions in team member relationships. *Group & Organization Management, 33*(2), 194–215.
166. Maltarich, M., Greenwald, J., & Reilly, G. (2015). Team-level goal orientation: An emergent state and its relationships with team inputs, process, and outcomes. *European Journal of Work and Organizational Psychology, 37*, 1–21.
167. Van Woerkom, M., & Croon, M. (2009). The relationships between team learning activities and team performance. *Personnel Review, 38*(5), 560–577.
168. Schein, E. (1990). Organizational culture. *American Psychologist, 45*(2), 109–119.
169. Schein, E. (1985). *Organizational culture and leadership: A dynamic view*. Jossey-Bass.
170. Lounsbury, M., & Glynn, M. (2001). Cultural entrepreneurship: Stories, legitimacy, and the acquisition of resources. *Strategic Management Journal, 22*(6), 545.
171. McPherson, C., & Sauder, M. (2013). Logics in action: Managing institutional complexity in a drug court. *Administrative Science Quarterly, 58*(2), 165–196.
172. Weber, K. (2005). A toolkit for analyzing corporate cultural toolkits. *Poetics, 33*(3), 227–252.
173. Giorgi, S., Lockwood, C., & Glynn, M. (2015). The many faces of culture: Making sense of 30 years of research on culture in organization studies. *The Academy of Management Annals, 9*(1), 1–54.
174. Hannerz, U. (1969). *Soulside: Inquiries into ghetto culture and community*. Columbia University Press.

175. Swidler, A. (1986). Culture in action: Symbols and strategies. *American Sociological Review, 51*(2), 273–286.
176. Small, M., Harding, D., & Lamont, M. (2010). Reconsidering culture and poverty. *Annals of the American Academy of Political and Social Science, 629*(6), 27.
177. Lamont, M., & Thévenot, L. (2001). Rethinking comparative cultural sociology: Repertoires of evaluation in France and the United States. *American Journal of Sociology, 107*(2), 529–531.
178. Bourdieu, P. (1990). *The logic of practice*. Stanford University Press.
179. Swidler, A., et al. (2001). *The practice turn in contemporary theory*. Routledge.
180. ICF. (2015). *Definition of coaching*. International Coaching Federation.
181. Swidler, A. (2001). *Talk of love: How culture matters*. University of Chicago Press.
182. Lamont, M. (2000). *The rhetoric of racism and anti-racism in France and the United States*. University Press and Presses de la Maison des Sciences de l'Homme.
183. Molinsky, A. (2013). The psychological processes of cultural retooling. *Academy of Management Journal, 56*(3), 683.
184. Maurer, C. C., Bansal, P., & Crossan, M. M. (2011). Creating economic value through social values: Introducing a culturally informed resource-based view. *Organization Science, 22*(2), 432.
185. Seidel, V. P., & O'Mahony, S. (2014). Managing the repertoire: Stories, metaphors, prototypes, and concept coherence in product innovation. *Organization Science, 25*(3), 691.
186. Weber, K., Heinze, K. L., & DeSoucey, M. (2008). Forage for thought: Mobilizing codes in the movement for grass-fed meat and dairy products. *Administrative Science Quarterly, 53*(3), 529–567.
187. Dutton, J. E., et al. (2006). Explaining compassion organizing. *Administrative Science Quarterly, 51*(1), 59.
188. Zald, M., et al. (2005). *Social movements and organization theory* (pp. 253–279). Cambridge University Press.
189. Davis, G. (2005). *Social movements and organization theory*. Cambridge University Press.
190. Meyerson, D. (2009). Tempered radicals: How everyday leaders inspire change at work. *Equal Opportunities International, 28*, 536–537.
191. Morrill, C., Zald, M., & Rao, H. (2003). Covert political conflict in organizations: Challenges from below. *Annual Review of Sociology, 29*(1), 391.
192. Scully, M., & Segal, A. (2002). Passion with an umbrella: Grassroots activists in the workplace. *Research in the Sociology of Organizations, 19*, 125.
193. Evered, R., & Selman, J. (1989). Coaching and the art of management. *Organizational Dynamics, 18*(2), 16.
194. Olivero, G., Bane, K., & Kopelman, R. (1997). Executive coaching as a transfer of training tool: Effects on productivity in a public agency. *Public Personnel Management, 26*, 461–470.
195. de Haan, E., et al. (2016). A large-scale study of executive coaching outcome: The relative contributions of relationship, personality match, and self-efficacy. *Consulting Psychology Journal: Practice and Research, 68*(3), 189–207.
196. Kilburg, R. (1996). Toward a conceptual understanding and definition of executive coaching. *Consulting Psychology Journal: Practice and Research, 48*(2), 134–144.
197. Bozer, G., Joo, B., & Santora, J. (2015). Executive coaching: Does coach-coachee matching based on similarity really matter? *Consulting Psychology Journal: Practice and Research, 67*(3), 218–233.
198. Trathen, S. (2011). Executive coaching: Implications for developing leaders in the Middle East and Africa. *Career Planning and Adult Development Journal, 27*(1), 138–154.
199. de Haan, E., et al. (2013). Executive coaching outcome research: The contribution of common factors such as relationship, personality match, and self efficacy. *Consulting Psychology Journal, 65*(1), 40–57.

200. Grant, A., Curtayne, L., & Burton, G. (2009). Executive coaching enhances goal attainment, resilience and workplace well-being: A randomised controlled study. *The Journal of Positive Psychology, 4*(5), 396.
201. Gray, D. (2006). Executive coaching: Towards a dynamic alliance of psychotherapy and transformative learning processes. *Management Learning, 37*(4), 475–497.
202. Grant, A. (2012). ROI is a poor measure of coaching success: Towards a more holistic approach using a well-being and engagement framework. *Coaching: An International Journal of Theory, Research and Practice, 5*(2), 74–85.
203. Schlosser, B., et al. (2006). The coaching impact study: Measuring the value of executive leader coaching. *International Journal of Coaching in Organizations, 4*(3), 8–26.
204. Young, K., & Mack, R. (1959). *Sociology and social life* (p. 472). American Book Co.
205. Geertz, C. (1973). Thick description: Toward an interpretive theory of culture. In C. Geertz (Ed.), *The interpretation of cultures* (pp. 3–30). Basic Books.
206. Jenks, C. (2005). *Subculture: The fragmentation of the social*. SAGE.
207. Schneider, B., White, S., & Paul, M. (1998). Linking service climate and customer perceptions of service quality: Tests of a causal model. *Journal of Applied Psychology, 83*(2), 150–163.
208. Schneider, B., et al. (2017). Organizational climate and culture: Reflections on the history of the constructs in the Journal of Applied Psychology. *Journal of Applied Psychology, 102*(3), 468–482.
209. Schouten, J., & McAlexander, J. (1995). Subcultures of consumption: An ethnography of the new bikers. *Journal of Consumer Research, 22*(1), 43–61.
210. Agency, I. A. E. (1991). *Safety culture series*. In Safety Series No. 75-INSAG-3.
211. Beitelspacher, L., Richey, R., & Reynolds, K. (2011). Exploring a new perspective on service efficiency: Service culture in retail organizations. *The Journal of Services Marketing, 25*(3), 215–228.
212. Ridnour, R., Lassk, F., & Shepherd, C. (2001). An exploratory assessment of sales culture variables: Strategic implications within the banking industry. *Journal of Personal Selling & Sales Management, 21*(3), 247–254.
213. Clarke, S. (1999). Perceptions of organizational safety: Implications for the development of safety culture. *Journal of Organizational Behavior, 20*(2), 185–198.
214. Parker, D., Lawrie, M., & Hudson, P. (2006). A framework for understanding the development of organisational safety culture. *Safety Science, 44*(6), 551–562.
215. Antonsen, S. (2009). *Safety culture theory, method and improvement*. Ashgate Publishing Ltd..
216. Caldwell, C. (2018). *Safety culture and high-risk environments: A leadership perspective*. Ebscohost, CRC Press, Taylor & Francis Group.
217. Smircich, L. (1983). Concepts of culture and organizational analysis. *Administrative Science Quarterly, 28*, 339–358.
218. Alvesson, M. (2002). *Understanding organizational culture*. Sage.
219. Passmore, J., & Jastrzebska, K. (2011). Building a coaching culture: A development journey for organizational development. *Coaching Review, 1*(3), 89–101.

Chapter 3
Process Model of Coaching Culture Development

Coaching of organisational leaders, managers and employees has grown in popularity over several decades. During this time, researchers have demonstrated the effectiveness of coaching as a valid organisational practice to improve performance, foster employee engagement and promote wellbeing. Subsequently, leaders and practitioners proposed that the benefits of individual coaching could be more widely applied to developing a coaching culture within an organisation to increase team effectiveness and productivity, and contribute to competitive advantage and sustainability. In this chapter, the extant individual and organisational approaches to developing a coaching culture are detailed and arguments provided for why these approaches are insufficient to guide organisational leaders and practitioners in their attempts to implement transformational cultural change through coaching. With extensive practitioner interest yet little empirical, academic evidence of how to achieve cultural change through coaching, my research study investigated the question: *How do organisations develop a coaching culture?* A theoretical model of coaching culture development over four stages was derived from the research findings, and the strategies that promote and hinder progression across stages identified. The model not only guides successful implementation of a coaching culture but also contributes to the emergence of coaching as a discipline in its own right.

Extant Models of Coaching

Extant models of coaching are either individually or organisationally oriented. Only two individually oriented models were found in the academic literature: (1) the earliest conversational GROW model [1] and, (2) a more recent, generic process model based on a cycle of self-regulation [2]. In addition, a study that illustrates a specific outcome of coaching known as the "ripple effect" [3] informs our understanding of how these models may transition to an organisational orientation.

S. Knowles, *Coaching Culture*, https://doi.org/10.1007/978-3-031-09050-9_3

The first GROW model of coaching [1, 4] delineates a sequence of four discrete steps in the coaching process: (i) identification of the coachee's short- and long-term goals; (ii) reality checking to explore the current situation; (iii) exploring options, alternative strategies, and actions; and (iv) wrapping up the sessions with what needs to be done, by whom, and when. Choice and self-motivation are critical to success. This process facilitates individual coaching and can even be used for self-coaching.

The second model utilises self-reflection and self-review during coaching to develop self-awareness and insight, leading to goal-centred behaviour and actions [2]. Coachees cycle through awareness, responsibility, commitment, action, and results. According to this model, the basis for effective coaching is the successful formation of a collaborative working relationship based on mutual respect. The coach guides the coachee towards increased awareness of the issue and helps them accept their responsibility for change. An outcome or goal which is explicitly linked to the coachee's needs and situation is collaboratively established. The coach then motivates the coachee to take action and be committed to achieving the desired result. A trusting, meaningful relationship expands the coachee's development, performance or skill set, pacing the process according to the coachee's ability and readiness to change, and considering the coach's personal ability to deal with any potentially emotive issues that may arise during the coaching session.

Extant Models of Coaching Culture Development

There are no models of coaching culture development in the extant academic literature. However, from their practitioner experience, a number of researchers have listed the stages/steps and strategies by which a coaching culture may be developed to stimulate systemic, cultural change. Research has been concerned with the stages organisations go through as they progress towards achieving a coaching culture and the strategies leaders use to enact that progression. However little, if any, attention has been given to the theoretical dimensions that underlie the development of a model of coaching culture development and the dynamic process mechanisms by which a coaching culture progresses or may regress under changed circumstances, which emerged from my research findings.

Within the management literature, researchers have identified a number of stages or steps to develop a coaching culture [5–7]. These organisationally-oriented approaches have been derived from consideration of the systemic factors that influence organisational culture and are outlined below.

First, Clutterbuck and Megginson [7] proposed four stages in the development of a coaching culture, namely:

1. Nascent: The organisation shows little or no commitment to creating a coaching culture. Coaching activity is occasional and uncoordinated.

2. Tactical: The organisation recognises the value of establishing a coaching culture but there is little understanding of what it means.
3. Strategic: The organisation invests resources into educating staff about the value of coaching as well as training, and top management accepts the need to demonstrate good practice.
4. Embedded: People at all levels are engaged in coaching in such a way that the organisation can tackle difficult issues and focus on improvement.

Drawing from Schein's [8] work, these researchers [9] later depicted their approach to coaching culture development as a tree with the roots representing the unconscious beliefs, assumptions and mindsets that underpin the coaching philosophy, the trunk representing core principles reflecting the unwritten rules of *being* and *interacting,* and the leaves as visible manifestations of behaviours that result from the coaching as new skills or improved processes and systems are developed. The four stages are diagrammatically presented as four progressive illustrations of the growth of the tree from an early bud (nascent) to developing a trunk (tactical) to sprouting leaves (strategic) to becoming a fully grown tree (embedded).

Second, Hawkins [5] also drew from Schein's [8] model of culture to graphically depict five levels of culture as a tree whose roots represent the emotional ground and motivational roots on which organisations are founded. The third level is the trunk which represents the mindset of organisational members. The fourth, visible leaf, level is the pattern of behaviour enacted by organisational members, and the fifth level, organisational artefacts, is symbolic of the culture. Hawkins proposed seven steps to develop these five levels of a coaching culture, namely:

1. Developing a panel of external coaches.
2. Developing the internal coaching and mentoring capacity.
3. Organisational leaders actively support coaching endeavours and align them with cultural change.
4. Coaching moves beyond individual formal sessions to team coaching and organisational learning.
5. Coaching becomes embedded in the HR and performance management processes of the organisation.
6. Coaching becomes the predominant style for managing throughout the organisation.
7. Coaching becomes *how* an organisation does business with all its stakeholders.

Third, Passmore and Jastrzebska [6] proposed five stages in the development of a coaching culture, namely:

1. Informal external coaching.
2. Professional external coaching.
3. Coaching for all.
4. Coaching as a management style.
5. Coaching across the network.

The reason why these three approaches to developing a coaching culture were chosen for comparison with the model built from my research is that their underlying framework is consistent with the Schein [8, 10] culture framework of assumptions, values and artefacts which I adopted as the cultural foundation for my research study.

Deficiencies in Current Approaches

The established literature on, and these three approaches to, the development of a coaching culture reveal deficiencies in three significant areas: (1) they are prescriptive lists of stages, steps, levels or strategies which suggest a linear progression to a coaching culture; (2) the linear representation does not reflect the dynamic nature of how a coaching culture develops in a volatile, uncertain, complex and ambiguous environment [11]; and (3) the methodological basis for their research is not provided to validate the rigour and quality of the findings. Let me explain. First, whilst the extant lists of stages, steps, levels or strategies are intuitively logical, they prescribe static actions that leaders and organisations need to take to develop a coaching culture. A second, consistent deficiency is the complete lack of detail concerning the movement within and between stages, steps or levels to develop a coaching culture. Mention is not made of activities that might facilitate forward movement or may cause possible regression. The third notable deficiency in extant approaches is the lack of detail of the methodology in the research that led to the development of the stages, steps, levels or strategies. Inadequate detail does not allow the reader to identify from where the approach originated. Thus the findings in the extant literature are prescriptive and lack the academic rigour necessary to replicate the research or ensure the findings are trustworthy, authentic and credible. The lack of methodological detail points to the inadequacy of the approaches as *models* which provide the academic rigour required on which to base future research to test their veracity. These deficiencies compromise current understandings of what a coaching culture is or how to develop one, highlighting the need for a more dynamic and comprehensive process for theoretical clarity and practical application. They clearly indicate the need for a more rigorous model of coaching culture development to be derived from a sound methodological basis.

This need provided the impetus for my research study to develop a *model* of coaching culture development which acknowledges the dynamic nature of the organisational environment yet provides a structure, processes and strategies that CEOs and senior executives, organisational leaders and HR professionals can implement to bring about transformative cultural change.

A Theoretical Model of Coaching Culture Development

The methodology* used to investigate my research question "How do organisations develop a coaching culture?" was guided by a research paradigm of social constructionism which assumes a relativist ontology and subjectivist epistemology [12]. The research design was an inductive qualitative study that sought to build theory about the empirical phenomenon of coaching culture by interviewing two types of informants: (1) senior managers who were associated with a coaching agenda inside a single organisation, and (2) executive coaches who had experiences of delivering coaching to people employed across multiple organisations. The focus was on the way these informants, as "knowledgeable agents" [13], experienced the phenomenon of coaching and gave it meaning rather than on numbers, measurement, frequency of occurrences, and any other measures of coaching activity and organisational culture [13]. Data were primarily collected through semi-structured interviews and analysed iteratively and inductively to generate theoretical insights into the emergence, development, and transitions as organisations are enabled and constrained in progressing towards a coaching culture. * Details are available from the author.

The findings of my research study were captured in a multi-staged, process model which shows how an organisation develops a coaching culture, as depicted in Fig. 3.1. The model portrays a dynamic process of four stages which are analytically discrete for the purposes of theorisation although in practice the stages may overlap. Each stage is characterised by a distinct combination of conceptualisation, motivation, driver, and delivery.

The barriers that inhibit progression and the enabling factors that support forward movement were also identified in my research. As shown in Fig. 3.1, an organisation's progression from one stage to the next is facilitated by enablers depicted by curved arrows across the top of the figure. As organisations progress through these stages, they retain elements of the previous stages. Conversely, the boxes below the model portray how barriers may act to anchor the organisation at its current stage, halt its progression to later stages, and even detract the benefits that were previously available or embedded from coaching.

The model contributes to both theoretical and practical understandings of how a coaching culture is developed.

Theoretical Contributions of the Theoretical Model

Three key theoretical contributions to the coaching literature emerged from my research study. Principally, the model of coaching culture development derived from the research findings may be the first methodologically derived, empirically based, theoretical model reported in the coaching literature. The model is grounded in insights that deepen understandings of the processes by which coaching is

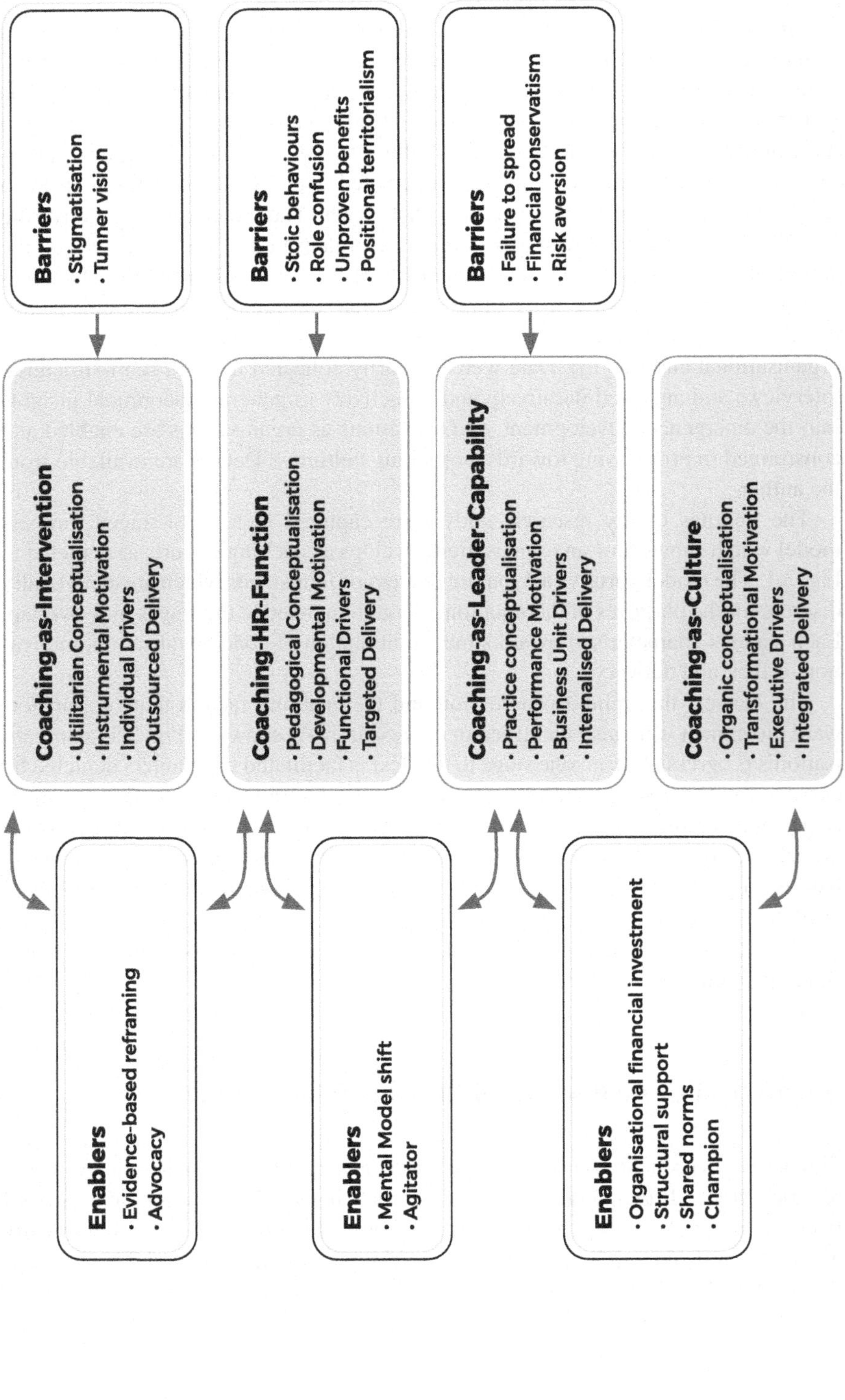

Fig. 3.1 Process model of coaching culture development

conducted inside organisations over time. It highlights the inter-connected and multi-dimensional, dynamic nature of coaching. The model goes further than existing approaches by identifying specific behaviours and processes that may inhibit the capability of an organisation to progress to the next stage of coaching culture development. Both barriers and enablers to progression across the four stages have been identified in the model.

Second, the theoretical process model that emerged from my research, as presented in Fig. 3.1, makes important advances on the process approaches that have been proposed by other researchers. The extant literature on coaching has tended to focus on the micro-processes and practices of coaching rather than on organisational and systemic-level factors that allow or inhibit coaching to be delivered within organisations [14]. With its four distinct stages, the model offers evidence of how the coaching activities conducted at each stage progressively transverse the individual-organisational divide. The first two stages of the model reflect individual-level coaching targets which are more comprehensive than the published individually-oriented approaches to coaching [2, 4] and show how coaching is used at the personal level for individual psychological or performance outcomes. The latter two stages address the gap between individual and organisational effects, as highlighted by research which not only considered the inter-personal effects of coaching but also explored the "ripple effect" on others in the organisation [3]. They provide a deeper understanding of how organisationally-oriented coaching cultures differ from individually-oriented coaching cultures. The four dimensions that characterise each stage evolve progressively over time as organisations move towards systemic and organic-level factors that underpin a coaching culture, giving deep insights into the essential shifts that have to happen *together* for a coaching culture to develop.

Third, my research findings may make an important contribution to the coaching literature by adding clarity to the definition of a coaching culture and expanding on the limited set of process approaches to coaching culture development that researchers have proposed. As reported in the previous chapter, there is no shared understanding or agreed definition of what constitutes a *coaching culture* [15]. The findings of the final, Stage 4, *Coaching-as-Culture*, of the model in Fig. 3.1 suggest that the definition of a coaching culture should include an organic conceptualisation of coaching, a transformational motivation for implementing coaching, and coaching initiatives being driven by executives throughout the organisation using integrated delivery mechanisms. Hence, from these research findings, the definition that I propose is this:

> A coaching culture is a way of being, relating, and transacting in which teams and team members transform through shared norms and social support structures, and executives integrate coaching delivery to motivate organisational members to increase productivity, outperform the competition, and achieve organisational, cultural change.

In summary, the model generated from my research goes further than existing approaches by identifying specific behaviours and processes that may inhibit the capability of an organisation to progress to the next stage of a coaching culture.

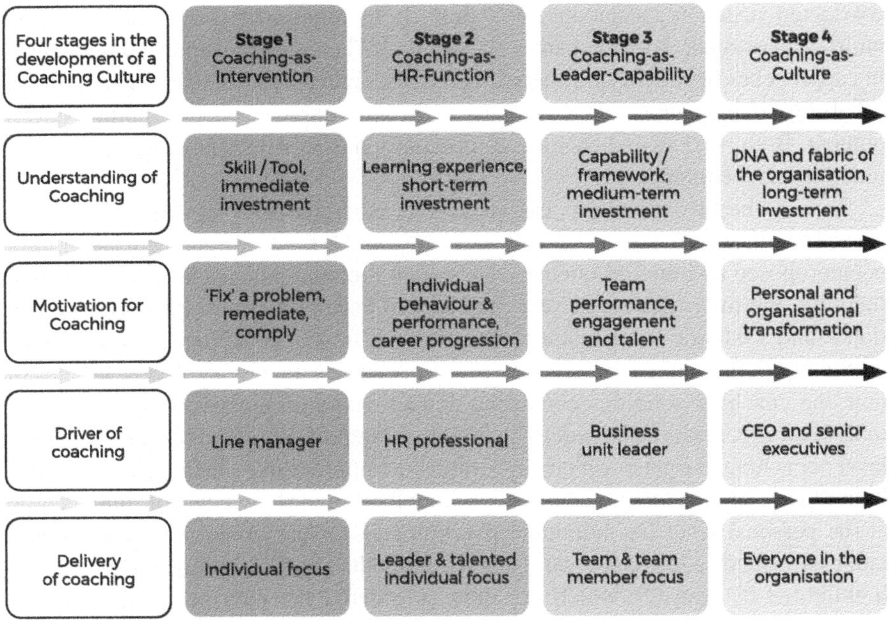

Fig. 3.2 Four stages in the development of a coaching culture

Barriers and enablers are particular to each stage. The barriers may indicate pre-work that is necessary for organisations to address to ensure that the required foundations are in place for progression to occur. The enablers in the model represent pre-conditions that are necessary to progress to the next stage.

Stages Identified in the Theoretical Model of Coaching Culture Development

My research study revealed four stages in the development of a coaching culture: *Coaching-as-Intervention*, *Coaching-as-HR-Function*, *Coaching-as-Leader-Capability*, and *Coaching-as-Culture*. Each stage is characterised by the understanding that organisational leaders have of coaching, their motivation for coaching, the key drivers of coaching, and how coaching is delivered throughout the organisation (see Fig. 3.2). Each of these stages and the four characterisations is explained in Chaps. 4–7 that follow.

***

This chapter has provided details of my research study and revealed the model of coaching culture development that resulted from the findings. The next chapter explains the four key dimensions of Stage 1 – *Coaching-as-Intervention.* The following three chapters address Stages 2, 3 and 4.

References

1. Whitmore, J. (2002). *Coaching for performance: GROWing people, performance and purpose* (3rd ed.). Nicholas Brealey Publishing.
2. Stober, D., & Grant, A. (2006). *Evidence based coaching handbook: Putting best practices to work for your clients*. Wiley.
3. O'Connor, S., & Cavanagh, M. (2013). The coaching ripple effect: The effects of developmental coaching on wellbeing across organisational networks. *Psychology of Well-Being: Theory, Research and Practice, 3*(2), 1–23.
4. Whitmore, J. (2017). *Coaching for performance: The principles and practice of coaching and leadership* (5th ed.). Nicholas Brealey Publishing.
5. Hawkins, P. (2012). Creating a coaching culture. *Strategic HR Review, 11*(6), 364.
6. Passmore, J., & Jastrzebska, K. (2011). Building a coaching culture: A development journey for organizational development. *Coaching Review, 1*(3), 89–101.
7. Clutterbuck, D., & Megginson, D. (2005). *Making coaching work: Creating a coaching culture*. Chartered Institute of Personnel and Development.
8. Schein, E. (1985). *Organizational culture and leadership: A dynamic view*. Jossey-Bass.
9. Clutterbuck, D., Megginson, D., & Bajer, A. (2016). *Building and sustaining a coaching culture*. Chartered Institute of Personnel and Development.
10. Schein, E. (1990). Organizational culture. *American Psychologist, 45*(2), 109–119.
11. Rodriguez, A., & Rodriguez, Y. (2015). Metaphors for today's leadership: VUCA world, millennial and "cloud leaders". *Journal of Management Development, 34*(7), 854–866.
12. Lincoln, Y., & Guba, E. (2000). Paradigmatic controversies, contradictions, and emerging confluences. In N. Denzin & Y. Lincoln (Eds.), *Handbook of qualitative research* (2nd ed.). Sage.
13. Gioia, D., Corley, K., & Hamilton, A. (2013). Seeking qualitative rigor in inductive research: Notes on the Gioia methodology. *Organizational Research Methods, 16*(1), 15–31.
14. Western, S. (2016). The key discourses of coaching. In T. Bachkirova, G. Spence, & D. Drake (Eds.), *The SAGE handbook of coaching* (pp. 42–61). SAGE Publications Ltd.
15. Gormley, H., & Van Nieuwerburgh, C. (2014). Developing coaching cultures: A review of the literature. *Coaching: An International Journal of Theory, Research and Practice, 7*(2), 90–101.

Chapter 4
Stage 1: Coaching-as-Intervention

This chapter addresses the first of four stages in the development of a coaching culture as depicted in the model of coaching culture development (Fig. 3.1). During this stage, line managers arrange for individuals who are behaving inappropriately or not performing to role expectations to be coached. This first stage is characterised by a *utilitarian conceptualisation* of coaching as a skill set or tool, an *instrumental motivation* for coaching to remediate an underperformer, and an intervention driven by *line managers* within a line management structure but delivered by an *outsourced* external coach.

Utilitarian Conceptualisation

In the *Coaching-as-Intervention* stage, coaching is a skill set or tool that is used to fix a problem or issue. The coaching initiative is driven by a line manager who has first-hand knowledge of the employee and the circumstances surrounding the presenting concern. It is a one-off investment to achieve an immediate result. Managers at this first stage *send* the employee to be coached because they believe that coaching is a skill set in the hands of specialised experts and therefore "it's not my role to coach". The focus of coaching in this stage is to assist the coachee improve their performance or behave in more appropriate ways with colleagues and others in the workplace. When behaviour is a problem, the coach explores ways that the coachee can develop better interpersonal and relationship skills to interact more effectively with their manager and others in the team (Fig. 4.1).

In this first stage, managers may have tried to fix the problem themselves but been unsuccessful and now are at their wits' end. Hence, referral to an external coach is seen as the answer. Managers see external coaches as skilled at helping employees break down the problem or issue into smaller chunks against which actions can be taken to better manage the situation and achieve their desired

S. Knowles, *Coaching Culture*, https://doi.org/10.1007/978-3-031-09050-9_4

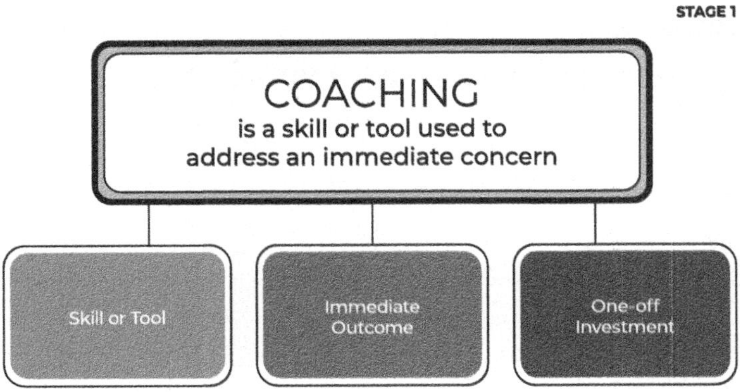

Fig. 4.1 Stage 1 - Coaching is a skill or tool

outcome. In every job, there are a multitude of tasks to be completed and, whilst the coachee may have both the motivation and the skill to complete some of those tasks, they don't necessarily have the motivation and skill to complete all the tasks. This is where a coaching programme can fill the gap.

In this stage, coaching is seen as a one-off investment to achieve a particular outcome. When viewed in this way, it can be likened to a *fast-burn fire* which brings about an immediate outcome. The fire is lit, burns quickly, turns around the situation, and can be put out just as quickly. In an organisational context, coaching at this early stage in the development of a coaching culture is aimed at bringing about quick changes in an employee's behaviour or performance. Like a fire, employees who are coached in this first stage are expected to only need one coaching session and learn from it. The outcomes of the *fast-burn fire* approach to coaching are obvious both on the sporting field and in an organisational context. Using the sporting analogy, employees who are coached are offered insights that are outside of their own head and physical experience because, when "in play", they are totally "in the moment" and there's no time to self-reflect. Coaching provides them the time to self-reflect. From their new awareness as a result of being coached, employees can make the changes they need to make almost immediately to save their job or career. Alternatively, they may decide to exit the organisation voluntarily or, if there is no improvement in their situation, be involuntarily exited from the organisation.

Overall, when an organisation is at the first stage of developing a coaching culture, coaching is conceptualised as a skill set or tool of a professional external coach. An immediate outcome is required from the coaching.

Instrumental Motivation

In this first stage, managers who arrange for their difficult or problem employee to be coached use coaching as an instrument to "fix" them and resolve the situation. The issue often relates to someone who is underperforming because of their behaviour which may be causing conflict in the workplace. Their underperformance may be impacting on the team's ability to achieve its targets, causing additional work and stress. In this first stage, misbehaving or underperforming employees are typically sent to coaching for *remedial* purposes which sometimes is just a "box-ticking" exercise so that the manager can say they have complied with the requirements of the organisation's performance management system or with legislative requirements before exiting the employee from the business (Fig. 4.2).

An employee who is sent to coaching approaches it with trepidation knowing that, as an underperformer or badly behaved individual, this may be their last chance to redeem themself or be exited from the organisation. For this reason, when coaching is used as an instrument to address poor performance or bad behaviour, there is often a *stigma* attached to being sent to coaching. External coaches typically refuse to "fix" an employee who has been sent to coaching but they may undertake *remedial* coaching if the individual is considered to have the potential to improve. The role of a coach is to assist the coachee identify barriers or constraints to their performance or behaviour and find ways to resolve these roadblocks. They may be performing well in a number of areas but they're not "firing on all cylinders". In this instance, an external coach works with the coachee to identify the issues holding back their performance or affecting their behaviour and helps them address these issues step by step until the situation is resolved.

Unfortunately, this instrumental motivation for coaching does not take into account other factors that may be impacting on the employee's ability to perform, for example, the organisational context, systems and processes, interpersonal relationships or team dynamics. If the organisation is to progress to the next stage in developing a coaching culture, all of these factors must be unpacked by the coach as possible areas of concern to assist the coachee gain clarity in relation to their situation and how to resolve it. Fortunately, the view of coaching as a "fix it" instrument

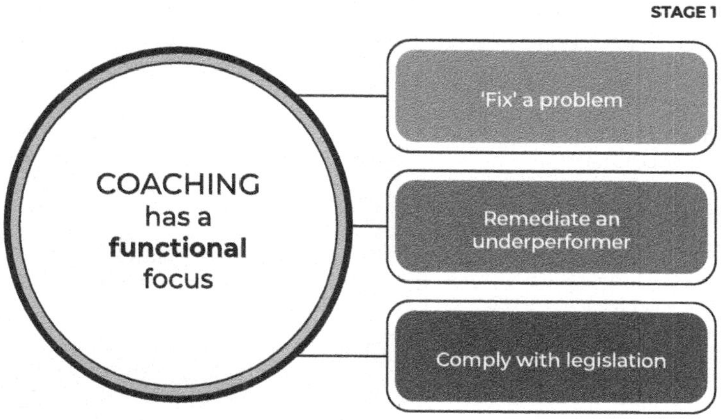

Fig. 4.2 Stage 1 - Coaching is used to "fix" a problem

of change is becoming less prevalent in organisations today, as this story from an external coach illustrates:

> *When I first started coaching it was seen as* remedial. *It didn't have a development focus. The thinking was:* 'There's something wrong. Can you fix this person?' *Nowadays, coaching is seen as almost like exercise – as a fundamental part of professional development.*

When organisations use coaching as a "box-ticking" exercise or a way to announce to the world that "we do coaching", there's often no real meaning behind the coaching because neither manager nor employee is held accountable for any improvement. In such instances, coaching is simply seen as an intervention of "last resort" before exiting the employee from the organisation. However, as managers progress in their understanding of coaching and how it can benefit them when they have the capability to conduct the "tough discussions" with their direct reports rather than avoiding them, the *instrumental* motivation for coaching may change to *developmental*, which is the next stage in the development of a coaching culture.

Overall, when an organisation is at the first stage of developing a coaching culture, the motivation for coaching is instrumental. Employees are coached to fix a problem that the line manager has been unable to resolve. Alternatively, the motivation for coaching may be to comply with legislative requirements before exiting the employee from the organisation.

Individual Drivers

The key drivers of coaching in this first stage of developing a coaching culture are managers positioned within the line management structure. They identify an employee who is underperforming and *send* them for coaching. Sometimes, however, they avoid the whole situation by having the employee transferred to another department which doesn't solve the problem but actually reinforces it (Fig. 4.3).

The line manager may have already tried to resolve the situation by using the organisation's performance management policies and procedures but without

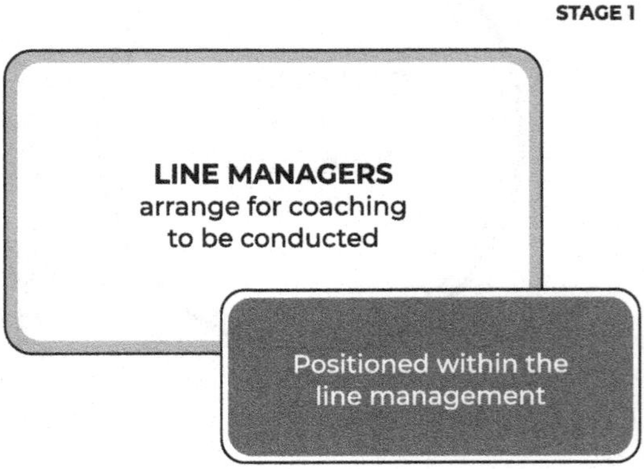

Fig. 4.3 Stage 1 - Line managers drive coaching

success, or their efforts may have been thwarted by legislative impediments. For example, in a unionised environment in which "the legislation is so rigorous around getting rid of someone that you have to go through a lot of hurdles to do that", both the manager and the problem employee may become increasingly stressed as time goes by if the situation is not resolved quickly.

On occasions, employees may claim harassment or bullying by the line manager who tries to have them change their behaviour or performance, as the following story illustrates:

> *So when it's a difficult person, what could happen is that the person could turn around and say*: 'I'm being bullied.' *So managers are running scared. And I'm not saying this is rife but it's an element that exists in many organisations. So, some managers just flick the problem over to someone else because they don't want to manage it themself.*

Problems with underperformers are identified at the line management level by managers who recognise when employees are not pulling their weight, causing disruption within the team, or behaving rudely or aggressively. Consequently, team morale may slip and there may be strained relationships or conflict within the team. The line manager wants the employee's performance or behaviour to improve so they can return to being a fully functioning member of the team and so that good working relationships can be restored within the team. Dissatisfied with their own attempts to rectify the situation, line managers in this early stage in the development of a coaching culture may form the opinion that only an external coach can provide an objective perspective or insight around the challenge because they're too close to the individual in their team. Hence, they believe that an external coach is the only person who can deal with the employee and fix the problem. If the employee needs to make drastic changes in the way they perform or behave, they may need to develop a completely new set of behaviours – a different style of engaging with people – as an outcome to be achieved through coaching within a very short time.

In this first stage, employees may be *sent* to coaching by managers who just don't see that they have had any part to play in bringing about the situation and definitely have no intention of remediating it. They don't see that they are part of the system which created the problem. They see the employee's performance as separate from their own and *sending* an employee to coaching is the only part that they have to play in making things right. Line managers who behave in this way leave the responsibility to fix the problem to an external coach when, in fact, it may be the manager who also needs coaching. Managers in this stage may know that coaching is a good thing because the research says that it is but they don't want to coach or be coached. They tell themselves that they don't need coaching but that others do. Transferring their responsibility to fix an employee to an external coach is a completely different approach to that of managers in more advanced stages of developing a coaching culture who want to learn how to coach and consider coaching to be a core capability that they require as a leader.

Overall, when an organisation is at the first stage of developing a coaching culture, line managers are the drivers of coaching. They send employees to coaching and do not see themselves as in any way responsible for the situation even though they are part of the system that created the problem. They arrange for coaching to be conducted by an external coach to resolve the situation.

Outsourced Delivery

In this first stage, coaching is outsourced to external or executive coaches who have the requisite skills to work with coachees to achieve the outcomes that the line manager desires. However, engaging an external coach to conduct a number of coaching sessions with an underperforming employee can be expensive particularly if the coachee decides to leave the organisation during or after the coaching, in which case the return on investment (ROI) to the organisation has not been realised (Fig. 4.4).

Managers in this first stage do not usually have the motivation or skills to undertake individual coaching unless they have been formally trained as a coach. So, when an external coach is to be engaged to coach a problem employee, the manager generally approaches HR who sets up an initial meeting with a coach and together they establish the basis on which the coaching will be conducted. Once a coach is engaged, they meet with the line manager to gain details of the problem and desired outcomes. Are they realistic? How will personal issues be handled if they arise? What are the ethical principles around coaching, confidentiality, accountability and trust? The external coach also wants to obtain a clear understanding from the line manager as to the outcomes that are expected. Fully qualified coaches who behave ethically and professionally will establish dates for triangulation meetings to occur at agreed intervals. Afterwards and before the coaching commences, the coach will usually informally contract with the problem employee in addition to the formal

Fig. 4.4 Stage 1 - Coaching is outsourced to external coaches

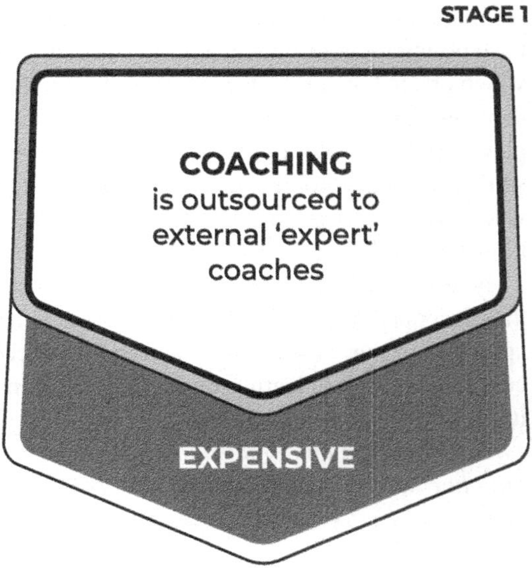

contract they have with the organisation, to make sure they are both on the "same page" before coaching commences.

A 360-degree assessment may be conducted and the results debriefed with the coachee before the coaching commences. Thereafter, the coach guides the coachee towards self-awareness and insight, leading to behavioural and performance change. A close, working relationship is formed as the coach gets to know the coachee and understand their coaching needs. Four to six sessions may be conducted to start with, and, provided the behaviour or performance improves, the number of sessions may be extended since it often takes longer to shift mindsets and consciousness. In the next stage of developing a coaching culture, these extended coaching sessions have a developmental focus. They elicit the coachee's concerns, hopes and dreams before establishing learning goals and action plans to achieve them. To assess the success of the coaching programme over say, a 12-month period, the 360-degree assessment may be re-administered at the end.

Delivering coaching to individuals can be expensive especially when many coaching sessions are required or many individuals are to be coached. The cost of the coaching comes out of the line manager's budget. However, their budget may not have an allocation for coaching, and hence, it may stretch business unit resources. Perhaps for this reason or when alternative motivations come into play, the organisation may take steps to progress to the next stage of developing a coaching culture where the cost of hiring external coaches is born by the HR budget.

> In summary, when an organisation is at the first *coaching-as-intervention* stage of developing a coaching culture, coaching, is delivered by an outsourced, professional, expert coach who has the required skill set to "fix" an underperforming employee and resolve the situation. However, coaching can be expensive and may not be included in the line manager's budget.

Stage 1: Illustrative Examples: *Coaching-as-Intervention*

Illustrative examples were extracted from my research dataset to "paint a picture" of each stage in the development of a coaching culture. These examples offer compelling illustrations of the different characteristics of each stage, highlighting the four dimensions of how managers conceptualise coaching, their motivation for requesting coaching to be conducted, the people who drive coaching within the organisation, and how coaching is delivered at each stage as a coaching culture develops.

The examples in this chapter illustrate organisations at Stage 1 of a coaching culture. Examples of organisations at Stages 2, 3 and 4 are included at the end of the following three chapters. The examples are included so that the reader can reflect on whether these stories resonate with your knowledge and experience of working in your organisation, hence serving as a way to assess which stage of development your organisation is at in terms of developing a coaching culture. The examples may also be used in an academic setting for students to discuss the different characteristics of organisations at the different stages and ways that the organisation can progress to a more advanced stage. Readers should note that the learnings accumulated at each stage in progression are cumulative as long as there continues to be forward movement. However, whilst the stages are ideally progressive, they are, in fact, dynamic. That is, an organisation can regress to previous stages if significant events cause progress to be halted, for example, by the exit of a committed CEO, lack of funding, or an organisational restructure or takeover.

These illustrative examples were developed from my research participants' reports of activities being undertaken in their organisations to develop a coaching culture. Readers will note that the number of examples presented to illustrate each stage diminishes from the first to fourth stage which, from anecdotal reports, is consistent with the number of organisations in general which have been able to commit to, fund, and maintain a coaching culture. Pseudonyms are used in all illustrative examples.

Illustrative Example 1

TotalCare is a not-for-profit organisation in the aged care/disability sector. The organisation has approximately 500 support workers. Bella worked in *TotalCare* as a learning consultant for 6 years but left the organisation 10 months ago as a result of unresolved bullying. She claimed that she was unfairly treated and bullied by her manager, Lisa, who was a peer before being promoted. Lisa's adverse behaviour included having conversations with the team and not including Bella, and cancelling the training that Bella had organised and not telling her. Lisa was treating another team member the same way. Bella did her best to "stay out of her way". As a result of this treatment, the relationship between Bella and Lisa became "non-existent". Bella knew that the CEO, Megan, was aware of Lisa's behaviour but didn't do anything about it so there was "no point in putting in a complaint". However, when she couldn't take it anymore, Bella went directly to Megan and asked for assistance. Megan engaged an external coach whom she had used before and who was, in fact, her coach (but Bella didn't know that at the time).

The external coach, Maryanne, had worked as a consultant/coach to *TotalCare* for a number of years. Megan had used her services before with staff who were experiencing issues. For example, the manager previous to Lisa, Eliza, was promoted to the manager role when she didn't have the skills or experience to do the job. As a consequence, Eliza did not provide all the necessary information to her team members, undermined certain staff who didn't agree with her, and created divisions within the team between those she favoured and those she couldn't control. As a result, one team member had developed mental health issues and was "let go" rather than the organisation dealing with the problem. Another example was when Maryanne coached a "delightful manager", Dave, but someone with poor management skills who was "sent to coaching" to be remediated as a result of complaints from team members. However, the coaching was ineffective and "didn't end well" with Dave being "managed out". A third example was in relation to the manager of *TotalCare's* day service, Trevor, who was dysfunctional and aggressive. He was "sent to coaching" but the problem was "not fixed" and is still ongoing – after 7 years!

Six coaching sessions were arranged for Bella, to be conducted at Maryanne's home which was being renovated at the time. The first session was all about the renovations that were being undertaken. As Bella continued her "supervision" with Maryanne, the mention of possible dismissal was "turned back on me". They talked about "how Bella approached the world" and she vividly remembers Maryanne telling her that she had "angry hair". From Bella's point of view, the best thing that came out of her coaching sessions with Maryanne was when she said, "every day, we paint a picture of who we are in the workplace" and people either say, "Wow", or "It's not a good place to be". Maryanne did mention, in passing, that when Bella's line manager, Lisa, was "pushed", she would "come out firing" which confirmed to Bella that she was "not going nuts". Bella found out later that Maryanne had also coached Lisa on other matters but, even so, she "made it my fault that we were in conflict". Bella derived no benefit from the coaching because her concerns were constantly "swept under the carpet" by Maryanne.

When another executive took over running the department, Lisa's behaviour "accelerated" which resulted in a "huge altercation" between her and Bella and there was talk of Bella being made redundant. The new executive, Jack, took over Bella's management and she got more out of working with him than she did from working with Maryanne because, even though Jack was "trying to performance manage me out", he did it in a way that Bella could "leave on my own terms".

Jack left *TotalCare* 6 months later because his numerous attempts to implement different practices, policies and procedures had failed since the CEO, Megan, was unwilling to make any changes.

Illustrative Example 2

BLGC Corp. employs approximately 400 people and services 5 regional communities across its extensive, isolated, outback government jurisdiction. Tricia worked for *BLGC* for two and a half years in the role of workforce planning coordinator responsible for organisational capability, succession planning, and current and future workforce scenarios. An incident occurred whilst she was in the role of acting HR director for 2 weeks when the HR director, Rosy, was on leave. It involved the senior manager in charge of the asset team, Bill, who had approximately half the staff reporting to him. Ever since he was appointed 12 months ago, Bill had been badly behaved – shouting at staff, not giving balanced feedback, embarrassing staff in front of others, and swearing. These behaviours were accepted by the organisation as "that's just the way Bill is" and "Don't worry about it . . . just get on with your work". As a result, some of his bad behaviours had filtered down to managers and team leaders in his department.

However, as new employees were appointed to teams within Bill's department, they began to question some of these behaviours. They were not used to this kind of management and enlisted the help of the union organiser, Mike, to "push it up to HR". Mike phoned Tricia "in confidence and off the record" to see what could be done. They arranged to meet and Tricia committed to "get some more information and insight" into the situation.

Over the following week, Tricia met with the team members who had complained about Bill's behaviour and then brought the situation to the attention of the General Manager, Ted, who acknowledged the concern but said, "That's the way Bill is. He's very passionate but gets stressed". Tricia told Ted that she had spoken to Bill and informed him that there were "lots of concerns about his blow-ups" and that his behaviour was not appropriate. As Bill was well-known to Rosy, who would be back to work the following week, Ted decided to leave it until then so that she could address the situation.

When Rosy retuned to work, Tricia completed a handover with her and one of the top items to address was Bill's behaviour. She provided Rosy with the details that had emerged from her investigation of the situation, to which Rosy responded, "This has happened before and it was not managed well". Tricia was "pretty shocked about this". She was concerned that, with union involvement, "this could go pear-shaped and go further in terms of its effect on *BLGC*". Tricia suggested the option of coaching to "fix" the situation, a suggestion which was "taken very positively" by Rosy. It took a month or two to gain an appointment with Ted (because of internal "politics" – if Bill was more senior, the situation would have been dealt with more quickly) after which Tricia was asked to seek providers of professional coaching services.

Tricia met with a few external coaches to "vet" them because the situation was sensitive and the coach would be dealing with someone with a "strong ego" who had not been managed well in the past. It was important to get the right "fit" – someone who "understood his ego" and would make a good connection with him. At the same time, Tricia had identified some team leaders who were showing promise from a talent management perspective and arranged for them to be coached as well. She admits that she may have been trying to defuse the situation in relation to Bill's behaviour, although she did recognise the need for "that type of intervention" (coaching) as a talent management strategy that would be proactive in helping the team leaders "take the next step", and an especially good opportunity for them to develop "self-awareness and insight".

Meanwhile, Ted spoke with Bill to see if he was "happy to give it [coaching] a go". When Bill agreed, an external coach, Mitchell, was engaged to conduct the coaching with him. Mitchell was very subtle in his approach but he also "called it as it was", got Bill to see the bigger picture, and worked with him over the next 9 months. Afterwards, they continued to meet for coffee for a while. Tricia admits that "it was a risk . . . it could have gone either way". Bill could have just been "ticking the box" to say that he had complied with the coaching intervention.

Towards the end of the coaching, Tricia asked Mike, in confidence, how things were going. She didn't mention that Bill had received coaching as it was something new to the organisation and, if the "grapevine" got hold of this word, it would be associated with counselling which was not highly regarded. Mike reported that there had been no concerns or complaints raised by staff about Bill's behaviour over the past 6 months. Hence, Tricia concluded that "as an intervention, it [coaching] was very good". In addition, she reported that "the organisation thought it was great too". However, coaching did not continue within *BLGC* as, shortly after the coaching with Bill ended, the organisation underwent a series of restructures.

Illustrative Example 3

HealthBubs provides specialist, medical intervention services to patients using state-of-the-art technology and equipment. The organisation employs 500 people in Australia and overseas. An external coach, Craig, was contracted to assist a team leader, Elias, who had a problem with one of his direct reports. It was a behavioural issue concerning how one of the scientists, Sharon, interacts with others in the laboratory environment. Scientists do not, in general, have good "people skills" but this individual was even worse – rude, abrupt and verbally aggressive. She railed at and questioned everything that was requested of her and wanted to know how everything was done.

In the first two coaching sessions, Craig let Sharon vent and waited until she had offloaded all her issues. She complained about everything, pushing blame onto everybody else. She was an "angry young lady". In the third session, Craig asked her, "What are you trying to achieve?". There was a long pause and Sharon started to cry. She said, "I have so much to offer, and no one's listening to me. I can add so much value so we can get ahead of the game". Craig asked her what she had done to get people to listen to her and what she could do differently. She replied that no one takes her seriously and that her team leader, Elias, doesn't respect anything she says. However, the coach discovered that Sharon did have the respect of another team leader, Melissa. He prompted her to meet with Melissa and chat about her ideas.

In the next coaching session Sharon beamed, "You would be so proud of me!". She had met with Melissa who was impressed with her innovative ideas and said that she would speak with Elias about them. Sharon then met with Elias who was "gobsmacked" that she was "laughing not attacking". They discussed her ideas and talked about the process of creating innovation. As a result, Sharon came to understand how things are done from an organisational perspective. As the weeks went by, Craig continued to work with Sharon to change her "victim, attacking, aggressive" behavioural style into more appropriate ways of behaving so that she would be heard in the future.

As a result of her changed behaviour, Sharon was appointed to head up a new innovation team and sent to the USA to compare ideas and learn best practice. She is now presenting to the national scientific community. From a person with aggressive behaviour, she has changed into a team leader working with innovation. *HealthBubs* was amazed at how personally transformative coaching can be even in the technical space.

Craig subsequently discovered that even when Sharon was growing up, no one heard her, and her voice didn't count. He concluded that the value of the coaching programme and the turning point for her was when she realised that, "I create my behaviour". Consequently, as a result of her improved behaviour and interpersonal skills, people now listen to her. The benefit to the organisation was that they retained a talented scientist and team morale lifted, as did the organisation's reputation when they started working in the innovation space.

Illustrative Example 4

StateTrans delivers state-wide transport solutions. It was created 12 months ago as an amalgamation of a number of government departments with the intention of breaking the culture of existing "silos" to form a modern, customer-focused organisation. The new entity inherited a large number of engineers who were "old school" and not "people persons". They had never worked in another job and continued to be fiercely loyal to their previous department, holding onto old ways, traditions and expectations. To them, coaching is a tool to "fix" a problem or exit an individual, with no thought being given to identifying the underlying cause. Peppered within this "old school" group of employees are new leaders who have been recruited since the new entity was formed, who are supportive of coaching for developmental purposes.

The continuing problem for the new CEO, Dennis, is that the "old school" employees will remain in the new organisation until retirement age to ensure they receive all their entitlements and defined benefits. Hence, cultural change will be 5 to 10 years away. An additional concern is that his 2IC, Brian, who was retained from a previous organisation, has a bullying style. Hence, whilst Dennis is supportive of people's development and very approachable, Brian continues to display an aggressive management style in his interactions with everyone in the new organisation including key external stakeholders.

Worrying for Dennis is that Brian's aggressive style has been remarked on in government circles over the past 20 years but no one has ever done anything about it. His behaviour has been accepted and gone unchallenged. The dilemma for Dennis is to decide if, how and when, he challenges Brian's behaviour before it starts to affect *StateTrans'* recently formed good standing in the community. Or should he just hope that, as the new organisational leaders "make their mark", they will have a significant impact on Brian and the organisation's culture? Realistically, Dennis knows that this scenario is unlikely and that cultural change is going to be a long way off and won't happen until Brian and the "old school" brigade have retired.

Illustrative Example 5

ConCare is a small government department of approximately 1500 employees who are mainly scientists in various fields relating to nature and conservation. The scientists are highly intelligent and well-educated people focused on their job and how they preserve the natural environment but their "soft skills" are limited. In *ConCare*, coaching is positioned within the culture and performance team which is responsible for organisational culture and leadership development. *ConCare* has a long-standing mentoring programme with senior executives as the mentors. The organisation is at the stage of delineating how coaching is different from mentoring. A few senior executives have been coached by external coaches so they understand the value and benefits of coaching as opposed to mentoring. They are open to being coached and already informally coach their direct reports.

Within *ConCare*, employees understand that leadership is not necessarily hierarchical but behavioural and therefore, everyone can lead. Coaching is considered to be a highly effective way of developing people to be high-achieving as well as supporting a workplace culture that empowers individuals and enables success. Managers believe that coaching is about unlocking an individual's potential by asking the right questions. Hence, coaching is an opportunity for employees to look both inside and outside of themselves so that they're uncovering their inner wisdom to manage themselves and others more effectively.

ConCare has a performance framework which includes coach-type conversations to give employees formal one-on-one feedback which helps them perform better in their role. However, as it's early days, anyone searching for coaching on the organisation's intranet would find no reference to this opportunity at all. When required, formal, matched coaching relationships are arranged for nominated employees so that developmental coaching can occur. The cultural performance team knows that their task is to become more purposeful in developing more employees – giving them the skills to coach and understanding the value of it. And because the organisation will soon have five generations in the workplace who need to be coached, team members are considering instigating "reverse" coaching, that is, more senior people being coached by junior people – but that's just talk at the moment. If *ConCare* makes a decision to proceed with coaching, the culture and performance team will develop the infrastructure for coaching and establish a register of coaches from whom all employees can proactively seek to be coached.

***

This chapter has detailed the four key dimensions of Stage 1 – *Coaching-as-Intervention*. The next chapter explains the four key dimensions of Stage 2 – *Coaching-as-HR-Function*.

Chapter 5
Stage 2: Coaching-as-HR-Function

This chapter addresses the second of four stages in the development of a coaching culture as depicted in the model of coaching culture development (Fig. 3.1). During this stage, coaching resides within the HR function which is responsible for the training of managers in coaching skills and the delivery of coaching to employees in the organisation. In Stage 2, coaching is characterised by a *pedagogical conceptualisation* as a training and learning experience. The motivation for coaching is *developmental*, designed to change managers' mindset and behaviour, improve individual performance, and support career progression. The *functional drivers* for coaching are positioned within the HR function which builds the infrastructure and support for coaching skills training to begin. HR professionals arrange for the *targeted delivery* of coaching to leaders and talented individuals within the organisation.

Pedagogical Conceptualisation

In the *Coaching-as-HR-Function* stage, coaching is conceptualised as a training and learning experience. HR professionals, selected organisational leaders and talented individuals are trained in coaching skills or formally qualified as coaches by external coach-training providers, and experience being coached. The training and coaching experience allows them to build stronger and deeper relationships with others. It is a short-term investment in valued employees who are committed to building the organisation's human capital as they transfer their skills to others in the business (Fig. 5.1).

Organisations which invest in formally training HR professionals, selected organisational leaders and talented individuals as coaches have made a decision to bring coaching skills into the organisation in the most cost-effective way. From their formal coach-training, these individuals have learned what coaching is all about, developed coaching competencies and are able to coach others to help them resolve

S. Knowles, *Coaching Culture*, https://doi.org/10.1007/978-3-031-09050-9_5

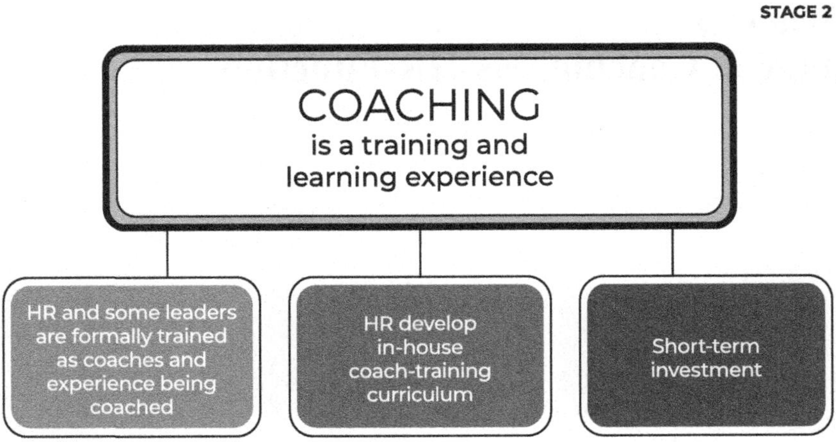

Fig. 5.1 Stage 2 - Coaching is a training and learning experience

their own problems, goal set and action plan. The formal coach-training programme in which they enrolled should be approved to international standards established by professional associations such as the ICF. An essential component of formal coach-training programmes is usually the delivery of individual coaching sessions so that participants experience being coached and come to understand how coaching can benefit themselves and others. From their experience, they "get it in their heart and guts" as well as in their *head*, which makes all the difference in terms of their understanding of how powerful coaching can be and their subsequent advocacy for coaching as a valid developmental process for change.

During their formal coach-training, HR professionals develop an understanding of coaching as an instrument that promotes self-development by consistently, in every interaction, encouraging self-awareness and insight. Utilising coaching skills allows HR professionals to engage more personally with individuals to meet their specific needs, play to their strengths and bring their best to the table. Through reflective listening, questioning for exploration and discovery, and periodic summarising, coaching facilitates improved communication, collaboration and cooperation among individuals and within teams. It enables conversations based on trust, motivation and positive intent, which allows deeper issues to surface for discussion.

Organisations in this second stage of developing a coaching culture want to become self-sufficient in training managers in coaching skills which is understandable from a financial point of view. Hence, they fund HR professionals to become formally qualified as coaches, who then design in-house coaching skills curriculum for organisational managers based on what they have learnt and experienced in their formal coach-training. The coaching skills training curriculum they develop for the organisation may consist of, say, three key training programmes based on leaders' tenure, functionality, or anticipated career progression within the organisation. The design of such programmes takes time because there are many stakeholders to consider and functional groups within the organisation whose specific needs must be accommodated within these programmes. Over this and the next two stages, HR professionals provide follow-up support until coaching practice is fully embedded within the organisation.

In this second stage, the formal coach-training of HR professionals and selected others is a short-term investment in increasing their ability to coach and subsequently developing the leadership capability of the organisation. When HR professionals train managers in coaching skills, this strategy doesn't require the major investment that would have been necessary if the coaching skills training was conducted by an external coach-training provider (although an external provider may be contracted to deliver additional expertise and support). Unfortunately, in many organisations, once the HR budget for coaching skills training is exhausted, the programmes cease and the funding must be renewed year-on-year to keep the initiative alive. At this second stage, it is rare that an organisation will allocate recurrent funding to the provision of coaching skills training unless it is on the path to developing a coaching culture.

The in-house delivery of coaching skills training to organisational leaders may take longer to be approved when the responsibility for coaching remains within the HR function rather than in a customer-facing business unit as it does in the next stage of developing a coaching culture, because of the many policies and procedures that need to be taken into account within the HR environment. When the responsibility for coaching is positioned within a business unit, there is a sense of urgency to gain approval because every interaction counts towards a business win or loss.

Overall, when an organisation is at the second stage of developing a coaching culture, coaching is conceptualised as a training and learning experience for HR professionals, selected organisational leaders and talented individuals to be formally trained as a coach and experience being coached. HR professionals then go on to design in-house coaching skills training curriculum which they deliver across the whole organisation.

Developmental Motivation

In this second stage, the motivation for coaching is *developmental*. Coaching is specifically focused on assisting individuals develop greater self-awareness and insight so that they shift their mindset from a *management* style of interacting with their direct reports to a *coaching leadership style.* This style supports employees to change their behaviour, improve their performance and enhance their career progression. It's only in the last decade or so that coaching has started to become accepted as a valid developmental process in organisations, often associated with its earliest use as a sports-related intervention (Fig. 5.2):

> I've been a rugby coach at the highest level – first grade. I can't play the game for my players. What I have to do is equip my team or individuals within the team with the necessary skills, attributes, and standards of proficiency in terms of the profession that they had chosen.

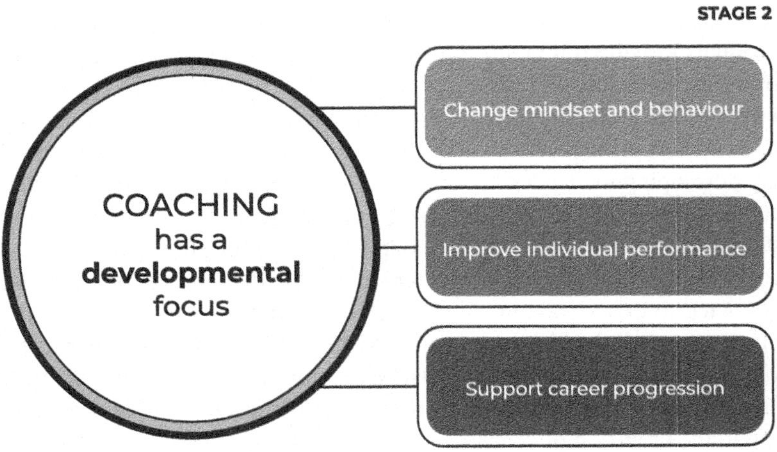

Fig. 5.2 Stage 2 - Coaching changes individual behaviour

The first *developmental* motivation for coaching is to stimulate self-awareness and insight so that individuals learn and grow, and change their behaviour. Behavioural coaching is based on reinforcing the behaviours that lead the coachee to be personally and professionally effective, and then asking what's going to stop them from being successful. Before coaching begins, a behaviour profiling assessment may be used to identify the coachee's strengths, weaknesses, and leadership style. Behavioural coaching can be revelationary, helping coachees achieve their goals and progress in their career faster than they normally would. The following story from an executive coach illustrates the reaction that some managers have when it dawns on them that they need to change their behaviour:

> *The guy basically was having massive behavioural issues, massive anger issues, and as he turned around he said:* 'OMG! I've been doing harm. I've affected my team. Please show me how to support them.'

Assessment is typically conducted with senior executives before coaching is undertaken to improve their performance through behavioural change. It's also commonly administered to managers who have recently been promoted into a leadership role particularly if they are transitioning from being in an operational to a strategic role or a technical into a more general management role. Coaching supports them to *lead* as well as *manage* employees. However, before a coachee can change their behaviour, they may need to shift their mindset. This is especially true of managers who use a *command-and-control* style with their direct reports. They may find it difficult to embrace a *coaching leadership style* of interacting with them instead, since managers who were brought up in the "old school of management" may see coaching as a sign of weakness.

During the coaching skills training, managers are encouraged to let go of their *command-and-control* style and replace it with a *coaching leadership style*. Some managers readily change their style and thrive on the new challenge. However, many struggle when they are required to change from a *telling* to an *asking*, enabling, empowering, and supporting leadership style. Some may comply on the surface but their *command-and-control* is still very much in-play as an inherent, underlying behaviour – even though very few employees have ever responded positively to such an approach. Hence, for those managers whose *command-and-control* style was previously an issue within their team, it may still be an issue after the training – just dressed up as coaching – and still problematic. This is especially the case when the training programme is short (e.g. a few hours) and when managers have resisted being personally coached.

When managers adopt a *coaching leadership style*, instead of *telling* employees what to do and how to do it, they *ask* open and powerful questions which support discovery so that direct reports identify their own solutions. Managers engage with employees in more meaningful conversations which enable and empower them to perform better and use their initiative. Unfortunately, the *command-and-control* management style is still very much alive in organisations today. A number of examples support this claim. First, a large national telecommunications company was bought out by an overseas firm which comes from a *command-and-control* cultural background. The new CEO had multiple strengths but no real understanding or appreciation of coaching. Hence the coaching initiative, which had been ongoing for 2 years, was starved of funds and died. The second example illustrates what happened when a new CEO was appointed to an organisation which had been coaching for 5 years. She had no knowledge of coaching – what it is, how it is conducted, and what it can do. However, she allowed the coaching initiative to continue which it did, supported by the dedicated HR professionals who knew and appreciated coaching. A third example illustrates the confusion of staff within a military organisation when the new commander, a leader who had just completed a formal coach-training course, used a coaching approach with his team: "They were a bit taken aback. The guy who was in the position before me was very directive, commanding control, had a short temper, and would go ballistic at times with people". So when this leader sat down with his direct reports it was like, "Wow! Nobody's ever done this before". It took team members some time to adjust to the new style because they didn't know how to respond to a more personal and empowering approach from their leader. They didn't know whether or not they could trust him based on their experiences with the previous leader.

Fortunately, some organisational leaders are aware that the *command-and-control* management style is not effective. For example, the leader of a HR function in a government department in which a coaching initiative has continued to be funded for 5 years describes coaching as "exciting territory which is really shifting the public sector management and leadership from the old-school archaic command-and-control to where we need to be, to drive value for money and engage a motivated, adaptable workforce". He believes that coaching has the capacity to spread across the entire public sector in his State to influence and improve whole-of-government effectiveness.

> I think that to move away from the old-school, public sector mindset and really build that coaching environment is critical to neutralise the preciousness and sensitivity of the government environment, and goes a long way to us being organisationally effective.

The second *developmental* motivation for coaching in the second stage of developing a coaching culture is to *improve individual performance* so that employees achieve their KPIs. When KPIs are not being achieved or the employee is not performing in a certain area, a scheduled coaching session or coaching conversation identifies what the employee needs to do to better perform in their role because that's how they will be measured, and to discuss the impact on the team dynamic of their non-performance. Moreover, for coaching to continue even when leaders are busy, conducting coaching sessions or conversations with direct reports needs to become a KPI in their position description because, as one organisational leader explains: "If there's no KPI or report required, or nothing that I have to give to anyone to prove that I've done something, I might get to it if I have time". Measuring coaching as a core competency of the leader's role shows how they are progressing towards meeting this performance objective. If non-performance is detected, a conversation with the leader's "one-up" may need to be conducted to address ways in which they can support the busy leader continue coaching whilst still meeting their business KPIs.

A major responsibility of leaders who coach is to actively remove business or systemic roadblocks or barriers to employee performance. As employees start to better perform in their role, the focus shifts to identifying the factors that support behavioural change and those that hold coachees back. Hence, coaching is more than just helping employees meet their KPIs. It's also about recognising their needs as people. An organisational leader who is responsible for the HR function of a multinational corporation at a state level explains: "You have to actually have people on board. You can't have everyone putting in complaints about you, on stress leave, and leaving, but heck – you met your KPIs, so we don't care about that". Moreover, coaching to improve performance doesn't have to be conducted within a scheduled coaching session. Coaching conversations can occur as part of any interaction during which a leader asks insightful questions to guide the employee to find their own solutions.

When leaders learn how to motivate their staff developmentally through coaching, coaching conversations flow through all aspects of daily business including how employees relate to their colleagues, resolve differences, manage problems, and run meetings to improve their own and others' performance. Hence, coaching which has a developmental motivation also has an operational component in the day-to-day when leaders provide constructive feedback on individual performance. In organisations which do not train their managers in coaching skills, feedback is typically transactional particularly in front-line services functions. The supervisor listens to calls made to the operative, gives feedback on their performance, and engages in a conversation with them which is "probably not what I would consider coaching – just feedback on performance and a performance management type of conversation, which has the beginnings of having a coaching conversation with staff but it's not the real thing". To encourage the take-up of coaching as defined by the ICF, organisations need to consider providing supervision for leaders who coach to maintain the quality of the coaching they deliver.

A third *developmental* motivation for coaching in the second stage of developing a coaching culture is to support career progression and retain valuable staff. Leaders at all levels of the organisation need to understand that coaching is not a "nice to have" but an essential component of a leader's responsibility because if employees are not engaged and don't feel that they're valued, staff turnover generally increases. Leaders who don't coach their direct reports may end up with complaints because employees are not able to receive the support they need. Leaders who conduct regular developmental coaching conversations with employees prevent resignations from occurring by providing specific feedback on their performance, exploring ways to unlock their potential, and providing opportunities to improve their career prospects. Together, they develop a plan that's related to the employee's personal journey. The leader guides them to find their own solutions because they have all the answers. They just need help getting there.

Some organisations in this second stage of developing a coaching culture use coaching as a reward for high achievers who, like elite athletes, go on to become even better performers, entering the organisation's talent pool and becoming part of the succession plan. For these talented individuals, organisations are prepared to find the money to develop them and their careers. Members of the executive team sometimes automatically qualify for a coach when they enter the executive level: "We take the development of our senior leaders seriously and find them mentors or coaches". An example of the importance of coaching in a peak performance environment is of an organisation which experienced the loss of a highly valued employee (and others) to an international competitor, as this story illustrates:

> Ten years ago, a well-known law firm had a partner candidate who wanted to become their managing partner but he was passed over for that promotion. Within three months, a law firm from overseas started an office here. The partner took twenty lawyers and their client lists and moved to the new law firm. At that point, his previous firm started investing in coaching because they realised that he had not been coached or communicated to properly regarding the promotion and his career cycle. So, it has to be a significant crisis for an organisation to take investment in coaching seriously. It's an expense but, in my personal experience, organisations are willing to spend the money if they can see a return on investment quickly.

This example illustrates the need for organisations in this second stage of developing a coaching culture to not just claim they are motivated to develop talented individuals but also to demonstrate this motivation through the timely and targeted provision of coaching focused on individual employee needs and opportunities for growth. Coaching from a developmental motivation removes the "stigma" of *remedial* coaching interventions in the first stage of developing a coaching culture and the resistance of "old school" *command-and-control* managers in this second stage. Indeed, the developmental motivation for coaching shifts employees' views to the extent that being coached may seem more acceptable and even *prestigious*. The example also suggests that an enabling mechanism for progression towards developing a coaching culture beyond the second stage is the conversion of a developmental motivation for coaching into a business performance motivation in which the organisation is able to see and calculate an economic return on their coaching investment.

A significant challenge to progressing the organisation beyond the *Coaching-as-HR-Function* stage arises when systemic factors undermine realisation of the developmental motives for coaching, such as when certain individuals have demonstrated really poor behaviour and they have not been held accountable for that behaviour. For example, coaching of a talented financial controller in an important small division of a federal government department was unsuccessful because the individual held such an important role in the system that his aggressive attitude to staff was continually accepted. Hence, there was no real meaning to the behavioural coaching that he received. If the wrong behaviours are rewarded, there will be insufficient improvement in the coachee or commitment by the system to progressing beyond this second stage in the development of a coaching culture. This is especially likely when *command-and-control* manager behaviours are rewarded.

Overall, when an organisation is at the second stage of developing a coaching culture, the motivation for coaching is developmental to assist individuals shift their mindset and behaviour, improve their performance, and support career progression.

Functional Drivers

In this second stage, coaching is positioned within the HR function and driven by HR professionals as a centralised process because, in organisations with a "strong people function", HR professionals are usually the ones who know most about people and coaching. However, not all organisations have a transformational HR focus. Some are primarily transaction-driven and, whilst transactional HR professionals have an important role to play within organisations, they may have no, or very little, desire to coach or learn about coaching. Some may even believe that coaching will "do them out of a job". In organisations with a transactional rather than transformational HR approach, the organisation may be held back from moving to the next stage of developing a coaching culture for this reason (Fig. 5.3).

In this second stage, when a *transformational HR professional* displays passion for coaching and the benefits it can bring to individuals and teams, they are encouraged to drive the coaching initiative from within the HR function. However, critics of HR taking this responsibility believe that it should lie at a more senior level with someone who has significant oversight of the strategic agenda as it does in a later stage. They believe that the function responsible for coaching needs to have a strategic overview of systemic factors and the business context so that the outcomes of coaching can make a significant difference to achieving organisational objectives. They suggest that if HR is to be the responsible function, it needs to partner with other functions like Workforce Development or People & Culture since these teams

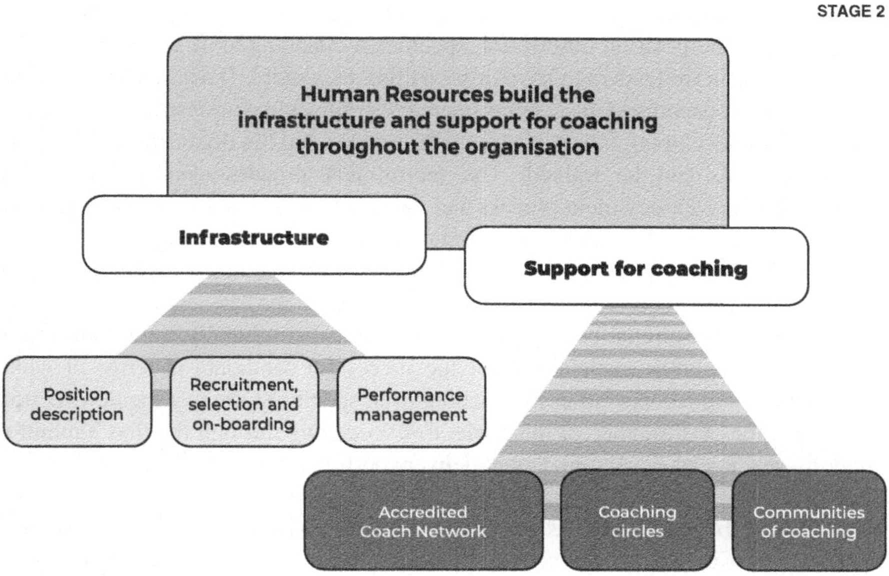

Fig. 5.3 Stage 2 - Human resources build the infrastructure for coaching

are instrumental in the design and development of organisational structures and assessing the requirements of the organisation to deliver on its strategic objectives. Plus, these functions may be driving some broader cultural agendas that can be supported by the uptake of coaching throughout the organisation.

Because coaching falls within the HR function in this second stage, the responsibility for developing the infrastructure to support coaching throughout the organisation lies with HR. HR professionals enact this responsibility by incorporating coaching within the organisation's HR policies and procedures which apply from the time that leaders are recruited until the time they leave. The infrastructure that supports coaching throughout the organisation includes the establishment of specific mechanisms to support leaders who coach as well as fundamental changes to documentation relating to the leader's position description, recruitment and selection procedures, and performance management systems.

Position Description In this second stage of developing a coaching culture, the requirement for leaders to coach is written into their position description and becomes a KPI which is measured and reported against. In addition, the leader's span of control should be realistic to allow sufficient time and opportunity for them to coach. For example, if a leader's position is responsible for 100 people with no supervisory direct reports, the organisation is saying, "We don't care. You have to coach all your direct reports anyway" which is an impossible task given the large number of direct reports. So it's important that the requirement to coach is written into the position description of leaders and reflected in the position's span of control.

Recruitment, Selection and On-Boarding In this second stage when recruiting for a new leader, the position description specifies a coaching skill set as one of the selection criteria for leaders to have or be willing to acquire. If a suitable candidate doesn't have a coaching skill set but is open to learning and demonstrates an attitude conducive to developing others, these attributes are what the organisation hires for. Coaching skills can be trained. The recruitment process usually includes a behavioural-based assessment process and interview questions so that the selection panel can ascertain the candidate's degree of alignment with the organisation's values and coaching philosophy. After selection, an induction programme covers "common ground" requirements of the organisation and the role, as well as expectations about organisational behaviour and professionalism. Ideally, the organisation has the first 6 months mapped out for the successful candidate in terms of what training they will receive either in coaching or in specific skills that the new recruit requires in the performance of their role. *Role coaching* through the first 3 months supports new leader development and delivers performance results more quickly.

Performance Management As well as the requirement to coach being written into the leader's position description, other non-performance-based indicators of performance may also be included such as the requirement for leaders to develop their people and remove roadblocks to their performance. Team-based performance indicators may include the requirement for leaders to support the development of colleagues as well as demonstrate support for organisational decisions and direction. When a *coaching leadership style* is adopted by managers, the performance management process becomes a meaningful exchange rather than a "tick and flick" exercise which, at the very least, can be distressing and, at times, almost destructive when managers save all their feedback for this one hour in a year and then offload their negative feedback onto an unsuspecting employee. Sometimes, uninformed or untrained managers simply use this hour to gloss over any concerns which leaves the employee with no valid feedback on which to base performance improvement. Rather, a coaching leader devotes regular four to six weekly coaching sessions to deliver constructive feedback to their direct reports and motivate them to keep doing more and better, resulting in increased self-confidence as their performance improves.

In this second stage, the HR function also provides significant support for leaders who coach. They do this by establishing: (1) an *Accredited Coach Network* for HR professionals and others who have been formally trained as coaches and who volunteer to coach back into the organisation in addition to their "day job"; (2) *Coaching Circles* of leaders who have been internally trained in coaching skills to support the delivery of coaching to their direct reports; and (3) *Coaching Communities* which provide supervision for the coaching practice being delivered throughout the organisation. These three coaching support systems are explained below.

Accredited Coach Network HR professionals and selected others who have been formally trained as coaches by external coach-training providers volunteer to coach individuals who request to be coached, in addition to their "day job", as coordinated by HR or the Learning and Development function. This internal, volunteer coaching service delivers coaching to employees at all levels of the organisation. Executives and senior leaders may be funded to undertake formal external coach-training and then invited to become volunteer coaches. This establishes the credibility of coaching as an important developmental process within the organisation. Gaining access to senior executive coaches is a privilege because of the impost on their time and, for some employees, it is an incredibly powerful experience; the relationships that form may continue well beyond the coaching programme.

Coaching Circles A second way that the HR function provides ongoing support for coaching is by establishing Coaching Circles as a follow-up to in-house coaching skills training programmes or leadership development programmes which include a coaching skills component. After the training, leaders are assigned to cross-organisational groups to coach each other and continue their learning: "I was part of the pilot three years ago. My coaching circle lasted longer than most. We came together, sort of ad hoc, and we just coached each other". However, for this leader, there was no follow-up to ensure that the Coaching Circle continued so, after 12 months, his was the last remaining Coaching Circle. Unfortunately, there were no recorded benefits or sustainable embedding of the coaching within the organisation as a result of the short-term investment in the coaching skills training of leaders, so the coaching initiative floundered.

Coaching communities A third way that the HR function provides ongoing support for coaching is by establishing *Coaching Communities* to provide coaching supervision and maintain the quality and currency of internal coaching practice. Leaders who coach their direct reports are encouraged to self-audit their coaching delivery and receive supervision on their coaching process and outcomes. Formally coach-trained HR professionals are injected into those discussions at various times to provide the supervision and facilitate the extension of coaching into other areas of the business. In addition, HR may develop an online forum to propagate the research conducted by, and support the learnings from the work of, the *Coaching Communities*.

The challenge in this second stage of developing a coaching culture is to convince managers that it is a requirement of their role that they coach. Unless this requirement is written into their position description and placed upfront during the recruitment interview, some managers may resist learning how to coach. However, as a KPI of their role, coaching practice is monitored and measured. Organisations which make attendance at in-house coaching skills training programmes voluntary may find that progression to the third stage in developing a coaching culture will take a lot longer to effect – if it is at all possible – unless they make the coaching skills training mandatory. In organisations which do mandate leader participation in coaching skills training programmes, those who do not attend may find that their absence impacts on their performance results and, on occasions, may actually lead to their employment being terminated.

Overall, when an organisation is at the second stage of developing a coaching culture, the drivers for coaching are HR professionals. Coaching is positioned within the HR function, and HR develops the infrastructure and support for coaching to occur. However, there is some controversy as to whether HR professionals are the most appropriate people to drive the development of a coaching culture throughout the organisation given that many HR professionals are not formally trained as coaches and may, in fact, be transactional rather than transformational in their approach. Both these factors may hold the organisation back from progressing to the third stage in the development of a coaching culture.

Targeted Delivery

The final aspect that characterises the *Coaching-as-HR-Function* stage concerns the two ways that coaching skills and the ability to coach are developed and delivered within the organisation by: (1) *Manager-as-Coach* or *Leader-as-Coach* programmes delivered by HR to organisational leaders and talented individuals, and (2) external coaches contracted to coach individual employees for performance improvement or behavioural issues and talented others on a developmental career path (Fig. 5.4).

In this second stage of developing a coaching culture, HR professionals conduct standalone *Manager-as-Coach* or *Leader-as-Coach* programmes for organisational leaders to train them in coaching skills and how to coach. Alternatively, a coaching skills training component may be incorporated within the organisation's regular leadership development programme. As a standalone programme, the *Manager-as-Coach* or *Leader-as-Coach* programme is typically of 2 or 3 days' duration and may be embedded into a more extensive leadership development training programme.

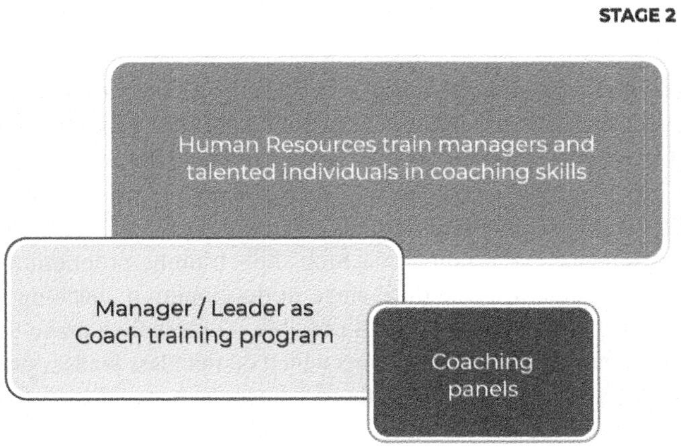

Fig. 5.4 Stage 2 - Human resources train managers and talented individuals

Participants are typically paired across leadership divisions or cohorts to conduct hands-on coaching with each other and experience being coached. This approach starts a process of *peer coaching* within the organisation. Alternatively, HR may contract the services of an external coach-training provider to deliver the programme to increase the capability and resilience of their leaders, as this story illustrates:

> The CEO took the stance that the bench strength of our leadership team was too weak and they wouldn't be able to cope with the messages that had to be delivered across the organisation. Now, this organisation was important to this country because it had 80 per cent of the nation's customers so it couldn't fail. It couldn't just fall apart and become dysfunctional. So the CEO's view was to address this weakness in our leadership – in our line management.

Coaching skills training allows managers the time to reflect on their role and how they interact with their direct reports so they can make the changes necessary to develop a *coaching leadership style*. These programmes have the flexibility to be implemented consistently across the organisation but also to be tailored when they need to be, to meet particular business needs. Where possible, the line manager is included as a member of the training delivery team so they can more quickly assist participants transfer the learnings back into the workplace. When individual coaching sessions are included as an essential component of the coaching skills training programme, participants report that being coached is the part of the programme they value most.

One of the desired outcomes of conducting *Manager-as-Coach* or *Leader-as-Coach* programmes is that managers who participate in coaching skills training and experience being coached shift their awareness of self and others and come to an understanding that they are human beings just like everyone else. This realisation may happen gradually as the training progresses or it can strike a participant like a "thunderbolt out of the blue". By whatever process, the manager's views on the world change during the training, and they realise that people are human, people make mistakes, and people are fallible – including themselves. With this realisation comes an acceptance of their own and others' imperfections and an acknowledgement that mistakes are really opportunities for improvement, provided they are handled constructively with specific feedback in mind. After their coaching skills training has concluded, the leader's role is to practice their new competency by coaching their direct reports to develop their own self-awareness, better self-manage, and discover their own solutions within the responsibilities of their role.

Some in-house coaching skills training programmes are more successful than others in changing the mindset of managers, for several reasons: (1) although a major motivation for conducting coaching skills training is to facilitate managers to become more developmentally focused and less *command-and-control*, 2 or 3 days of training is often insufficient to bring about a long-term, mental mindshift and produce real cognitive and behavioural change; (2) in-house coaching skills training programmes, whilst an important first step in developing a coaching culture, are unlikely to produce the desired change unless supported by the experience of being coached as part of this programme; (3) managers are very busy – "stretched to the max" – and cannot give their undivided attention to changing the way they already operate; and (4) why would managers change the way they have been interacting with their teams for so long when they have been successful in gaining promotion and being rewarded time and again for getting results for doing what they are doing right now?

Critics of in-house coaching skills training programmes delivered by HR professionals believe that the outcomes of these programmes are suboptimal because they are only as good as the understanding and experience that the HR professionals have of coaching. Some critics have even described the in-house coaching skills training delivered by (not formally trained) HR professionals as a "car wash" – the "take-out", "fast food" version of leadership: "I'm going to send you through the coaching car wash to clean you off, and you'll be clean for a little while. I'll spend some time buffing everybody's emotions and their abilities – but you'll still get dirty down the track". To formally trained coaches who know and understand the benefits of the behavioural and performance shifts experienced during coaching, the programmes designed and delivered in-house by HR professionals can appear "weak" – as if they've been "dumbed down" to appeal to a broader group of leaders with varying skill levels, backgrounds and histories. They note that a "caring conversation" is important but not sufficient to bring about behavioural or performance improvements.

The second way that coaching is delivered in this second stage of developing a coaching culture is by external coaches who are appointed to a coaching panel as a result of a procurement process conducted by HR. External coaches are engaged to coach executives and selected employees who need more skilled coaching than can be delivered by internal coaches. The procurement process identifies a number of vendors and then shortlists a company to deliver the coaching. Executive coaches are typically hired to coach the executive team and individuals in situations where an experienced coach is required. However, it is often difficult for organisations to know which external coaches to select onto a coaching panel because there are no standard criteria that organisations can use to guide their decision. Their criteria are usually based on the background and experience of the coach. However, because the coaching industry is self-regulating, selection should also be based on whether the external coach has been formally trained to international standards and is a member of, or credentialed by, a professional coaching association such as the ICF.

To ensure that there is a "chemistry match" between the coach and coachee, before the coaching begins, a meeting is arranged to ascertain if a trusting coaching relationship can be established. Once agreed, an initial "deep-dive" goal-setting session is conducted to identify the employee's coaching needs and the specific goals to be achieved through the coaching programme. Conversation is around determining where the employee is now, where they need and want to be, what key milestones are needed to get there, specific timelines and measures of success – the tangibles of coaching that can be reported against as necessary. The next step is to gather information from a psychometric or similar assessment instrument to provide the coachee with a reality check on how they and their behaviours, communication, relationships, and leadership style are viewed by others around them including any direct reports. There are a number of commercially available 360-degree instruments in the marketplace that the coach can use to obtain a behavioural profile on the individual before coaching commences. Alternatively, the organisation may have a preferred instrument that they use.

In summary, when an organisation is at the second *Coaching-as-HR-Function* stage of developing a coaching culture, coaching, skills training programmes and coaching are primarily driven and delivered by HR professionals. Coaching allows individuals to grow and their performance to improve in a safe environment. It reframes failures into learning experiences and builds the capability of leaders whose resilience encourages others to keep trying, perfecting, and reinventing their best possible future. HR professionals who are formally trained as coaches are better able to assist the organisation transition to the third stage in the development of a coaching culture than those who rely on the "car wash" coaching skills training delivered in-house by HR professionals who are not formally trained as coaches.

Stage 2: Illustrative Examples: *Coaching-as-HR-Function*

Illustrative Example 6

ConnectHub is a large national technology company in an industry where the profit margins have been gradually falling for years. The "cash cow" that was the telecommunications infrastructure has been reduced to a utility. *ConnectHub* now has to rethink how to "monetise the pipe", that is, how to make money out of basically a dead electric pipe. Under the previous CEO who was keen on coaching, one of the Big 4 consulting firms was engaged at considerable expense to train leaders in coaching skills. *Coaching Circles* were established after the training was completed but because no one was coordinating them or monitoring their activity, they floundered after a few short months.

Then the company was bought out by an overseas firm. The new CEO was not interested in coaching. He was more interested in the "bottom line" and creating innovation in a market of declining revenues. Hence the "coaching" that was being conducted in the organisation returned to one-on-one conversations which were basically problem-solving exercises based on asking a series of questions to promote self-learning – which is helpful – but leaders trained in coaching skills would like to guide coachees to "go deeper, own their solutions" and learn from the experience. The reality now is that there is rarely the opportunity to coach direct reports because, in the new environment, there are more important priorities, no budget or resources for coaching, and the CEO is pushing a different agenda.

Illustrative Example 7

FedFinancial is a federal government organisation in the financial services industry with approximately 19,000 employees. The organisation is in its "infancy" in terms of creating a coaching culture. Some of the executive team have external coaches and other senior leaders can access coaching from the *Accredited Coach Network* which matches internal volunteer coaches with those who request to be coached. The *Network* consists of more than 200 volunteer coaches who have self-funded their formal coach-training through various private providers. Any senior staff member can request to have a one-on-one coaching relationship with one of these coaches. However, this type of coaching is more aligned to a mentoring relationship rather than coaching which, in this organisation, "doesn't really matter as long as it's about the person's development".

In addition, general staff with direct reports have access to a 2-day *Manager-as-Coach* programme which has been conducted in the organisation for some years. The programme is designed to train managers in how to use coaching conversations for developmental purposes particularly around some of the technical areas for development. The programme trains managers to ask, "What are your goals?" and "What are your strategies to get there" so that they can give direct feedback to their team members. Hence, the training is really in *performance* rather than *pure coaching*.

In their call centre operation, the "coaching" that occurs is completely transactional, simply providing feedback on operator performance much as would occur under a performance management system. Full-time call centre "coaches" listen to calls with the operative, give feedback on their performance and support development planning. They assist front-line team members establish their own goals and direction and keep them motivated and engaged to achieve their goals. In principle, the idea of *pure coaching* is still evident in that the "coaches" try to guide staff to understand their capability gaps and set their own goals but the actual "coaching" uses forms and templates so it's quite often just a step-by-step, formulated process.

In other (senior) areas of *FedFinancial*, the coaching is more traditional. One-on-one coaching sessions over 6 weeks are conducted, driven by the senior leader. For the past 12 months, the HR function has been trying to gain approval to develop and roll out a "middle of the road" coaching programme that sits between the performance management feedback currently delivered to front-line staff and individual one-on-one coaching sessions delivered at the executive level. This coaching programme would be delivered to all staff for development purposes on the understanding that the approach would be "a little bit more directive [than a client-led pure coaching agenda] in terms of building specific skills and capabilities" but less performance-directed. It was only when a consultant reviewed the work of the unit and recommended coaching as a high priority that executives agreed to conduct a pilot coaching programme at the middle management level.

A working party was established consisting of representatives from various sections of the business which co-designed the programme based on an analysis of the current situation and how the organisation wants coaching to be conducted in the future. After designing the generic components, the working party addressed: "What's the extra bit that's specific to each department? What is coaching actually going to achieve as opposed to whatever else [developmental tool] is out there?" The pilot was then conducted in one of their sites. People who volunteered to become coaches were those who were one level below management, typically at the level of technical expert, for example, full-time call centre coaches or team leaders with the intention of helping junior staff succeed. These volunteers wanted more information about how to improve the coaching they were already doing informally and to learn the coaching skills. Following the in-house coaching skills training, they were connected with employees who wanted to be coached.

As a result of the success of the programme, it "got on the radar of the executive" and will be extended across the business group but how and when this will happen has yet to be determined. What is necessary to do next is to set up an evaluation process to gauge the effectiveness of the programme, the coaches, and the coaching relationships and to determine if the coaching is actually developing the coachee. After that, it's looking at the bigger picture to ascertain things like: "How is the program actually delivering on our capability of the workforce as a whole?" and "How are we getting better at the types of things that we need to get better at?" As yet, the working party is unsure how to address these questions but at least they are part of the thinking and programme design moving forwards.

Illustrative Example 8

RRR Inc. is a government authority that delivers infrastructure services to the general public at a state level. It employs 2300 people directly plus numerous contracted staff. There's a strong mentoring culture and an emerging recognition of coaching which began 2 years ago when a new CEO was appointed. Since then, there's been strong encouragement for all senior executives to take on an external coach as modelled by the CEO and several executive directors. So, from the very top, there's recognition that coaching is a valid component of employee development and a methodology to be embraced in order to become a fully functioning member of the organisation.

RRR Inc. believes that coaching is a one-on-one opportunity to work closely with an employee to improve their performance and develop identified skills deficits. Coaching encourages coachees to be accountable for the decisions they make about how to do things differently within their leadership and collegiate teams. Coachees make a commitment to plan their learning so that when they meet with their coach again, they can discuss what worked, what didn't work, and how to move on to fully developing themselves and their people.

All the executive officers and senior leaders in *RRR Inc.* have been trained in the use and debrief of a particular "coaching" assessment instrument. In committing to fund this external assessment process and training, the organisation made a decision that they wanted to be self-sufficient and use internal accredited "coaches" rather than continue to engage external coaches. All those who undertook this external training were assigned a peer "coach" with a clearly defined objective – to develop a coaching plan over the next 6–12 months around how they could improve as a senior leader and how that would be measured. The five or six "coaching sessions" they received were structured in accordance with the "guide" that executives received during their training on how to deliver individual feedback in relation to the results of the assessment instrument.

In addition to this external training in how to assess and provide feedback on the results of the assessment instrument, *RRR Inc.* conducts internal *Leader-as-Coach* training programmes and provides support for leaders who coach. The facilitators who deliver the in-house coaching skills training programmes have been accredited in the "coaching" assessment instrument. The organisation is working towards embedding coaching as an understood requirement of leaders and an expectation that all employees will be coached at some time in their career. In the past, senior leaders who have not been able to focus their leadership on the development of others and become a contemporary, authentic leader have been exited from the organisation.

***

This chapter has detailed the four key dimensions of Stage 2 – *Coaching-as-HR-Function.* The next chapter explains the four key dimensions of Stage 3 – *Coaching-as-Leader-Capability.*

Chapter 6
Stage 3: Coaching-as-Leader-Capability

This chapter addresses the third of four stages in the development of a coaching culture as depicted in the model of coaching culture development (Fig. 3.1). During this stage, coaching is an expected capability of leaders and embedded within a leadership development framework. Coaching is conceptualised as a *practice* and an understood requirement of leaders who have a *performance* motivation to uplift team and business results. *Business units* are responsible for driving coaching throughout the organisation and coaching is *internally delivered* by leaders to their teams and team members.

Practice Conceptualisation

In the *Coaching-as-Leader-Capability* stage of developing a coaching culture, organisational leaders have a *practice* conceptualisation of coaching as a requirement of the leader role and an expected capability for leaders to progress in their career. Coaching is a "micro skill" in the leader's "kit bag" that they can draw upon not necessarily as a formal coaching session but as the need arises in any conversation. It is a medium-term investment in building leader capability and the human capital of the organisation (Fig. 6.1).

The first way that coaching is conceptualised as a *practice* is as a capability requirement of leaders in the performance of their role. In previous stages, it was difficult for some organisations to accept the value of coaching as an expected practice of leaders. In this third stage, coaching is a required leadership capability – like Leadership 101. Leaders have to be able to coach. Hence, coaching is included in the leader's position description which makes it crystal clear that leaders are required to coach their direct reports as part of their role. However, organisational leaders' conceptualisation of coaching is still not entirely well-formed at this stage. Hence, some coaching advocates may position *coaching* under the banner of *leadership*

S. Knowles, *Coaching Culture*, https://doi.org/10.1007/978-3-031-09050-9_6

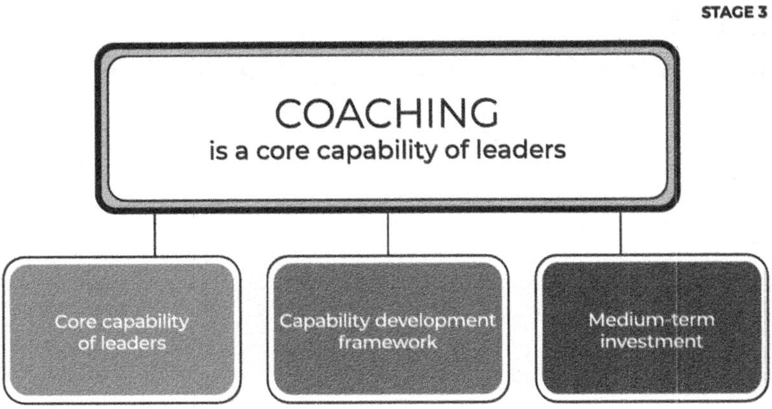

Fig. 6.1 Stage 3 - Coaching is a core capability of leaders

which employees are familiar with and see as being really important, whereas coaching is relatively unknown to them. Then, when leaders interact with their team as a coach, they may describe using the coaching skills as *leadership*, not *coaching*.

When leaders express a desire to develop their leadership capability through coaching, the business unit leader sits down with them to identify the outcomes they want to achieve and discuss options for doing that. Building the capability of leaders in coaching skills enables them to elicit better performance from their team as they create shared models of understanding based on the coaching language and process, and relationships built on trust, openness and honesty. That shared understanding promotes a common philosophy within the team and a way of interacting that team members accept as malleable, mouldable, and built on foundational principles. The coaching philosophy is the agreed understanding of how the team communicates the levels of cooperation and collaboration required within the team and the support that's available for team members' ongoing development and career progression.

Leadership capability is built on a coaching philosophy which supports leaders not only to lead for improved performance but also to nurture their employees' innate ability to grow. Building organisational capability has been described as "exciting, fertile ground" and a way of ensuring that individuals and teams are provided with regular, constructive, one-on-one formal and informal feedback on their performance. Leaders who coach, step back from the day-to-day "doing" and "hold the space" for others to lead, which is difficult for those managers who have not made the mental mindset shift from *command-and-control* to a *coaching leadership style*. If managers cannot achieve this transition to leader, they may be exited from the organisation because in this third stage, a coach "is not a person that you bring in to do it for you". The responsibility to coach lies with the leader as a requirement of their role.

In organisations which have the funds to deliver consistent *Manager-as-Coach* or *Leader-as-Coach* programmes, or ongoing leadership development programmes which include a coaching component, the expectation that leaders will coach is a mandated requirement of their role. In other organisations which do not have the funds to ensure the training of all leaders in coaching skills, the expectation that they will coach is just that – an expectation that is not enforced. These organisations have limited resources and, hence, limited places in their development programmes. In addition, the leadership development programmes may be competing for funds with other organisational initiatives. Hence, in less well-resourced organisations, it's often voluntary for leaders to attend a coaching skills training programme, and it will take longer for a coaching culture to develop. However, in organisations on a journey to develop a coaching culture in which coaching skills training is mandated, it's unacceptable for leaders to pass coaching onto an external coach unless the situation requires a degree of skill or expertise that the leader does not possess or the consequences of "getting it wrong" are significant.

The second way that coaching is conceptualised as a *practice* is as a capability requirement within the organisation's *capability development framework.* This framework guides the delivery of in-house coaching skills training programmes and establishes processes to monitor the quality of the coaching that is delivered – same way, right way – each and every time. Establishing a capability framework for leaders that includes coaching involves gaining executive agreement on what coaching means to the organisation (because each executive will have their own view) and the standards and quality of the coaching to be delivered within the organisation. It is in this third stage that organisations may decide to reshape their capability development framework to include an *employee life cycle* of which coaching forms an essential component, particularly at the middle management level.

As a designated leader capability within the organisation's capability framework, coaching can be applied to any conversation for any purpose among a leader, their direct reports, and others in the organisation. For example, in one organisation, their capability development framework for leaders has six competencies – all soft skills – with a strong emphasis on coaching, engagement, and connection to serve the organisation's broader goals. These leadership competencies underpin the roles of the approximately 850 leaders in the organisation, all of whom have participated in their leadership development programme which incorporates the coaching language and shared models of coaching as applied to the day-to-day leadership of their teams.

Another organisation has established a capability development framework for leaders that is a compilation of a set of principles around leadership and the expected behaviours of leaders in their organisation. Rather than conducting training programmes to inculcate these principles and behaviours, the organisation is filtering them down through monthly team discussions about what these principles mean to employees and how they should be enacted at the team level, and then following through with peer accountability thereafter. These principles are statements of intent as to how a leader behaves in relation to their direct reports and others in the organisation. They're framed as questions to stimulate discussion at the team level. One of them, for example, asks how leaders provide the opportunity for team members to input into decisions. Each month, a new principle becomes the focus for discussion as a way of investing in leaders to think about their role and encouraging them to approach their leadership responsibilities in the "right" organisational way.

A third way that coaching is conceptualised as a *practice* in this third stage of developing a coaching culture is as a capability requirement of leaders to advance in their career. Coaching is included within a *career progression framework*. Leaders who wish to promote are expected to possess coaching capability. Pathways are developed which identify the skills and capabilities required to make the important transitions such as from technical specialist to team leader to line manager to inspiring leader of people. Within a state government department, career pathways have been developed at the various leader levels which identify the "stepping stones" to executive leadership. These self-assessment tools give upwardly mobile team members the knowledge they need to make decisions about the capabilities they require to promote to their desired position within the organisation.

Within a clearly articulated framework for coaching and acknowledgement of its value, every leader new to the organisation in this third stage undertakes in-house coaching skills training and receives individual coaching if they haven't been coached before. Hence, every organisational leader develops their coaching capability – to different degrees for different levels. As part of the capability strategy for the organisation, the Workforce Planning function periodically "core reviews" coaching as a skill to ascertain the numbers that need to be included in future coaching skills training programmes. Investing in the ability of business unit managers to coach is one of the most important decisions that an organisation can make in this third stage of developing a coaching culture.

The in-house coaching skills training of managers in this third stage is typically a medium-term investment in building organisational capability. Organisations usually only invest a few hours to a few days in dedicated coaching skills training programmes; obviously, the more time invested, the better leaders will be at coaching. A few hours of training allows the organisation to say "We coach" but is an insufficient allocation of time for leaders to truly understand what coaching is all about and become proficient in coaching skills. Time devoted to coaching is what is needed for managers to practise coaching and become confident in their coaching ability. Some organisations offer a more comprehensive programme of training - for example, 3 days of training a month apart with practice in between. A 3-day programme may include say, one day on coaching skills, one day on coaching process and a third day on coaching practice around issues of real concern to managers. As part of the training, managers may be allocated an external coach to focus on their development needs during the programme and assist them embed their learnings back into the workplace post-training.

An example of an organisation that cost-effectively implemented coaching throughout a business unit is a large national organisation in the technology service sector. It successfully transitioned from using external coaches to train and coach employees, to providing the funding for a number of selected employees to be formally trained as internal coaches by an external coach-training provider. Because the organisation didn't intend to keep the external coaches coming back interminably, once qualified, these internal coaches started delivering training and coaching throughout the business unit, cascading it down from the senior leaders to team leaders. Now, they estimate that 90 per cent of their team leaders are far better coaches than most other leaders in the organisation. So, rather than relying on just five or six fully qualified HR professionals to do the coaching, or external coaches, there are now over 800 leaders in the business unit who have been trained in coaching skills and they coach their teams on a regular basis. This has allowed the call centre operation to shift mindsets and implement behavioural changes more quickly than ever before, which has resulted in a greater impact on business results. An organisation gains traction in developing a coaching culture when it invests in the formal coach-training of HR professionals and the subsequent coaching skills training of managers and team leaders who then deliver coaching to their teams within the business unit.

Overall, when an organisation is at the third stage of developing a coaching culture, coaching is conceptualised as a practice. It is a medium-term investment in building an organisation's capability by including coaching as a core capability of leaders and incorporating it into leadership development, capability and career progression frameworks.

Performance Motivation

Another characteristic of the *Coaching-as-Leader-Capability* stage concerns the motivation for why coaching *practice* is being undertaken by the organisation. In this third stage, coaching has a *performance* motivation as part of a suite of development tools at the leader's disposal so that leaders can improve the performance of their teams and team members, increase team engagement and retain talent (Fig. 6.2).

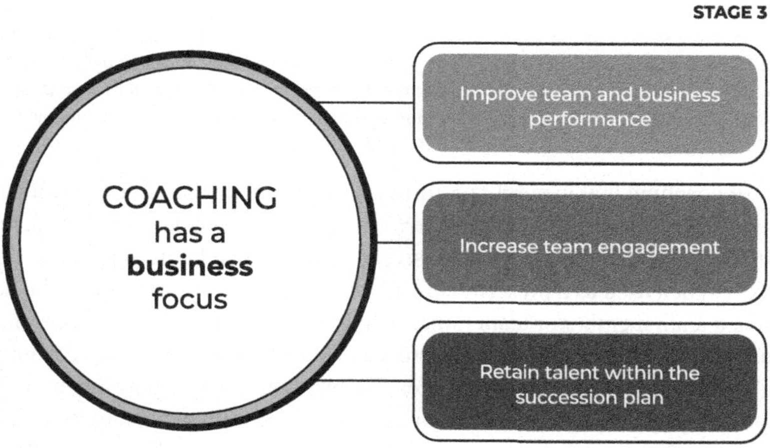

Fig. 6.2 Stage 3 - Coaching improves team and business performance

The first *performance* motivation for coaching is to enable employees to fulfil on the requirements of their role and deliver on their Key Performance Indicators (KPIs). This is *performance coaching* in which a leader works with a middle performer – where the leverage, opportunity, and potential sits – demonstrating an investment in that team member over and above the time that they've already spent with them. Performance coaching directs the conversation towards deliverables. How is the team member going to achieve their targets and what will be the impact on them and the team when they achieve those deliverables, or don't? Performance coaching also considers the external environment in which teams operate, to identify what might be holding team members back from delivering on the requirements of their roles - for example, the pressure that they're under, the sensitivity of the assignment or the complexity of changes in the team composition and roles.

The coaching that leaders conduct with their teams and team members in this third stage as a KPI of their role is scrutinised and the results input into their job contract renegotiations. However, if the expectations around how and when coaching will be conducted and to what standard have not been specified, the actual measurement of the KPI is less meaningful. Critics of individually based KPIs suggest that the focus should be on how individual performance and behaviours impact on the team rather than just on the achievement of individual KPIs. Non-individual KPIs could relate to team performance and business effectiveness and may include indicators of, for example, communication, relationships, collaboration and cooperation within the team as well as the demonstration of behaviours which are consistent with organisational values. Advocates of team-based KPIs believe that the focus of coaching should go beyond individual results into the achievement of collective outcomes at the team level.

Organisations advancing in their development of a coaching culture recognise that the annual performance review may cause anxiety and stress for many employees. They are moving away from the "redundancy of the annual performance review as an artefact of a performance culture" and replacing it with regular coaching sessions, as this organisational leader explains:

> So we have a system in place where we no longer get performance ratings at the end of the year but we are required as leaders to have monthly one-on-ones with our people. So you have KPIs, and then you have the development part of it. And every month, you'd have a look at it and see where that person is going and give them feedback, give them coaching. And like I said, it goes all the way from the CEO down.

Critics of coaching that is purely performance-driven note that it may become "prescriptive" and be used instead as a performance management tool. If coaching is used in this way, it could create defensiveness rather than being seen as "reflective practice". When used as a prescriptive tool, coaching is all about shaping the performance of a team member or team rather than it being about "*who* we are … and *how* we are in the workplace". However, there may be times when a prescriptive approach has value as an enabler of performance - for example, in an environment in which the business requires the achievement of specific tasks or financial targets. A "coaching to revenue" approach may, for example, use performance-enabling software in a sales-driven environment. If the performance needs to be lifted in certain business areas, “prescriptive” coaching can be applied within those areas to improve overall performance, as this story illustrates:

> So we’re working in the back-of-house with our finance team and our analysts to produce data, produce reports, and then we feed them up to the sales leadership team to help them make decisions, to help them drive performance to enable the sales leadership team to have meaningful conversations with their sales teams.

This story highlights how coaching practice is used to support a performance motivation for improved economic returns to the business. The expectation is that, after receiving training in coaching skills, leaders go to a “coaching place” first before they adopt a “performance management” stance. An example is of a managing director of a large company who establishes relationships with team members first before going to performance management:

> *He’s a guy I admire a lot because, in his early forties, he’s got an enormous job and high energy levels. He walks the talk around* ‘the most important thing I can do is deliver profitability, which comes through people’.

The second *performance* motivation for coaching is to increase team engagement and improve business outcomes. Identifying the strengths of team members is a good first step to increasing job satisfaction but insufficient to ensure increased team engagement and business improvement. Rather, when team members are coached within a capability framework that supports and affirms individual and team performance, the business benefits from the increased productivity generated from the team’s collective efforts. Leaders who use the coaching language within a productivity framework integrate coaching into everything they do with the team and team members including how they communicate, relate and interact with each other on a daily basis. When leaders adopt a *coaching leadership style*, it demonstrates that the business cares about the team members who work for them, and they have an objective and a goal to help them develop and do more to reach their potential. This ultimately leads to more engaged team members who perform better, which impacts on the organisation’s “bottom line”. In all aspects of the business relationship, coaching enables consideration for the people involved in driving and delivering the business transactions.

Team morale improves when team members are enabled and empowered to perform their best and contribute significantly to the performance and productivity of the team. An example of team collaboration is when team members participate in co-designing their own coaching skills training programme. When this design method is used, organisations establish a working party of key stakeholders who represent the interests of different departments or sections of the business. They design not only for commonalities but also for differences pertaining to the areas they represent. The key is always to discover the “additional extras” that should be incorporated into the flexible part of the programme specific to a particular group or team to ensure that the learnings are tailored and applicable to that group or team’s business performance.

Some areas of importance to the organisation that may need a specific design modification include how to coach team members who work in different locations including overseas, and how to coach teams with specialist or technical expertise that is of particular value to the organisation. For example, a team leader in an international logistics firm who wants to become more engaged with his team and have team members feel more connected to each other requires infrastructure to support coaching his team members at a distance such as internet-enabled group forums and interactive webinars. A second example is of a leader attempting to create an empowered team when there are a number of high-performing team members each with their own "ego on display". Coaching these individuals can prove challenging in itself. Coaching them as a team may require additional coaching capability because of team-related issues such as how to achieve collaboration and cooperation among individuals, especially if the team is very much a "group" and not a team.

Another example that illustrates this situation is of a large federal government department where the work is fast and high-pressured. Each team member has a discrete area of responsibility and, at worst, they may be immediately dismissed for any errors of content or judgement since such errors have a significant impact on key stakeholders and the reputation of the department. Team members are usually recruited because they are "stars" in their own right, used to working alone in their particular area of expertise with little direction and making huge judgement calls on a daily basis. These teams often have a very big remit. However, because team members are all "stars", they're not used to working together as a team. Therefore, the focus of coaching is to transform this "group" into a team with interdependencies and support systems in place. The leader's role is to use a coaching leadership style to assist the "group" members identify the ways they can improve the overall team performance by developing awareness of each other's role and responsibilities. The leader can then outline the areas of expected team performance and explore options to transition individual "stars" into team members.

The third *performance* motivation for coaching is to retain talent within the team or business unit. Coaching is particularly effective in developing people and recognising their true potential, enabling them to flourish, step into their greatness, and make a significant difference to their life and the lives of others with whom they interact. Organisations which develop the coaching capability of their leaders and talented employees are well-positioned to utilise their skills and expertise as the organisation grows. Such individuals are included in the organisation's succession plan and receive coaching to prepare them for future positions within the organisation. The aim is to achieve a talent pipeline of employees who have the potential for development over time, whom a talent champion can steward through the organisation until they reach the executive level. Employee surveys may be used to gauge the extent to which an organisation needs to support talented individuals whom they wish to retain within the organisation, as this HR professional explains:

> In my nine years with this organisation, nothing gets done just because it's a good idea. You have to have a reason. So the reason they've put in place is the Intention to Leave survey. From the results, we identify people where a coaching conversation may help reduce their intention to leave.

When talented individuals are identified, resources are allocated to provide the potential leaders with opportunities that recognise their abilities and enhance their career prospects. A *Leader-as-Coach* programme is something that aspiring leaders identify as of particular benefit and support to them in their process of transitioning to a more senior role. Individual career coaching may be offered to support employees in making the transition from one position to another. External coaches may be used to work with talented executives who have confronted the "glass ceiling" for a range of reasons or who may be competing with younger talent identified for promotion. An "outside" perspective may be just what they need to help them transition into their next role. In fact, in some organisations, the only reason that external coaches are engaged is to support talent. Coaching by an external coach is an opportunity for the talented individual to have the "impartial ear" of someone to whom they can speak confidentially, which they may be reluctant to do with an internal coach who may not be seen as completely confidential. However, this level of external coaching support can prove expensive when large numbers are involved in the coaching to retain talent within the organisation.

Aspiring leaders may be recruited into the organisation via a graduate entry programme which aims to identify potential in the early phases of an employee's career. Such individuals may be "fast-tracked" within a talent management cycle as they transition from one position to the next based on a series of talent metrics driven by HR. "I'm working with five early leaders who've just gone through psychometrics and, for want of a better word, developmental opportunities", reports an external coach. The talent management cycle looks at the "end-to-end" processes from the policies and procedures surrounding how the organisation recruits new employees through to how it plans for the workforce of the future and manages organisational talent through that cycle.

A challenge when promoting talent from within, and especially when appointing an external candidate, is to manage the expectations of unsuccessful internal candidates. External appointments may negatively impact staff morale and possibly lead to resignations of team members who were overlooked for the position, as illustrated by the story of a very large organisation which provides essential utility services to customers nationally. Initially, it only produced the product but then the decision was made to move into distribution and retail of the product rather than using partner distribution networks and resellers. As the organisation grew the distribution arm of the business, the growth could be managed by existing staff supplemented with a manageable number of new recruits in a few specific areas. However, to develop and grow a completely new retail arm of the business in which the organisation had no expertise required some talent to be "bought in from outside" because no one in the organisation knew how to run a retail business. Growing the retail business from almost nothing to four million customers necessitated successive rounds of recruitment of people who had the expertise to fill these new roles. This proved to be a particularly challenging time for existing employees who were not selected for the available roles. The morale of some unsuccessful team members plummeted and some talent left the organisation. Those who remained needed to be supported by coaching to understand the reasons for their non-selection to these roles.

Overall, when an organisation is at the third stage of developing a coaching culture, performance motivations for coaching combined with practice conceptualisations of coaching have progressed organisational leaders from an emphasis on individual performance and motivation to team motivation and business performance. There are two challenges for organisations wishing to incorporate both developmental and performance motivations for coaching. First, leaders need to work out how to combine individual human capabilities with strategies to embrace the diversity and different skill sets available within their team, to drive improved performance. Second, leaders need to decide whether their approach to talent management will include the provision of opportunities for more than the select few to receive coaching and identify ways to do this when large numbers of employees are involved. A sceptic of a talent management strategy quipped that "it really amuses me because, once you have a talent management pool, you're telling everyone else in the organisation that they're not talented."

To progress to the next stage in the development of a coaching culture, leaders need to intend that all team members will be coached, not just a few talented individuals, so that everyone's performance can improve as much as possible, resulting in increased engagement and work performance because of the personal attention they receive. Not everyone can be included in the organisation's succession plan but if all team members lift their performance, it will result in improvements across the entire business unit.

Business Drivers

In this third stage, the leaders of *business* units drive coaching as an expectation of their role to increase the performance of their teams. They use their coaching capability to motivate team members to greater levels of engagement, collaboration and teamwork. However, when coaching is positioned within business units, the *performance coaching* may initially be "formulaic" and "procedural" to provide consistency and ensure product quality and "same way delivery" each and every time. Hence, leaders in this third stage need to focus not only on achieving business outcomes but also on ensuring "care and concern" for individuals as they drive team performance towards achieving the designated business targets. Balancing the need to look after people but also deliver on role expectations illustrates how leaders in this third stage of developing a coaching culture coach from a *performance* motivation to improve business outcomes (Fig. 6.3).

The first element relating to the business drivers of coaching in this third stage involves leaders coaching their team members as an understood *expectation of their role*. In a digital economy, the workforce needs to respond quickly to changes in the marketplace. Reports on digital workforces point out that leaders need to optimise their "people skills" – the "soft skills" – to capture future opportunities, and critical

Fig. 6.3 Stage 3 - Business unit leaders drive coaching to increased performance

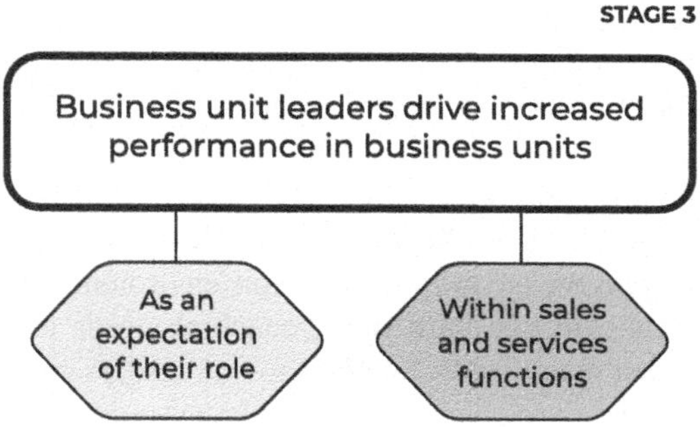

to doing that is to adopt a coaching skill set. Increasingly, workforces are required to become more agile and adaptable. Coaching programmes that work with front-line staff assist team members build resilience to change and, by removing barriers that are holding them back from delivering on the expectations of their role, leaders enable employees to work "better, faster, and stronger".

When coaching is a mandated requirement of a leader's role, the way that it is enacted is explained by one organisational leader thus: "I set the scene from the very beginning when we recruit new leaders that part of their role is the coaching of their team and others - not just their team - from a 'pay it forward' perspective". In other words, the leader asks: "What have you learnt from others, and how can you share that with somebody else?" In addition, if the function has, say 500 employees, the question is asked: "Is the leader able to manage that well, and are they actually able to coach within a leadership framework to make sure that people are performing?"

Leaders are also expected to meet the needs of key stakeholders. For example, governments expect the workforce to respond to megatrends in the marketplace, adapting and responding quickly to the changing environment in which they work. Departments are increasingly expected to move towards a one-government approach to whole-of-government issues and challenges, working in multidisciplinary, multi-agency teams. If coaching is not a core capability of departmental leaders, "we'll never meet the expectations of Ministers in Parliament". Governments require a workplace culture that supports sharing, working with each other, learning from each other and guiding employees towards higher performance. Unless leaders coach their teams and team members, the expectations set by key stakeholders may not be met.

The second element relating to the business drivers of coaching throughout the organisation at this third stage involves coaching initially being positioned *within sales and services business units* to improve team performance. These business units have accountability for the achievement of business targets focused on the generation of revenue for the organisation as a whole. Hence, the coaching initiative may start within the front-line sales and services functions which are directly customer-facing as these are the functional areas most likely to see an immediate financial return to the business from coaching. Within these business units, coaching is used to support team leaders and front-line staff land sales deals of substantial proportions. Leaders of these business units recognise how important it is to get the best performance from the teams they lead because the revenue they generate supports not only their business operations but also the corporate services and regulatory functions of the organisation.

In a revenue-generating distribution or retail sales environment, things are fast-paced. There's urgency to the interaction. Decisions must be made quickly or even on the spot. Problems emerge which must be dealt with immediately. Front-line employees are familiar with this environment and trained to respond appropriately. Hence, in this third stage, coaching needs to be positioned within business units rather than the HR function so that leaders are ready to respond to emerging opportunities or to counter potential threats quickly. Organisations which continue to have coaching reside within the HR function with a learning and development focus will find that their organisation will have difficulty progressing to this third stage of developing a coaching culture unless the responsibility for coaching is transferred and positioned within business units. Business unit leaders have a wealth of experience in front-line roles so they can focus their coaching on both the behavioural aspects of interacting as a member of a team as well as on the performance aspects of meeting business targets. Behavioural coaching breaks down the "silo" mentality that can develop in organisations and tends to negatively impact performance because of internal disagreement and conflict.

Within sales and services functions, teams which use the coaching language and philosophy listen to customer concerns and support each other to ensure that they are on track for a sales win and to review the win thereafter. Hence, teams which embrace coaching are more than just utilising the strengths of individuals and the team as in *performance coaching*. They engage team members at a personal level as integral contributors to team performance. A business unit leader comments that, in his organisation, he found there was "a real appetite for people to just really start a personal development conversation and create some self-awareness" and that coaching was the answer he was looking for to take his team to that place. Coaching provides the vehicle to enable his leadership team to have meaningful conversations with their sales teams around the information that is generated from data analysis and reports, which promotes better decision-making and drives performance improvements. By coaching both personal and professional issues, leaders discover that there's a whole other layer to coaching outside of a one-dimensional, strengths- or performance-based conversation to develop their teams and team members.

Overall, when an organisation is at the third stage of developing a coaching culture, they have progressed from functional drivers of performance being centrally located within the HR function where their remit is to develop a training and learning experience for managers and talented employees, to business drivers of coaching positioned within business units where performance has a direct impact on revenue generation. The performance motivation in this stage focuses on economic returns to the business from behavioural change and improved team performance. Combined with a practice conceptualisation of coaching, leaders in this third stage foster team engagement and the retention of talent, which makes central to this stage the business environment and business performance.

Internalised Delivery

The final aspect that characterises the *Coaching-as-Leader-Capability* stage concerns how coaching is delivered *internally* by organisational members. In this third stage, coaching is delivered in four ways by: (1) *leadership coaching* so that business unit and team leaders can more effectively coach their direct reports to change their behaviour and improve their performance; (2) *team coaching* as leaders use coaching skills to increase their team's performance; (3) coaching by *specialist coaches* who coach teams and team members to increase business and sales performance; and (4) coaching by fully qualified *internal coaches* who coach within business units and *internal coaching teams* who coach across business units to increase productivity and competitive advantage. Coaching by leaders, specialist, and internal coaches is a cost-effective way to spread coaching practice throughout the organisation (Fig. 6.4).

The first way that coaching is internally delivered in this third stage is by business unit and team leaders who coach individual team members as a requirement of their role. Business unit and team leaders are the ones who are accountable for meeting business objectives within budget. They're also the ones who spend the most time with their direct reports. They direct the energy and focus activities within their area of responsibility. External coaches have their value but are nowhere near the centre of action when it comes to the immediacy that can be exerted to change behaviour and performance almost immediately, as this business unit leader emphasises: "Coaching's got to sit with the line managers. No one else can do it".

Business unit and team leaders improve the performance of their direct reports by conducting individual coaching and feedback conversations with them every 4–6 weeks. Before coaching commences, team members may undertake behavioural profiling to identify their strengths and opportunities for improvement. When all team members are profiled, the leader can also map the dynamics of the team. When a team member displays behaviours which are inconsistent with organisational values, a coaching conversation is conducted and, as a result, the individual

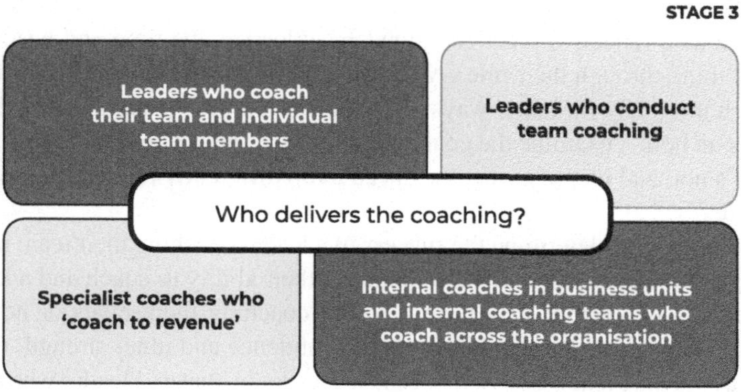

Fig. 6.4 Stage 3 - Internalised delivery of coaching

may decide to change their behaviour so they better relate to other members of the team and the team functions more effectively. However, if change is not forthcoming, a decision may be made to exit them from the organisation. The following story illustrates how important it is that all business unit leaders recognise their responsibility not only for staff performance but also for their job satisfaction and team morale:

> *I remember a company once where the director of HR was a friend of mine. Every Monday, they had a directors' meeting. If the director of building and construction said* 'I've saved a million dollars out of that building in the city', *they would go,* 'Wow, isn't that fantastic! How did you do that?' *He said, if I said I've saved a million dollars through staff turnover they'd go,* 'Well, isn't that your job?' *He said the only reason staff turnover reduced in this company was that he got the CEO to tie staff turnover into individual director's performance bonus. Everybody had to have their staff turnover below 20 per cent or it affected their bonus. That's the only reason why they even looked at staff turnover.*

Organisational leaders who want to optimise the opportunities for employees in their team know that the coaching skill set is critical to their success: "It's the engine room, I think, this skill set—the engine room of actually unleashing that discretionary effort and engagement." However, one of the biggest barriers for leaders to coach their team members is having time to coach. They are often so busy with their role and delivering on their responsibilities that they don't have or make the time to coach. However, when coaching is a requirement of their role and their span of control is realistic, the environment is set for them to fulfil on their coaching obligations. Their coaching is not just a "car wash" approach to say that "I've done coaching". It's an investment of the leader's time in increasing organisational capability. An example of the turmoil that leaders can encounter on a daily basis is illustrated by the story of a leader who wants to coach his direct reports and starts to, but then gets "sucked back" into the "doing" and urgency of daily priorities. This leader likens his situation to "someone swimming in an ocean called coaching, but then there's this whirlpool of the daily reality of dealing with priors. I can be coaching for a while but, inevitably, I get pulled back into the reality of problem-solving". When the urgency of the daily priorities has abated, the leader has to recreate his coaching headspace and recollect his thoughts to get back into the mindset of coaching – out of the day-to-day turmoil that seems to happen all too often. Coaching, when used as a reflective practice, allows busy leaders the time and headspace to relax and think through their role – what they are doing and how they are doing it – and search internally for better ways of operating. It allows leaders to "hit the pause button for an hour", examine the goals and challenges ahead, look at what's working and what's not, and identify what they need to do differently to create a more desirable future.

A factor that may determine the success of a leader coaching their team members is the degree to which they have confidence in their ability to coach and a key component of this is whether they have received coaching themselves or not. Those leaders who have been coached have more confidence and inner strength to transition into a *coaching leadership style* because they know that as a leader who coaches, they don't have to have all the answers, whereas as a manager of the business unit, they do. Leaders who are very comfortable with themselves and understand the relative vulnerability of being a coach within a business environment will succeed in greatly assisting those whom they coach to find that comfort and inner strength within themselves which enables them to step forward and achieve their individual and team targets.

The second way that coaching is internally delivered in this third stage is by leaders within business units who coach their team at the collective level. The motivation is to increase team engagement and ownership of performance outcomes. Leaders who coach use an *ask* rather than *tell* methodology with their teams to generate ideas and options for improved performance. *Team coaching* can occur every day or every week as leaders focus their team on achievement of their 30/60/90-day plan, highlighting opportunities for forward movement. It's an ongoing discussion that incorporates coaching as an embedded skill in the day-to-day leadership of their team. Intelligence is shared, ideas for improvement encouraged and options for action examined. Leaders use the team's perspective to identify if a new idea will be embraced and if the team is equipped to execute it. Team coaching is about helping each team member understand how they can leverage each other's strengths rather than "hedging their own turfs". If team members view coaching as a means to enhance their personal and professional improvement, it's likely they will shift the way they behave with each other which will influence changes in interaction within the team, and the result will be "phenomenal".

When leaders model team coaching, they expect that each team member will go back to their team and do the same. In this way, coaching cascades fluidly down the business unit with very little effort and no call on the unit's budget for external coaching services. The response of team members may initially be mixed because they may not be familiar with coaching or may not have been exposed to a *coaching leadership style* before. However, over time, coaching practice becomes a regular feature of team and business interactions. An example of team coaching is of a leader who has coached his team for the past 5 years. In that time, team members have changed but he has remained the constant factor in promoting the coaching agenda. When they meet, team members ask themselves: "Is this the best value way that we, as a leadership team, can be spending our time at this moment for this business unit?" As new recruits enter the team, a team member is assigned to "bring them up to speed" on the *coaching leadership style* and how the team coaching sessions operate. Using this approach, team interactions have moved from "reactive to dependent, to independent, to interdependent" over the 5 years, even with multiple changes in individual team members.

Another example is of an executive director who meets one-on-one with each of her direct reports every 4–6 weeks. Their individual coaching sessions focus on work-in-progress but also include discussions around how the team member is developing themself through the work that they're doing and identifying any issues that may be holding them back. The coaching conversation asks: "Have you thought about …?" "Tell me how you see that." "Oh, that's interesting." "How would you play that?" "What would be the effect of that sort of decision?" In this way, the coaching is simultaneously motivated by performance and development intentions which demonstrate to the employee that they are a valued member of the team.

A third example is of a high-performing team in the hospitality industry which had "dissention within the ranks". The business owner was a talented general manager but someone who gave his team a little too much freedom. As they pushed the boundaries of that freedom, team members started to "tread on each other's toes" causing even more trouble. Adopting a *coaching leadership style*, the business owner conducted individual coaching sessions with his team members and then brought them together for 2 days of team coaching in which he reinforced the one-on-one individual coaching with "team work". As a result, the "group" came together as a team and started supporting each other to achieve improved business outcomes.

The third way that coaching is internally delivered in this third stage of developing a coaching culture is by specialist coaches who are appointed to business units to coach team leaders in specific performance aspects of their role, for example, how to win more sales. These specialist coaches are well-experienced business operatives. They know their customers' needs and wants and are intimately acquainted with how the business works. They use their specialist knowledge and skills to identify the significant business levers that will make a huge difference in terms of identifying the best prospects to approach and how to approach them to ensure the best chance of success in winning a sales deal.

An example is of a specialist coach who works in a revenue-generating business unit of a very large telecommunications company with national and international clients whose leaders are knowledgeable about, and support, coaching. He works in an $8 billion division of a $30 billion organisation, concentrating on international opportunities particularly in the Asia-Pacific and US regions. In Australia, his division manages the top 1000 enterprise and government accounts including the major banks. With 35 years of sales experience in this industry, he is able to examine a deal impartially and objectively which gives him the authority to coach account executives in areas that they hadn't thought of before because they have "emotional blinkers" on. As a coach, he explores options with them about how to approach existing and potential clients in different ways to increase their organisational engagement and generate increased sales revenue.

This specialist coach uses proprietary organisational software with pre-set criteria which allow the user to determine the likelihood of success of a particular strategy or action to generate increased sales. He relies on this software tool because, whilst opinions are good, they need to be tested and, in his experience, the only legitimate way to test an opinion is to use coaching as a tool that puts a science behind a major opportunity. He trains account executives in a qualification and validation process before they engage with either an existing or new client. In a disciplined coaching session, they review the particular vulnerabilities of any deal and look closely at the relationships the executives have within those acquisition accounts. He uses the software tool to assist account executives decide how best to approach a particular client or target market. They appreciate his support because he uses a coaching approach and a sports analogy to motivate them to perform better in their field of work without actually doing it for them. Following the success of his employment as a full-time specialist coach, his organisation is now training a number of selected leaders as specialist coaches who will work in other areas of the business, as part of their "day job", to support the generation of increased revenue in these business units. He explains the rationale for specialist coaching thus:

I'm there because they can't see their swing – bit like a golf coach, you know. They're too 'into the trees and the bushes', and I need to bring them out and show them that the maze is not that scary and that if we do all the right things, we can orchestrate ourselves to go from point A to point B, which is a successful sale. But there's a lot of stage gates that we've got to get through to lift our performance and execute against an agreed set of goals.

The fourth way that coaching is delivered within business units in this third stage is by *internal coaches* or an *internal coaching team* to support front-line staff through behavioural coaching to resolve issues that are holding them back from improving on their performance. Internal coaches are formally trained by an external coach-training provider in *pure coaching* techniques as well as *performance coaching*. Within a particular business unit, they may address relationship, interpersonal, or behavioural issues that are impacting on a team or member's ability to perform, and then work with them to determine actions to remove these roadblocks.

Interviewer: What would you say to somebody who suggests that if you've got internal coaches in the business unit, you don't need the leader to be a coach because the dedicated coaches will do all the coaching?

"Yeah, it's not true. Not true at all. Having a dedicated coach, in my belief and opinion, is in addition to any leader-based coaching. It's a very different conversation because it's an impartial conversation. A leader as a coach will always be perceived and bring content to that conversation in a different way than an internal or external coach will. So I would see a dedicated coach as an addition to leader coaching. This coaching might focus on a specific area of need over a particular length of time. It would complement the coaching that the leader as-coach is doing. And the leader-as-coach would actually tap into that. They'd tap into that in their own coaching and their own conversations with their team member."

Internal coaching teams may be created to support a particular business unit or deliver coaching across all business units in the organisation. As a dedicated coaching team, they have an opportunity to operate impartially and almost independently since they are not involved in the day-to-day machinations of the business units and can function akin to an external coaching service. This approach has many advantages in terms of confidentiality and the way that employees perceive the service being delivered. Coachees see coaching more as an investment in them rather than an imposition on their "day job" which makes it easier for them to respond positively to the coaching process. Being able to report into a senior executive *coaching champion* gives the internal coaching team a different level of engagement and enablement.

An organisational leader reports an example of an internal coaching team which sits within a front-line sales and services business unit of a large international organisation. It was embedded in this business unit so that the coaching it delivers to individuals and teams can be leveraged immediately to maximum effect. However, in a previous restructure, the internal coaching team was located within the HR function where their brief was very different. It was to develop coaching skills training programmes for all leaders based on whether they were new to business, middle performers, or moving from the middle to executive band. Over a 12-month period, the team became disillusioned and was nearly disbanded because of the amount of red tape, sign-off and "hoops to jump through" when positioned within the HR function versus when the team was in the distribution area of the business where decisions are made more quickly. In the next restructure, the team was transferred back into the distribution area where they continue to have a greater impact on business results and "show it on the scoreboard" sooner.

In summary, when an organisation is at the third *Coaching-as-Leader-Capability* stage of developing a coaching culture, coaching, is delivered within business units by leaders to their teams and team members on a regular basis. Specialist and internal coaching teams support the leader-led coaching particularly to front-line, customer-facing business unit teams who generate increased revenue for the business.

Stage 3: Illustrative Examples: *Coaching-as-Leader-Capability*

Illustrative Example 9

GenAdvance is a large public sector organisation that delivers basic utility services to the general public. It is on a journey to support individual leaders to improve their performance and change their behaviour. A leadership framework which incorporates coaching as a required leader capability has been built based on a values-led leadership style. The leadership framework is underpinned by the agreed understanding of senior leaders that values-based leadership behaviours are expected at every level of the organisation and that these behaviours are as important as management skills, technical skills, and experience – an appreciation that leadership has technical elements particularly at the team leader level but not especially at the senior leadership level where technical skills are often so diluted as to be completely redundant.

The leadership framework is balanced by a real understanding of *who* leaders need to be and *how* they need to "show up" in the organisation in terms of their behaviour. The framework is focused on behaviours like "connection" and the ability to manage diversity, how to manage change effectively and communicate the changes in a humane way, and the ability to coach and develop employee capability. It's heavily weighted towards *behaviours-in-action* that flow through to every aspect of the business including the language that leaders use, the way that performance conversations are conducted, and how behaviours affect team members as well as team culture.

GenAdvance uses the language of *leadership* in their development programmes and promotional materials rather than *coaching* because their employees find *leadership* a more acceptable term than *coaching*. Hence, the conversations in which leaders engage have a strong coaching element but principally, they focus on the "bigger picture" leadership framework which leads to improved performance and increased employee engagement. *GenAdvance* believes that the coaching initiatives they have put in place have made a real difference in achieving business and organisational goals more quickly and effectively than ever before.

Illustrative Example 10

InnovationOne is a leading telecommunications and technology company offering a wide range of services within Australia and South-East Asia from programmable networks to enterprise collaboration tools. Their Global Services Division (GSD) manages the top 1000+ enterprise and government accounts worldwide and has an annual turnover of $25+ billion. The division creates transformative, innovative solutions for businesses using the most advanced technologies to liberate the workforce, reach growth markets and secure new business. Using cutting-edge technologies and ideas, *InnovationOne* runs critical systems around the country dealing with the "top end of town" – very senior executives and senior public servants going right up to the Prime Minister. These sales engagements are critical to *InnovationOne*'s business success. Not every deal needs to be coached but the critical ones do, particularly "if you're bringing in junior people and putting them in development roles in sales organisations because if you don't coach them, you're just going to constantly be doing their job" which Ben, a specialist coach, notes a lot of *InnovationOne*'s sales managers "end up doing and that's why they don't have time for coaching. It's a vicious cycle".

Ben coaches sales account executives to win deals, some of which are worth hundreds of millions of dollars. He equips sales account executives with the necessary skills, attributes and standards of proficiency to perform in their role. With years of experience in sales, he knows selling and he knows what customers want. Headquartered in Australia, Ben regularly liaises with counterparts in other locations in the South-East Asia rim. As a specialist coach in the GSD, Ben's role is to give the sales team "the confidence that the strategies, tactics and techniques surrounding a particular deal" will win *InnovationOne* the deal. He works with the sales team to help them see where they are going and how they can execute against an agreed set of goals.

As an essential component of how the GSD does business, a coaching methodology is used to facilitate analysis of the business intelligence and research that is made available to the team from *InnovationOne*'s finance division. The sales team are not the usual "spreadsheet jockeys, sitting there looking at the numbers, punching out reports, doing the cadence" to generate sales. Rather, with Ben's coaching, the sales team data-mine the research on each client and create value propositions that will sell. But it's the "coaching to revenue" that raises ideas and options to maximise the acquisition of new and existing deals, supports the achievement of specific sales goals, and exploits revenue opportunities.

The account executives who are responsible for meeting sales targets meet with Ben whenever there's an important conversation to be had with a new or existing client – which is frequently as they're constantly sourcing new deals. The coaching approach that he uses has been so successful that 12 organisational leaders at the middle management level who are advocates for coaching have been selected to participate in the launch of a dedicated "boot camp" to show them how to coach and to certify and accredit them in the use of the proprietary software tool that *InnovationOne* uses, in order to meet the additional demand for the coaching that Ben does with sales teams. When trained, these new specialist coaches, who also have "day-job" leadership roles, will undertake "deep dives" with their teams into prospective deals. They will also have the opportunity to "cross-pollinate" their coaching services within other revenue-generating divisions in Australia and overseas. To ensure the quality of their coaching, they have to undergo annual certification of their coaching skills so that they are "absolutely at the top of their game". In developing additional specialist coaches, *InnovationOne* is "raising the tide to raise all the boats" not only to increase revenue generation but also so that the organisation is less reliant on external coaches.

The business drivers for coaching in *InnovationOne* are the sales executives who support team leaders and front-line staff to "win sales deals that make a quantifiable contribution to revenue". The coaching methodology was adopted by business leaders to qualify and validate major deals better. It is now well-entrenched in all the GSD's sales divisions in Australia and the South-East Asia region which is so very important because "we can spend hundreds of thousands if not millions of dollars on the pursuit of a deal and lose it". Hence, the account executives have been quick to grasp the coaching approach and use it with their teams. However, non-revenue-generating divisions of *InnovationOne* have yet to adopt coaching to support the achievement of their particular goals.

***

This chapter has detailed the four key dimensions of Stage 3 – *Coaching-as-Leader-Capability.* The next chapter explains the four key dimensions of Stage 4 – *Coaching-as-Culture.*

Chapter 7
Stage 4: Coaching-as-Culture

This chapter addresses the last of four stages in the development of a coaching culture as depicted in the model of coaching culture development (Fig. 3.1). During this stage, coaching is an essential component of the cultural change process which aims to develop all employees in the organisation to reach their potential. This final stage is characterised by an *organic conceptualisation* of coaching as naturally occurring and a *transformational motivation* to achieve personal, business and organisational change. The CEO and senior executives are responsible for driving coaching *top down* throughout the organisation via the *integrated* delivery of coaching into everything everybody does as they communicate and relate in daily business transactions.

Organic Conceptualisation

In the *Coaching-as-Culture* stage of developing a coaching culture, organisational leaders' conceptualisation of coaching is as an organic and naturally occurring activity – just part of "how we do things around here". Coaching is part of the DNA of the organisation and a lens through which to analyse all business transactions to achieve increased productivity and competitive advantage. Coaching is given meaning as part of the fabric of the organisation and a platform for cultural change (Fig. 7.1).

When coaching is conceptualised as *organic* and naturally occurring, it becomes part of the DNA and fabric of the organisation. Coaching conversations happen in the course of a day's work. They may be conducted formally on a scheduled basis

S. Knowles, *Coaching Culture*, https://doi.org/10.1007/978-3-031-09050-9_7

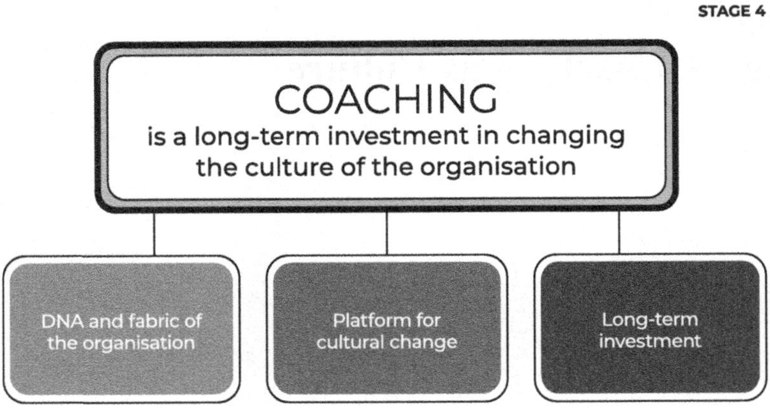

Fig. 7.1 Stage 4 - Coaching is a long-term investment in cultural change

or informally as the need arises. Formal coaching sessions are usually of an hour's duration; however, informal coaching conversations could last for just a minute or two, or maybe ten to fifteen minutes, depending on the issue or concern. As leaders are "slow to speak" and really listen to team members, they guide them on a journey to discover their own solutions. Leaders recognise the human side of their people assets and pay attention to the intent and potential of all employees, recognising them as "human beings first and then they do their work". With that recognition, leaders pay attention to *who* their employees are, *how* they function in the workplace, and *how* that shapes their performance, rather than the coaching conversation just being about the task.

As an accepted organisational practice in this final stage of developing a coaching culture, coaching assists employees do what they need to do to meet their individual, team and business goals and objectives. Coaching is not something special or something that leaders do in addition to their daily responsibilities – it's just part of *how* they do business and *how* they lead their teams. In a coaching culture, every conversation is an opportunity for coaching in one way or another. Everybody is sharing as a normal part of the work that leaders do – just a little piece of everything that fits together with something else within organisational activities. Organic coaching is a standard inclusion in normal daily activities – a "come to work" part of the job – "almost like exercise".

A second way that coaching is *organically* conceptualised is as a platform for cultural change. In this final stage, coaching is an integral part of the culture of "*who* we are and *what* we represent" and "the way we do things around here". Culture emerges from the stories that are told about the history of the organisation – whether that's culture in the sense of art, music, language, food or people. That culture is reflected in the workplace because employees are recruited from different walks of life and ethnicities and together, they form an organisational culture based on their shared experiences. The word *culture* is about "our story – and coaching should just be part of that story – part of *how* we are".

A coaching culture is developed from the common and shared understandings of organisational members in relation to *how* work is done and *how* they interact with each other as they perform their duties. When leaders and employees coach each other on a daily basis in this final stage, a philosophy is developed which guides all personal and business transactions and sets the foundations for a platform that supports human flourishing and business sustainability. The platform is the common coaching philosophy, coaching language, and shared coaching approach. There's a way of coaching that everyone understands, accepts and adheres to, which includes compassion and a shared interest in outcomes which are of benefit not only to the organisation as a whole but also to individuals and teams within business units. Coaching is about "what's done around here" rather than "what's done out there, for here" (i.e. outsourced). A coaching approach guides and pre-empts the thinking before actions are taken. Once a platform for coaching has been developed, it can be applied to every situation including how decisions are made, how problems are solved and how communication flows throughout and external to the organisation. When the business has a problem, coaching is recognised as the vehicle that enables the organisation to overcome it.

Leaders who enter an organisation with big aspirations and dreams about how they will shift the culture may become frustrated when they realise that all the history of that business may make it difficult to implement change. Take, for example, an organisation in the manufacturing industry with national service centres. The organisation is heavily losing money in its manufacturing arm. To change the culture, senior executives need to change the business model and how leaders interact with their staff. They decide to split the 30-year-old manufacturing side of the business which is highly industrialised from the services side which is showing promise of profitability so that it can become more nimble and responsive to customer needs and then work with staff in the production plant to change the leadership style and culture. However, changing the DNA of an organisation isn't something that happens just because executives say: "This is what we're going to do now". They need to consult with shareholders, staff, and unions to broker a deal that's acceptable to all parties and will bring the majority of staff along with them to ensure continuity of production to feed their renewed services division after the deal is done.

The *fire* analogy presented in Stage 1 represents how conceptualisations of coaching have changed as organisations progress in their understanding of coaching and a coaching culture. In Stage 1, *Coaching-as-Intervention*, coaching is a *fast burn*. It's like lighting a match. It's gone out and forgotten very quickly. It's a transactional scenario within the organisation. In Stage 2, *Coaching-as-HR-Function* where coaching is a training and learning experience, coaching is a *slow-burn* fire. It's smouldering and ready to burst into flames but not quite yet. In Stage 3, *Coaching-as Leader-Capability*, coaching is a *moderate burn*, making an impact on some of the business units within the organisation but not all. In Stage 4, *Coaching-as-Culture*, coaching is a *raging bonfire* that keeps going and keeps everyone warm, creating light and comfort throughout the organisation. It's visible and can be seen, heard and felt by everybody. As a raging bonfire, coaching is sustainably embedded into the organisation and can be leveraged within any area to bring about cultural change.

Cultural change takes time – 18 months minimum, depending on the size of the organisation. To sustain cultural change takes a dedicated commitment, mindsets that believe in the potential of all employees, and an ongoing investment in training, learning and support for coaching practice. An example is of a CEO and senior executive team in a mining operation who were coached individually and as a group for 3 years during a cultural change process. The purpose was to build alignment across the organisation and a coaching culture. The executive coach worked with the team and then with each of the senior executive's teams including their high potentials around how to handle difficult situations and staff who had personal or professional issues to deal with but whom the organisation wanted to retain. She describes it as "a real privilege to be able to work with leadership teams who are committed to developing and being the best leaders they can be for an organisation". In every interaction with these leaders, her challenge was to help them understand just how powerful coaching can be within an organisational setting.

To progress a cultural transformation throughout an organisation, a significant investment needs to be made in coaching based on a sound business case that outlines the major benefits for individuals, teams and the organisation in terms of productivity and competitive advantage. The investment is related to the achievement of business outcomes and shows how these reinforce organisational values, leadership effectiveness and employee engagement. A business case specifies: "What are our expectations?" "What do we hope to achieve?" "Who are the key people who have experienced coaching and its benefits?" and "What are the gaps in our business that we are hoping coaching will fill?" As a narrative to drive change, a business case is powerful in the hands of a coaching advocate who invites executives to join in the conversation. The push for coaching comes from senior executives who are passionate and enthused about culture and capability as a whole and message the benefits of coaching throughout the organisation. Once the business case is approved, support from the top is mandatory since employees "look up and follow". The CEO and senior executives must make a commitment to developing a coaching culture and lead by example, role modelling the coaching behaviour.

Overall, when an organisation is at the fourth and final stage of developing a coaching culture, the conceptualisation of coaching is organic. Coaching is part of the DNA and fabric of the organisation and a platform for cultural change. Coaching conversations happen "in the moment" as the need arises to develop all organisational members. A coaching culture takes time to develop and is only embedded within the organisation when there's a "look and feel" of a supportive, encouraging and enabling environment, and coaching conversations happen naturally on a daily basis.

Transformational Motivation

A second aspect that characterises the *Coaching-as-Culture* stage concerns the motivation for *why* coaching is undertaken by the organisation. In this final stage, coaching is motivated by the CEO and senior executives' desire for *transformational* cultural change. Coaching transforms not only individuals because it is such an effective way of developing people but also the organisation as it attempts to increase productivity and create competitive advantage. Transformational cultural change is achieved when organisational leaders: (1) support the personal transformation of all employees; (2) identify the key business levers that increase organisational productivity; and (3) leverage the organisation's human assets to achieve competitive advantage (Fig. 7.2).

The first *transformational* motivation for coaching in this final stage is to unleash the potential of all employees not just leaders and high-performing individuals, to bring about personal transformation. Organisations with a transformational motivation send a clear signal to employees that they care as much about their people and helping them reach their potential as they do about the goal and objectives for the team and business. In a transformational coaching culture, leaders provide all employees with developmental opportunities that are "fit to role" and "fit to purpose" to support their professionalism and career development. This approach to team members ultimately leads to more engaged employees who are happier and more satisfied with their jobs and, when this occurs, leaders feel a greater level of job satisfaction too, as this executive explains:

> I think it's about having that growth mindset somewhere in the organisation where they realise people are able to be developed and wanting to be developed and the benefits of investing in them.

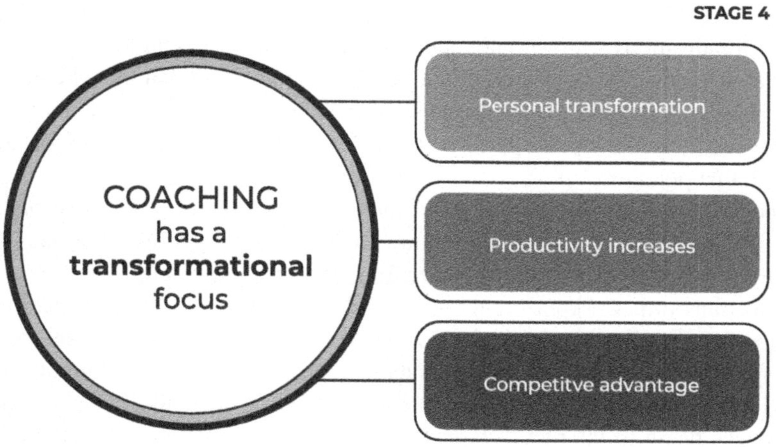

Fig. 7.2 Stage 4 - Coaching brings about personal and organisational transformation

A transformational motivation for coaching helps leaders shift their coaching practice so that it impacts on individuals and teams at both personal and professional levels. Coaching in this fourth stage supports individuals and teams to achieve a cultural shift which is really "about engaging the hearts and minds of employees as a visceral experience". To explain:

> It's a shift in culture where consistently, in every iteration, every interaction, you've got an approach to self-awareness and ongoing development, and leaders engage and develop people specifically.

In this final stage, coaching is used to unlock the potential of leaders who have attended a leadership development programme but who have not been able to fully realise the benefits. These leaders may need extra assistance in terms of not only their "people skills" but also their own self-management within the leadership space. They may have had feedback like, "You need to communicate more effectively" or "You need to build your reputation" but they have not had the follow-up support to achieve this. Or they may have attended generic coursework training programmes which have given them the knowledge about what they should be doing but not the ability to apply that knowledge into the everyday workplace. They need coaching support to translate what they have learned in their *head* into everyday *heart* practice with their team and team members.

Not only does coaching in this final stage bring about personal insight and confidence but it also helps resolve interpersonal issues. An example is of a leader working in a regional hospital where there was a "doctor/nurse-type issue" in which an individual caused a number of team members to file a complaint. The complaint was sent "two levels up from this team" to the director of nursing and the director of medical, neither of whom had been in leadership positions before. The problem was that their roles and how they would work together had not been clearly defined and so their professional relationship had to be sorted out first before the actual issue could be addressed.

Employees who are engaged and satisfied in their role perform better in the workplace which has a consequential, positive impact on the business "bottom line". Organisations which do not appreciate the value of all employees and are not motivated to develop the potential of all employees will find that they are held back from achieving cultural change because of their limiting belief in the ability of all employees to achieve peak performance. Coaching conversations are the way to unleash that potential.

The second *transformational* motivation for coaching is to improve organisational productivity. In a coaching culture, coaching is viewed as an organisational activity integral to everything that occurs in a team and business unit. Coaching aims to transform workplace culture to enable staff become more successful and high-performing. To do this, leaders who coach need to take into account the complex system that surrounds employees and the norming effect of culture. Coaching teams to increased productivity is a process that starts a chain of events in which employees begin to interact differently with their environment to co-create a new system, a new reality with new behaviours that foster increased cooperation and collaboration within teams. Leaders need to be aware of, and coach within, the different complex systems that are the team dynamic, the business environment and the organisational vision and mission. At the same time, they must be aware of team members' coaching needs and guide them towards consciously navigating the realities of each system so they can find their place as a force within each of these systems and influence the broader agenda.

At the organisational level, a coaching conversation with the executive team needs to identify the two or three key organisational levers that can be applied to reinforce business success and ways to consistently use them until they are embedded within the organisation's culture. These levers may include, for example, "people levers", such as the inclusion of a coaching component in all training programmes (not just leadership development) to ensure that the learnings are consistently applied thereafter in the workplace. A financial lever may be used to measure the impact of coaching programmes in business units in which coaching has been rigorously applied to leverage productivity improvement. Another lever may be the identification of underperforming yet potential new markets for exploitation or expansion and conducting a pilot programme to measure the success of leveraging coaching into one of these areas. Challenging existing thinking can broaden the application of coaching into different areas of the business that had not previously been considered significant to business productivity.

The third *transformational* motivation for coaching is to bring competitive advantage to the organisation. In a competitive market in which organisations have leveraged every physical asset including systems and technology, leaders start to consider leveraging their people. This is the hardest lever to pull because employees are not linear and cannot be manipulated. However, they can be encouraged and supported to look at things in a different way and embrace cultural change through coaching as a way of increasing their engagement and commitment to the organisation. Even organisations in downturn which have not invested in their people before will invest in hard economic times. There is no doubt that developing a coaching culture brings competitive advantage to the organisation during difficult times because, as one organisational leader believes:

> Any time people can feel like they're supported and valued, they will get to a point where they can do their best. And any organisation which recognises that will far outperform the competition. I don't care if you're washing cars, planting bushes, or running a bank.

Within the private sector, the main purpose of achieving competitive advantage is to obtain financial gain. However, from a public sector perspective, the reason is less obvious. It is to ensure a supply of talented individuals who can lead within the government sector, thereby achieving government priorities and improving on the outcomes from government spending for the benefit of the general public. Competition for talented individuals means that government entities try to position themselves as an "employer of choice" with wages and conditions comparable to the private sector to attract the most suitable candidates. These organisations need to meet the expectations of multiple stakeholders, including Ministers who have to report in Parliament on how public funds are spent. Senior executives of government entities don't want their performance to be "just average" – they want it to be "exceptional".

A coaching culture is particularly important when crisis situations arise in the external marketplace, and organisational leaders need to act immediately to seize the opportunity or eliminate a possible threat. It assists organisations *respond* to these situations rather than *react* to them. The crisis may have been precipitated by, for example, a rise in commodity prices or changes in legislation such as privatisation of a government entity. These externally driven, often unanticipated, events can have a major impact on an organisation by threatening its profitability or forcing it to change direction or priorities. External events are often the triggers for organisations to do something different so they can overcome the crisis and adapt to the changed situation. Coaching is a powerful way for leaders to address or indeed exploit a crisis for competitive advantage, as the following story illustrates:

> *I was working with a large well-known national organisation and they were given a report by one of the Big 4 consulting firms that said:* 'If you keep doing what you're doing, you're going to lose $12 billion in the next ten years.' *So it's those kind of punches that get CEOs to wake up and go:* 'We've got to do it differently. This isn't working.' *So they sent out a communication that said:* 'Look, we're not going to deliver [our product] every day.' *You can imagine the revolt:* 'What do you mean? That's our DNA. That's what we do.' *So they realised:* 'Oh, we can't just tell people. We've got to somehow win their hearts and minds.

Organisations generally accept the research that reports on the value and benefits of coaching. However, because budgets and time are limited, they have to make calls on where to focus their efforts. When margins are tight, they need to decide if coaching is one of the key skill sets to deliver on business targets. It's really a "catch 22–chicken and egg" situation. Productivity really needs to improve for the organisation to survive but they need to spend money to achieve the productivity improvement. In some organisations facing new entrants into the market with advanced technology, there is an urgent need to identify the key levers that can be better utilised to at least maintain their current standing in the marketplace if not improve it. Coaching may be the capability that organisations decide to utilise as they seek better ways to deliver on their vision and mission.

In the previous third stage of developing a coaching culture, coaching was recognised as a valuable capability of leaders who coach their team and team members. In this final stage, coaching is understood as the way to support all employees to achieve their best through coaching conversations that occur at any time, not just formally but informally as well. Anyone in the organisation can adopt a coaching approach to any conversation with any employee or colleague for any reason. Employees seek development, and if they cannot find it in their workplace, they'll look for it elsewhere. Like peeling back the layers of an onion, employees want to find out "what makes me [and others] tick". A coaching culture enables them to find the answers.

Overall, when an organisation is at the fourth and final stage of developing a coaching culture, the motivation for coaching is transformational. Coaching is an enabler of personal and professional growth for all employees and facilitates transformation of the entire organisation by improving the productivity of business units, creating opportunities for the organisation to gain competitive advantage in the marketplace, and achieving transformational cultural change.

Top-Down Drivers

A third aspect that characterises the *Coaching-as-Culture* stage concerns who is driving coaching throughout the organisation. In this fourth stage, coaching is driven by passionate and committed *CEOs and senior executives* who provide strong sponsorship for, and buy-in to, cascading coaching throughout the organisation. Coaching becomes a strategic priority. A *coaching champion* is appointed at the senior level. The CEO and senior executives speak publicly about the value of coaching and role model coaching behaviour. Coaching is positioned within all business units to deliver the greatest ROI for the organisation (Fig. 7.3).

Coaching, in this fourth stage, is positioned within all business units. The executives responsible for business units are fully committed to the coaching agenda and cascade it down their levels. The *top-down* drivers of transformational cultural change are the CEO and senior executives who are passionate about coaching and delivering coaching as a core capability of leaders. In this final stage, a committed executive team has defined what coaching means to the organisation and how it fits with their desired culture. They recognise not only the opportunities but also the limits of their employees coaching and being coached, which requires a degree of trust, transparency and confidentiality. They are clear on what their vision and values are and make explicit the kind of leadership they want and for why. Organisations which do not have *top-down* drivers for coaching will find that "pockets" of interest in coaching will spring up within various business units but they will have difficulty achieving transformational cultural change throughout the entire organisation.

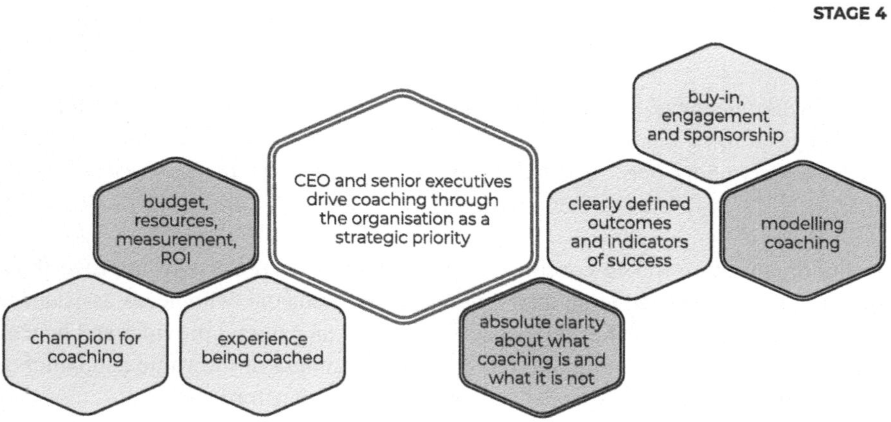

Fig. 7.3 Stage 4 - CEO and senior executives drive coaching through the organisation

Moreover, if the senior executives are not passionate about coaching or don't see the value in it, then:

It's gonna kind of die in the ... And we went through a period where we had a change of leadership and, you know, our senior leaders were people who just didn't believe in coaching. So it did die in the...

Interviewer: Who would be making that commitment [to develop a coaching culture] and deciding which place to start?

> *"The highest level possible in the organisation. Absolutely C-suite. So if it's not the CEO, it would be an executive general manager who is absolutely passionate about developing people. Not necessarily someone from HR but someone who has a big job, understands that coaching is not the only thing, but it's certainly something that can be used to leverage and get better return on investment of our other programs. You know, improve our engagement and our enablement, build resilience in people, and support them through the change, whilst at the same time helping them deliver on the expectations of their role."*

The most critical element in progressing to this final stage is the absolute and demonstrated commitment of the senior executives to being coached themselves. When senior executives talk openly about their experience of being coached and the benefits they have accrued, coaching takes on a credibility that wasn't afforded it before. If organisations do not have the top level displaying their commitment to coaching by coaching their team members and being coached themselves, there's little likelihood of achieving transformational cultural change. The experience of executives being coached has been described as "fertilising the ground" for others

> Interviewer: What do you see is the most critical element in getting a coaching culture together?

> *"It would be the absolute and demonstrated commitment from the top. I think they need to be equipped with the skills to be able to do it. And they would have had to have been coached themselves to understand the experience."*

in the organisation to see coaching as a developmental process to improve their performance as opposed to an intervention to "fix" someone who needs assistance. Some executives may be formally coach-trained by an external provider and hence, they may be even more committed to creating awareness of the value and benefits of coaching in achieving personal and organisational transformation.

When the CEO and senior executives are committed to developing a coaching culture, they are seen role modelling coaching, messaging the importance of coaching and being coached, and "walking the talk" among employees at all levels of the organisation. The senior executives are approachable, amenable to listening and learning, and open to change suggestions. CEOs who truly understand that business success comes through their people make themselves personally available to employees who want to interact with them, for example, by chatting to employees to understand where they're coming from and what their needs are and then starting to address those needs. Once employees overcome their initial apprehension about the CEO and senior executives' intention for introducing coaching into the organisation – which may be typified by, "What? Why is this guy talking to me? I'm in accounts and he's an MD" – they often commit to "walk over hot coals" to help the organisation achieve its goals.

Interviewer: Does the involvement of senior executives make a difference in developing a coaching culture?

"Absolutely, yes. And with the latest cohort of the leadership development program, they found the coaching was the most valued part of the program. And bearing in mind that a lot of them are outdoor workers who are working in isolated areas. They don't network. They don't get face-to-face contact with anyone. And we had a really positive take-up rate to receive coaching because these people were getting access to some very senior people who were very generous with their time. So, for some of them, it was incredibly powerful."

In order to change the culture of an organisation through coaching, the CEO and senior executives must have absolute clarity about what coaching is and what it is not, and what the organisation is trying to achieve by developing a coaching culture. Is it coaching or mentoring that the organisation wishes to engage in? Organisational leaders have become comfortable with the notion of mentoring but know less about coaching. They may not understand the purpose of introducing coaching into an organisation or know how coaching can change people's lives. Knowing about coaching and its capacity to impact powerfully on individuals, teams and the organisation starts with the CEO and top team. They are the organisational leaders who have to understand what *coaching* and developing a *coaching culture* mean and be fully committed to the coaching agenda for a coaching culture to develop, as this story illustrates:
An executive was sent to coaching by the CEO. In the first meeting with his coach, the steam was coming out of his ears and when he finally settled down, he said to the coach, 'Look, I honestly don't know what to do. I have been rewarded all my life in this organisation for working the way that I have and now my CEO gets up in a room and says', *Well, we don't want that, we want this*, and I have no idea how to be

this.' So, the executive had to unlearn past behaviours and learn a new set of behaviours more appropriate to how the executive role is expected to function today in his organisation. Unlearning behaviours can erode confidence, especially in the transition stage from manager to leader.

For a coaching culture to exist and sustain, there needs to be high-level buy-in, engagement and sponsorship of coaching by the executive team which requires passion and enthusiasm for coaching to truly deliver on the cultural change. Role modelling coaching has to come from the "heart not the head". There has to be honest, genuine buy-in and belief in coaching and its benefits. There are many reasons why change projects fail. However, when executives demonstrate total support for coaching and are seen to experience being coached themselves, there is less likelihood of failure. An executive coach tells the story of being engaged, together with two other external coaches, to coach the divisional executives of five geographic regions of a large, national organisation. These divisional executives had an understanding of coaching and had experienced being coached as had the CEO who engaged them. Of the five geographic divisions, two executives plus one other were enthusiastic about coaching, the fourth somewhat, and the fifth not at all. There was "no appetite for coaching" in the latter division. This executive even changed the name of the coaching conducted by the external coach in that division from *coaching* to *performance management*. Consequently, this external coach left because he couldn't get any traction for coaching within that division. Unfortunately, the organisation had not put measures in place to record the benefits of coaching. Hence, there were no real business results and when the money ran out so did the coaching. Moreover, when the executive coach who was coaching in two divisions returned to his first division 6 months later, all the benefits had been lost because the executive had been promoted and his replacement was not interested in coaching. This story illustrates that unless coaching is embedded in organisational activities with dedicated financial support, it will only be sustained as long as a supportive executive is in place and sponsoring the coaching. When they leave, it will lose its organic nature and be relegated to, at best, an intervention or, at worst, renamed as *performance management*.

When the CEO and senior executives are the *top-down* drivers of coaching throughout the organisation, they make coaching a strategic priority for the business and allocate a recurrent budget to developing a coaching culture. It is insufficient and will not achieve the desired outcome if only a year-to-year allocation of funds is made. The CEO may leave and a new CEO may not support coaching. Funds may be redirected to other priorities or new initiatives. Training funds may be slashed in times of reduced revenue. As a strategic priority, leaders know that an ongoing budgetary commitment will be attached to the coaching strategy to transform the organisation's culture and included in forward projections so that punctuated attempts to change the culture are not the result, as this story illustrates:

> We went one year from having a budget of $1.8 million to deliver a whole range of initiatives to help individuals and line managers to nothing the following financial year because there'd been a change of focus, a change of direction. I think there is an appetite for getting better at coaching but, like anything, it takes resourcing and it takes time.

In contrast, in another organisation:

> That vision was clear about developing the capabilities of the line and that stuck for many years. I could map out multiple programs that just, year after year, someone was able to find money in the budget to keep coaching going.

This is where the dedication and commitment of a *coaching champion* are required to conduct an ongoing, convincing conversation with the senior team about the benefits of coaching and steward the coaching initiative throughout the organisation. The higher up the organisation that this champion sits, the more successful the coaching transformation will be and the sooner it will be realised. If the champion is not the CEO, it should be a senior executive who is absolutely passionate about developing people, has a significant role to deliver on, and understands that if the organisation wants to assist people navigate in a constantly changing environment, coaching is a formidable vehicle for doing that. The impact of a senior champion promoting the merits of coaching demonstrates the importance that the organisation places on coaching. Alternatively, a strong, *transformational HR professional* could be the *coaching champion* if they have the full and demonstrated support of the CEO. The champion can gain agreement for continued expenditure on coaching by one of the most convincing ways that executives know – providing evidence of the positive and tangible outcomes from coaching. The ROI is so important to organisations because:

> Everybody is dollar-focused, so if they're going to spend $5, $10, $20 grand, it's a rare company that will spend that sort of money without expecting the executive you're working with to be more effective.

Organisations which put measurement criteria in place and record data in relation to each and every coaching programme are in an excellent position to display in hard facts, the benefits of approving the coaching expenditure and the expected ROI that executives can look forward to in the coming year. They use this data to monitor and benchmark the effectiveness of the coaching that is being delivered across all coaching programmes. One reason why organisations may be reluctant to invest in coaching is because they don't know how to measure the ROI from coaching since the outcomes of coaching are not always easy to quantify. Indeed, the ROI may take some time to materialise because coaching often involves helping an employee break down barriers that have been built up over years, so it's harder to ascertain the ROI until they have completed a coaching programme and are practising new behaviours. However, in a sales environment where quantification can mean the difference between survival and extinction, measuring the success of coaching is critically important, as this story illustrates:

> The issue we were grappling with was that we, as an organisation, were not very scientifically equipped to qualify and validate major deals, and that's dangerous territory to be in as a sales organisation. So we've moved the needle. We're qualifying the deals better. Our win rates are up. Our execution is more efficient and effective. And we're doing all this using a coaching approach to winning sales.

As organisations prepare to transition to a *Coaching-as-Culture stage*, the reality of the size of the investment to be made may be daunting. Developing the coaching skills of all organisational leaders requires a significant investment which many organisations cannot or may not be prepared to make. Investing in coaching within some business units is a good start. However, unless an organisation is fully committed to allocating the funds required to extend coaching into all business units, a lack of funds may starve the cultural change process. As well, unless organisations are prepared to take the time to identify the quantitative and qualitative measures of success from coaching including positive and negative indicators, they will never be able to determine if the coaching programmes have achieved the desired ROI. An executive coach explains how outcomes were measured in the organisation in which she was coaching:

> This particular organisation is coming to the end of a three-year program. We actually started doing a longitudinal study before the program started and then we've checked in with interviewees every six months. So the organisation's got quite a bit of data now in terms of before and after on a whole range of measures. They can say that, for example, the effectiveness of leaders being able to give feedback to their people has gone from this per cent to that per cent. And we've got a whole range of measureable matrix data points.

The momentum for coaching takes time to build – years even – to garner enough of a "ground swell" for it to cascade down all levels of the organisation. A cultural change project is not something that organisations "hire out" to external coaches to create alone, although executive coaches are often engaged to design and develop the cultural change programme from start to finish and assist with its implementation. When there is complete commitment, a strategy is devised to roll out the initiative and guide coaching culture development throughout the entire organisation. In other organisations in which executives are not so committed, or do not have sufficient financial resources, the decision to develop a coaching culture is often dependent on the CEO's appetite for coaching. Some organisations which do not have the full support and endorsement of the CEO may decide to just train their leaders in coaching skills rather than attempt to develop a coaching culture.

Overall, when an organisation is at the fourth and final stage of developing a coaching culture, the key drivers of coaching are the CEO and senior executives who are passionate about coaching and committed to driving coaching throughout the organisation. Coaching is designated as a strategic priority. The CEO and senior executives "walk the talk", speak publicly about coaching, role model coaching behaviour, and display buy-in and engagement for coaching by their sponsorship of, and dedication to, coaching programmes. A recurrent budget for coaching is allocated and the ROI is measured.

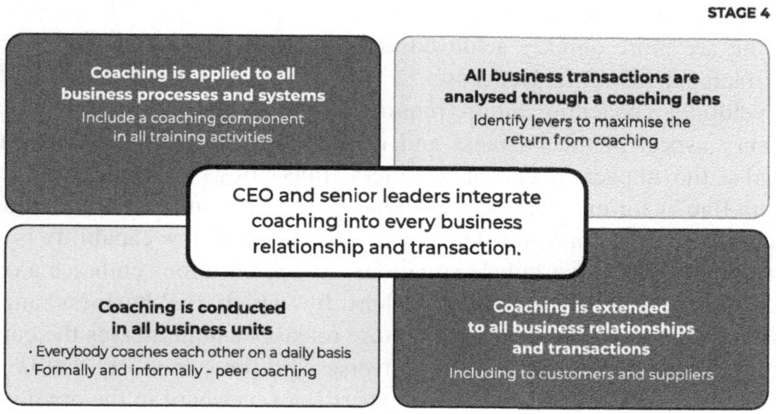

Fig. 7.4 Stage 4 - Coaching is integrated into all business transactions

Integrated Delivery

The fourth aspect that characterises the *Coaching-as-Culture* stage concerns *how* coaching is delivered. In this fourth stage, everybody coaches and is coached as the need arises or the opportunity presents. Leaders deliver coaching to their direct reports as an understood requirement of their role. Peers deliver coaching through informal delivery methods. Anyone, potentially, can be a coach or use their coaching skills to support others' development and/or career progression. By starting the development of a coaching culture within the senior executive team, a coaching culture is cascaded down the organisation as executives role model their support for coaching (Fig. 7.4).

When coaching is applied to all business processes and systems, a coaching approach is used to challenge existing thinking and extend coaching into other programmes and areas of the business. The coaching approach is used to "break free" of restrictive mindsets, neutralise potential threats and biases that constrain forward movement, and contribute to the achievement of organisational initiatives such as the introduction of diversity programmes and working with millennials. If an organisation is serious about making coaching a strategic priority, coaching sessions are included in all training activities – even training for commercial and business acumen – as an effective means of embedding the learnings and skills back into the workplace: "all of our training - no matter what the skill - comes with a coaching framework attached to it". Coaching that occurs post-training is closely monitored to see how much coaching actually occurs, ascertain the quality of the coaching conversations and gauge how the outcomes of coaching are being applied to everyday business relationships and transactions. Coaching can be utilised in any business function including corporate services. However, from a commercial point of view, the outcomes of coaching are more quickly achieved and visible in revenue-generating, customer-facing areas of the business.

Developing a coaching culture requires discipline and commitment to analyse every aspect of the business and identify how coaching can be used to maximise the impact of current business transactions on the organisation's "bottom line" - for example, analysing how coaching can increase the number and quality of deals done, how leaders are selected, and how capability is transferred and applied to workplace situations. As organisations embrace a coaching culture, coaching becomes the lens by which the business analyses everything that it does. A coaching culture releases and harnesses the capability, knowledge and perspectives of a diverse workforce in a way that is genuinely curious and exploratory. It sees expertise everywhere in the organisation and wants to build that up rather than turning everyone into a "cookie cutter". In a coaching culture, organisational knowledge is distributed rather than centralised and controlled.

In this fourth stage, coaching is conducted in all business units and can be delivered by anybody – leaders, peers, specialist or internal coaches. It's everybody's role to coach. It's an expectation that everybody will habitually and automatically coach each other meaning that, for example, if a situation arises in a meeting, there will be constructive questioning rather than combative challenge such as, "Okay, if we do this, what would that achieve?" or "How do you come to think that?", resulting in a much more collaborative and amiable approach to interacting at work. An example is of an AO5 HR adviser effectively using this approach in her daily activities as she just listened and used silence to help others work through their concerns and then assisted them break down those concerns into chunks. In a coaching culture, it's not just the leaders who are expected to coach. Everybody, "from the board chair to the gardener", is expected to conduct coaching formally or informally as the need or opportunity arises.

In this final stage, informal *peer coaching* occurs as a supportive learning activity no matter what the content or when or where the coaching is delivered. Peer coaching has many benefits since employees don't need to be formally trained as coaches but rather just in coaching skills and how to coach and exhibit *coach-like behaviours* as they interact with colleagues. In a coaching culture, peer coaching is just part of how the business operates on a day-to-day basis. As a result, employees don't go to be coached. They experience being coached in the course of their everyday interactions with others in the organisation.

The way that leaders promote peer coaching is by modelling it with their colleagues and supporting team members who practice it within their team.

As team members learn how to peer-coach, coaching occurs naturally and organically and the coaching philosophy becomes the normal way of interacting with others in the business. When this occurs, a coaching culture becomes embedded into the organisation which means that peer coaching, in particular, has been embraced and is working internally – which possibly implies that the organisation has reached a level of maturity to realise and accept that coaching is something important that people do right across the organisation.

Once coaching is conducted internally in all corporate and business units routinely on a daily basis across all levels of the organisation by leaders, peers, specialist and internal coaches formally and informally, the challenge is to extend coaching relationships to customers and suppliers. A coaching approach reduces the possibility that conversations deteriorate into a "talk fest" but rather achieves mutually beneficial outcomes. Coaching enables account managers to establish respectful yet robust and productive relationships with external customers and suppliers. To secure a business deal requires close attention to customer relationships, asking what the customer needs and negotiating how best to meet that need within a business framework. A coaching account manager is somebody who knows how to listen, has empathy, and is not afraid to engage in a tough conversation based on an exchange of information that is open, honest, truthful and concerned for the welfare of both parties. Coaching skills can be effectively used in every business transaction, as this executive explains:

> I think that most people don't realise the power of what coaching can provide. And that's unfortunate because, for me, it's had a huge benefit and I'm seeing that also in other people. It's challenging to both educate people in the value of coaching and then to have them recognise why it's useful or valuable to them, and then embrace it.

In summary, when an organisation is at the fourth and final *Coaching-as-Culture* stage of developing a coaching culture, everybody coaches everybody else. Organisations wanting to transition to this final stage broaden their approach to coaching to embrace the entire organisation so that not just leaders but everybody in the organisation knows how to coach and is encouraged to coach each other on a daily basis.

The key characteristics of the four stages in the development of a coaching culture are outlined in Table 7.1.

Table 7.1 Characteristics of the four stages in the development of a coaching culture

Stages	Stage 1: Coaching-as-Intervention	Stage 2: Coaching-as-HR-Function	Stage 3: Coaching-as-Leader-Capability	Stage 4: Coaching-as-Culture
Conceptualisation of coaching (i.e. understanding of *what* coaching is)	Utilitarian conceptualisation Skill Tool Immediate outcome One-off investment	Pedagogical conceptualisation Training and learning experience HR are formally coach-trained HR experience being coached In-house coaching skills training curriculum Short-term investment	Practice conceptualisation Leader capability framework Capability development framework Career progression framework Medium-term investment	Organic conceptualisation DNA and fabric of the organisation Platform for cultural change Long-term investment Cultural change takes time
Motivation for coaching (i.e. belief in *why* coaching is done)	Instrumental motivation "Fix" a problem Remediate an underperformer Comply with legislation	Developmental motivation Change mindset and behaviour Improve individual performance Support career progression	Performance motivation Business performance Team engagement Retention of talent Succession plan	Transformational motivation Personal transformation Productivity increases Competitive advantage
Drivers of coaching within the organisation (i.e. the *who* of coaching)	Individual drivers Line manager Positioned within line management structure	Functional drivers Human resources Positioned within HR Infrastructure for coaching Support for coaching	Business drivers Leaders as an expectation of their role Positioned within sales and services functions	Top-down drivers CEO and senior executives Absolute clarity about what coaching is and what it is not Clearly defined outcomes and indicators of success Experience being coached Buy-in, engagement, sponsorship Model coaching Strategic priority Budget, resources, measurement, ROI Champion for coaching

(continued)

Table 7.1 (continued)

Stages	Stage 1: Coaching-as-Intervention	Stage 2: Coaching-as-HR-Function	Stage 3: Coaching-as-Leader-Capability	Stage 4: Coaching-as-Culture
Delivered by (i.e. *how* coaching is done)	Outsourced delivery External coaches Expensive	Targeted delivery *Leader-as-coach* training programme Coaching panel/s	Internalised delivery Leaders deliver coaching to their teams and team members. Specialist coaches "coach to revenue" Internal coaches and coaching teams deliver behavioural and performance coaching	Integrated delivery Applied to all business processes and systems Analysed through a coaching lens Delivered in all business units Formally as scheduled coaching sessions Informally as peer coaching Extended to all business relationships and transactions

Stage 4: Illustrative Examples: *Coaching-as-Culture*

Illustrative Example 11

SecureWealth is a top 20 ASX-listed company with approximately 15,000 staff who deliver financial solutions to nine million customers in Australia and New Zealand through its network of banking, insurance and wealth creation services. Since the early 1900s, the organisation has created value for stakeholders whilst being a responsible and resilient business. *SecureWealth* is a diversified, simplified, low-risk financial services group that delivers both high yield and above average system growth. Their goal is to create value for customers through their portfolio of market-leading brands whilst benefiting from the efficiencies of scale achievable as a large organisation. Its mission is to help people live the life they want to lead and plan for the life they want tomorrow. Peter heads an internal coaching team of ten coaches who deliver coaching services to customer-facing business unit teams and team members. The organisation, headquartered in Australia, is 5 years into a strategy of embedding a coaching culture into the organisation.

In *SecureWealth*, coaching is regarded as *"just part of who we are and how we do business. It's not something special, or something we do* in addition. *It's just part of how we lead our people to accelerate results*". For Peter, coaching is co-achieving regardless of the environment, the business, or the individual. Coaching is concerned with understanding where an employee is performing now, helping them identify where they need to improve, and building a bridge between the two through powerful questioning. In recent years, *SecureWealth* hasn't needed to bring in external coaches for its business units and front-line staff because the growth of coaching conversations within the organisation has been organic.

Coaching was introduced into *SecureWealth* to deliver behavioural and performance improvements in individuals and teams to meet and exceed business targets. It was seen as the way to transform the business to create competitive advantage and facilitate cultural change. Peter is adamant that *SecureWealth*'s competitive advantage has been derived from the presence of his internal coaching team which works with front-line staff to remove barriers to their performance so they can deliver on the expectations of their role. The purpose of their coaching is to generate leverage within the organisation so that existing customers are retained and new business secured, with both strategies contributing to organisational sustainability.

The drivers of coaching in *SecureWealth* are the CEO and senior executive team who are absolutely committed to investing in coaching in the long term. The coaching initiative began from the enthusiasm and dedication of one senior executive who was instrumental in creating awareness of coaching and its impact at the organisational level. He's still a senior executive within *SecureWealth* and an influential member of the executive team who are all now passionate advocates for coaching. They have all been trained in coaching and role model coaching throughout the organisation. Peter's internal coaching team is sponsored by the initiating senior executive to whom they report. It gives coaching "some clout and an external feel". Peter believes that a senior level of sponsorship and buy-in is "absolutely critical" to developing a coaching culture.

There are three ways that coaching is delivered within *SecureWealth*. *Leader-as-Coach* training programmes occur at all levels of the organisation, starting with entry-level managers. *SecureWealth*'s policy is that all leaders are expected to coach their direct reports through scheduled one-on-one sessions. Peter's team assisted in designing all of *SecureWealth*'s coaching skills training and leader development programmes which are focused on embedding coaching within the organisation. His team has also contributed a coaching component to several other development programmes for leaders, for example, moving from front-line to business or business to strategic level based on employee tenure and capability. The second way that coaching is delivered in *SecureWealth* is as an important component of the training that talented staff, identified via talent metrics and leader recommendations, receive as members of the succession planning pipeline. Third, coaching is delivered by a select panel of external executive coaches to executive-level managers and above. These three methods spread coaching throughout the organisation to the extent that Peter believes coaching is now an "integrated part of what we do and how we do things here in our business". Coaching is also included to all extension programmes to increase employee engagement, support the application of key learnings back into the workplace, and obtain a higher return on investment.

Coaching by the internal coaching team is in addition to, and complements, the leader-led coaching that is routinely conducted throughout *SecureWealth*. Peter's internal coaching team works within the front-line stores with first-line leaders and business unit leaders who manage and oversee the regions to increase business sales. In this customer-facing area of the business, the impact of coaching can be seen almost immediately in the sales figures which have a major impact on the organisation's bottom line.

From the coaching initiative which started 5 years ago within the business sales and services function, a coaching philosophy now extends to how the entire organisation does business with all its internal and external customers and suppliers. Coaching practice is particularly embedded in the sales and services business units and there are "pockets" of coaching located in other areas of the organisation including the corporate functions. Peter's estimate is that the organisation is about 60 per cent of the way towards embedding a coaching culture across the entire organisation.

Illustrative Example 12

GlobalNetworks is a large international organisation steeped in hierarchy, bureaucracy and compliance. Given the type of industry, everyone understands and accepts the need for rules and regulations. Twelve months ago, as a result of an employee perception survey, the CEO issued a global directive that the organisational culture had to change. The HR function, which for many years has delivered leadership development training to all leaders in the organisation, was charged with this responsibility. Their leadership training now includes a coaching component so that leaders understand what coaching is and how they can better engage with their staff to not only perform to the required level but also exert discretionary effort as well to achieve even more.

Everyone in the organisation receives coaching on a monthly basis as a mandated requirement of leaders. Outcomes of these coaching conversations are recorded in a HR metrics system together with performance and action plans. The monthly coaching replaces the annual performance review. There is no doubt that the coaching is conducted as required; however, the quality of the coaching that is delivered is variable. Leaders are recruited into the organisation with coaching skills or they are trained during the induction period. Each business location has to submit a plan which details what the leadership team is going to do to shift the culture – one very specific thing that is tailored to shift the culture in that location.

GlobalNetworks's leadership development programme is delivered worldwide which signifies the importance that the organisation places on leader coaching. The training runs for a couple of hours and looks at what a successful leader does and then replicates that – whether it's how to conduct core routines or run a successful staff meeting. It trains leaders in how to engage staff and conduct one-on-ones with them so that they become excited about their work, solve problems more quickly, acknowledge the good things that their employees do, and improve in areas where they aren't quite meeting role expectations. Leaders take away a toolkit which has a number of items for them to refer to (which is also available online). Anybody who has a direct report must do the course. If a leader doesn't coach, it's considered a "negative". Everyone is coached even without asking for it.

A big part of the leadership development programme is training leaders not only in how to coach but also in how to give constructive feedback. Employees are used to getting mostly negative feedback. The constructive feedback is recorded in a real-time HR metrics system that is visible to, and interactive between, the employee and their manager and includes their performance plan and actions to be achieved.

Because the leadership team is highly experienced, the focus of coaching in *GlobalNetworks* is on the line manager and team leader levels as part of the Enterprise Agreement (EA) which dictates that operators have an individual development and performance review discussion with their manager every year. The way this review is conducted is also specified under the EA as a compliance obligation using a designated template rather than as a coaching conversation. However, line managers use their coaching skills to assist employees actively participate in the review process. To prepare for the review, HR team members meet with the operators to discuss any feedback they might have for their manager and how to give that feedback including, at times, writing it down for those employees who can't express themselves well particularly under pressure. Employees then go into the meeting feeling more confident.

Shadowing is another form of leader development in *GlobalNetworks* and something that's well-accepted. The HR team travels to a certain location, shadows the leaders and gives them immediate feedback on what they are saying and observed doing. The leaders being shadowed love this process and really relate to this form of personalised feedback.

To conduct any "heavy" individual coaching, *GlobalNetworks* engages the services of say, four or five professional coaches from an external consultancy company to travel to a particular location to deliver comprehensive coaching to front-line team leaders and operators. The individuals who are coached are assessed pre- and post-coaching to see what the shift is and to understand whether they're taking on the coaching.

***

This chapter has detailed the four key dimensions of Stage 4 – *Coaching-as-Culture.* In addition to identifying the four stages in the development of a coaching culture, the dynamic, process model (Fig. 3.1) also identified the strategies which, in practice, enable and inhibit progression from one stage to the next, which are addressed in the next chapter.

Chapter 8
Transitioning Across Stages

This chapter addresses the strategies by which organisations transition between stages as they develop a coaching culture. From academic research and practitioner experience, lists of strategies have been proposed as contributing to its development. In contrast, the strategies reported in this book are based on methodologically derived, empirically validated, theoretical underpinnings. These strategies relate to actions that line managers, HR professionals and organisational leaders can take as they learn and grow from being coached and trained in coaching skills, enact policy and procedural changes to support coaching in the workplace, and make coaching a strategic priority by which to effect transformational cultural change. A summary of the strategies that line managers, HR professionals and organisational leaders need to implement as an organisation transitions from one stage to the next in the development of a coaching culture is tabulated in this chapter and detailed in the next three chapters.

Strategies in the Extant Literature

Within the academic community, a review of the literature on how a coaching culture is developed revealed lists of strategies proposed by a number of researchers as follows:

Hardingham et al. [1]:

- Build experience of, and belief in, coaching among the leaders of the organisation.
- Capitalise on any experience of, and belief in, coaching.
- Get people talking about how coaching has helped them.
- Clarify what a coaching culture means.
- Explain the link between coaching and business.
- Provide evidence that coaching has an impact on performance.

S. Knowles, *Coaching Culture*, https://doi.org/10.1007/978-3-031-09050-9_8

- Acknowledge the difficulties of coaching people you work with.

Anderson et al. [2]:

- Seed the organisation with leaders and managers who can act as role models on coaching approaches.
- Link coaching outcomes to the business.
- Coach senior leadership teams in creating culture change.
- Recognise and reward coaching culture behaviours.
- Integrate with other people management processes.

Hart [3]:

- Ensure and promote alignment of organisational strategy with the use of coaching behaviour.
- Establish planned, formal, structured and long-term programmes for promoting coaching behaviour.
- Seek to create a cascade effect by developing internal coaching capacity through training programmes and follow-on coaching.
- Incorporate coaching behaviour as a job performance competency and link it to systems for advancement, rewards and incentives.
- Use external coaches as a positive developmental tool.

Gormley and van Nieuwerburgh [4]:

- Promote coaching throughout the organisation by the targeted efforts of senior leaders.
- Present coaching as an integrated part of the organisation or system (rather than an isolated activity).
- Role model coaching by leaders to demonstrate their strong personal commitment to developing their own capabilities.

Strategies to develop a coaching culture have also been derived from practitioner experience. These include, for example, developing psychologically based attitudes and behaviours such as a belief in managers' abilities and their continuous professional development [5], moving away from performance appraisals [6] and advice and support regarding the principles of a coaching culture [7]. Practitioner experience also informs how to choose external coaches and coaching skills training, launch a coaching programme, conduct informal coaching in the workplace, and manage the challenges of coaching in the workplace [7].

These practitioner and conceptual approaches to developing a coaching culture hint at the totality of what it takes to achieve a fully developed coaching culture. They provide lists of strategies based on intellectual rigour and practical experience. However, none is sufficiently grounded in empirical evidence to support their claims. Even collectively, they provide insufficient evidence for organisations to have the confidence to invest in developing a coaching culture. A comprehensive, staged approach to coaching culture development is required based on solid theoretical underpinnings together with identified strategies that CEOs, organisational leaders and HR professionals can use to progress the transition of their organisation to a coaching culture and minimise its regression under difficult circumstances. Hence, a comprehensive approach to developing a coaching culture was developed from the theoretical model derived from my research study (Fig. 3.1), as explained below.

Transitions Between Stages

To begin the process of transitioning from Stage 1 to Stage 2 in the development of a coaching culture, organisations need to implement strategies to assist the personal transformation of mindset, attitude and beliefs from *manager* to *leader*. To keep progressing, the organisation needs to transform its business policies, practices and procedures by leveraging coaching within selected business drivers. Finally, to achieve cultural change, the organisation needs all its members to transform by adopting a coaching philosophy and *coaching leadership style* (see Fig. 8.1).

Management research provides the *strategies* that organisations need to progressively develop a coaching culture. However, it is the *psychological mechanisms* that enable managers to transform their mentality, and the *educational mechanisms* that support personal learning, that have been identified in my research study as the "glue" that enables or inhibits strategy implementation at each transition. The ways that an organisation moves through these three transitions relate to the learnings, behaviour and actions taken by HR professionals, organisational leaders, and CEO and senior executives as they transition the organisation from one stage to the next (see Table 8.1). The numbers in Table 8.1 refer to the *strategies* and *mechanisms* that are detailed in Chaps. 9–11. But first, a word about the difference between *strategy* and *mechanism* as used in this book.

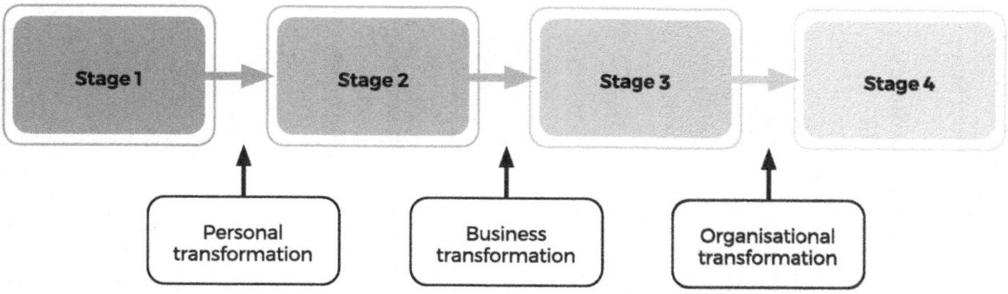

Fig. 8.1 Three transitions across the four stages

Table 8.1 Strategies and mechanisms to develop and embed a coaching culture

Coaching foundations	To *transition* from Stage 1, *Coaching-as-Intervention*, to Stage 2, *Coaching-as-HR-Function* (Ch9)	To *transition* from Stage 2, *Coaching-as-HR-Function*, to Stage 3, *Coaching-as-Leader-Capability* (Ch10)	To *transition* from Stage 3, *Coaching-as- Leader-Capability*, to Stage 4, *Coaching-as-Culture* (Ch11)
	Individual = individual change/transformation	Team = "pockets" of cultural change	Organisation = "whole" transformational cultural change
Learn (Education) Adding to what we know and finding ways to incorporate new discoveries into existing frameworks so that they make sense to us	**Mindset shift** 1. HR professionals are formally trained as coaches 2. In-house coaching curriculum is developed	**Malleable perspective** 1. Coaching is a core capability of leaders and is embedded in a leadership development framework 2. Managers are trained in coaching skills to become leaders (*leader-as-coach* programme) 3. Coaching is embedded in all leadership and executive development programmes	**Learning, growth, and development** 1. CEO and senior executives are formally trained as coaches 2. CEO and senior leaders have absolute clarity about what coaching is and what it is not 3. CEO and senior executives model buy-in, engagement and sponsorship for coaching
Grow (Psychology) Thinking differently, embracing new perspectives, experiencing change, behaving in different ways	**Cognitive restructuring** 3. HR professionals experience being coached	**Social restructuring** 4. Leaders experience being coached 5. Leaders let go of *command-and-control* and adopt a *coaching leadership style* 6. Any unwillingness of leaders to coach is addressed	**Self-regulation and emotional competence** 4. CEO and senior executives experience being coached 5. CEO and senior executives adopt a *growth mindset* 6. CEO and senior executives believe in the value and potential of all employees and identify opportunities to unleash that potential

Coaching foundations	To *transition* from Stage 1, *Coaching-as-Intervention*, to Stage 2, *Coaching-as-HR-Function* (Ch9)	To *transition* from Stage 2, *Coaching-as-HR-Function*, to Stage 3, *Coaching-as-Leader-Capability* (Ch10)	To *transition* from Stage 3, *Coaching-as- Leader-Capability*, to Stage 4, *Coaching-as-Culture* (Ch11)
	Individual = individual change/transformation	Team = "pockets" of cultural change	Organisation = "whole" transformational cultural change
Lead (Management) Leading people and managing change in new ways to enable, empower, and "hold the space" for others to lead	**Acquisition of coaching competencies** 4. Coaching is positioned within HR 5. HR develops the infrastructure for coaching 6. HR establishes the support for coaching 6.1 Accredited Coach Network 6.2 Coaching Circles 6.3 Coaching Communities 7. HR appoints a coaching panel to coach individuals throughout the organisation	**Motivation and performance improvement** 7. Coaching is positioned within business units 8. Leaders coach direct reports on a regular basis 9. Leaders create a safe environment in which to coach 10. Regular feedback coaching sessions replace the annual performance review 11. Specialist coaches are trained to coach within business functions 12. Internal coaches are appointed to work within business units 13. An internal coaching team is established to work across business units	**Interpersonal and relationship improvements** 7. Coaching is positioned at the organisational level as a strategic priority 8. CEO and senior executives align coaching with organisational vision, values and behaviours 9. CEO and senior executives define the purpose, organisational and business outcomes from coaching 9.1 A recurrent budget and resources are allocated to coaching 9.2 The return on investment from coaching is measured 10. A senior executive is appointed as a champion for coaching 11. A communication strategy is developed to introduce and sustain the coaching practice 12. CEO and senior executives analyse every aspect of the organisation from a coaching perspective 13. Organisational levers to maximise the impact of coaching are identified 14. Coaching is applied more broadly across the organisation 14.1 A coaching framework is attached to all training activities 14.2 Coaching is conducted throughout the organisation 14.3 Peer coaching is conducted throughout the organisation 15. Coaching relationships are extended to external customers and suppliers

Strategies and Mechanisms

Within the academic literature, *strategy* has been defined as a plan, ploy, pattern, position or perspective [8]. Strategic planning is undertaken by organisations to develop action plans to achieve business targets. A ploy is a manoeuvre to confuse the competition into thinking that a certain action will be taken but maybe isn't. A pattern is the habitual way in which business operates, often giving comfort to consumers but making an organisation's next actions predictable. As a position, strategy indicates where the organisation stands in the marketplace in relation to its competitors, possibly predicting what its next actions will be. As a perspective, strategy is the way that the organisation views the marketplace and how it takes actions in relation to that marketplace. All these ways that *strategy* can be conceived relate to the actions that organisational leaders take to maintain or enhance their position in the marketplace, their standing in relation to customers and key stakeholders and their competitiveness and sustainability in the long term.

Stepping back from strategy and action is the intention in the minds of organisational leaders in relation to what they believe is happening, or needs to happen, to promote the best interests of the organisation. In effect, *strategy* is the door through which the organisation exerts its influence on the world. The key to that strategy – the key that unlocks the door to allow actions to take place successfully – is in the pre-thought and motivation that goes into the creation of the strategy and how it will be executed for optimal outcome. That key is the *mechanism* that underlies every decision, every motivation to achieve and every desire to *be* and *do* the best by the organisations' customers, staff and shareholders. The key opens the door that allows action to take place. *Mechanisms* are the keys that unlock the doors to organisational *strategy* and success.

For the purpose of this discussion, the mechanisms are the experiences that people have and the learnings they gain from those experiences. The strategies are what people do to achieve a desired outcome. The learning generally comes after the experience of doing. However, when organisations are preparing a transitional plan, they need to work backwards from the *learning* (What has been done before and how can that work for us?) to the *experience* (How can I personally become involved so that I can see the benefits for myself?) to the *doing* (What do I need to do as a result of learning from my experience and the research that I have reviewed?).

Transition Strategies Identified from the Model

Table 8.1 outlines the strategies and mechanisms to develop and embed a coaching culture in organisations across the four stages as identified in the model of coaching culture development (Fig. 3.1). The strategies correlate with how CEOs and senior executives, organisational leaders and HR professionals *learn*, *grow* and *lead* as they enact these strategies to transition across the four stages. Details of each strategy in the three transition periods are provided in the three chapters that follow.

***

The next chapter outlines the strategies and mechanisms by which organisations transition from Stage 1, *Coaching-as-Intervention*, to Stage 2, *Coaching-as-HR-Function*.

References

1 Hardingham, A., et al. (2004). *The coach's coach: Personal development for personal developers* (Vol. 37). Emerald Group Publishing Limited.
2. Anderson, M., Frankovelgia, C., & Hernez-Broome, G. (2009). Business leaders reflect on coaching cultures. *Leadership in Action, 28*(6), 20–22.
3. Hart, W. (2005). Getting culture: Imbuing your organization with coaching behavior. *Leadership in Action, 25*(4), 7–10.
4. Gormley, H., & Van Nieuwerburgh, C. (2014). Developing coaching cultures: A review of the literature. *Coaching: An International Journal of Theory, Research and Practice, 7*(2), 90–101.
5. Waldman, J. (2009). Introducing a coaching culture. *Training Journal, 65*, 69.
6. Bawany, S. (2016). Time to stop performance appraisals? Reinventing performance management with coaching culture. In *Talent Management Excellence Essentials*. HR.COM.
7. Wilson, C. (2011). Developing a coaching culture. *Industrial and Commercial Training, 43*(7), 407–414.
8. Mintzberg, H. (1987). The strategy concept I: Five Ps for strategy. *California Management Review, 30*(1), 11–24.

Chapter 9
Transition from Stage 1 to Stage 2

This chapter details the strategies by which organisations transition from Stage 1, *Coaching-as-Intervention* to Stage 2, *Coaching-as-HR-Function*. The strategies start with HR professionals providing the opportunity for line managers to learn more about coaching (*Learn*) and how psychological mechanisms can change their mental perspective (*Grow*). Thereafter, they utilise strategies from management research to prepare the infrastructure for coaching and coaching skills training programmes to be delivered within the organisation, overcoming any barriers and enabling the transition from Stage 1 to Stage 2 (*Lead*). Line managers who believe in the value of coaching advocate for increased access to coaching services and coaching skills training. The chapter also outlines the mechanisms that may hinder an organisation from progressing to the next stage.

The process model of coaching culture development (Fig. 3.1) identifies three *barriers* which may hinder line managers' acceptance of coaching: stigmatisation, tunnel vision, and boundary entrenchment. The barrier of *stigmatisation* arises when employees are sent to coaching by line managers who do not understand what coaching is and how powerful it can be. They believe it to be a process by which an employee is remediated or "let go" from the organisation. They have a narrow, *tunnel vision* view of coaching as a short-term, technical "fix" and are unable to see other possibilities. *Boundary entrenchment* arises when the coaching is outsourced to external coaches because managers at this early stage in the development of a coaching culture believe that it's not their job to coach.

Two enabling strategies to progression help organisations overcome these barriers: evidence-based reframing of line managers' mental models and mindsets, and advocacy for a greater coaching presence within business units. The enabler of *evidence-based reframing* involves HR professionals accumulating and sharing sufficient evidence of successful coaching interventions to support the line manager's cognitive reframing of the purposes for coaching and the outcomes to be expected from coaching. It is their mental barriers and attitudes that HR professionals must assist line managers overcome if they are to support the progression of coaching

S. Knowles, *Coaching Culture*, https://doi.org/10.1007/978-3-031-09050-9_9

into business units. But first, HR professionals may need to know more about coaching and be formally coach-trained themselves. They can maximally accumulate such knowledge by enrolling in a coach-training programme with an accredited coach-training provider. During the formal coach-training, HR professionals experience being coached and come to realise its benefits. Those who speak publicly about their positive experience exhibit *advocacy* for coaching and actively seek increased coaching services within the organisation. When these two enablers for progression (*evidence-based reframing, advocacy*) are sufficiently powerful to outcome the three barriers *(stigmatisation, tunnel vision, boundary entrenchment)*, the model at Fig. 3.1 shows that the organisation progresses to the second stage of developing a coaching culture: Stage 2 – *Coaching-as-HR-Function.*

Let's look at how HR professionals accumulate increased knowledge of coaching and experience being coached so that they develop a greater understanding of the wider benefits of coaching for individuals, teams and the organisation. The new learnings enable HR professionals to design coaching skills training programmes and learning experiences for line managers (to be conducted in the next stage) and build the infrastructure for coaching within existing HR policies and procedures to support its introduction into the organisation. This process facilitates the extension of coaching beyond an individual intervention in Stage 1 into a learning and growth opportunity for line managers in Stage 2. The strategies and mechanisms to bring about this *personal transformation* are outlined in Table 8.1 and explained below.

Learn (Education): Mindset Shift

In this first transition period, to facilitate the adoption of the two enablers (*evidence-based reframing, advocacy*) and minimise the impact of the three barriers (*stigmatisation, tunnel vision, boundary entrenchment*), a *transformational HR professional* is identified to steward the organisation as it begins its cultural change journey. HR professionals are typically the people in the organisation with the most knowledge of coaching. Hence, they are the ones who usually take responsibility for promoting coaching as a development tool. They may have read about coaching or spoken to a colleague who has been coached; hence, they may want to know more about coaching – what it is and what it can do for organisational members. By becoming formally trained as a coach and experiencing being coached, HR professionals change their mindset about coaching from being just a skill or tool in the hands of external "expert" coaches, to understand it as a powerful vehicle that leaders can use to bring about behavioural change and performance improvement in many employees not just individuals who are "sent" to be remediated by coaching. They come to see the positive benefits of coaching which dispels any negative preconceptions they may have held previously.

HR Professionals Are Formally Trained as Coaches

Many HR professionals have not undertaken formal coach-training delivered by an accredited, external provider. They may have received in-house training in coaching skills ranging from a few hours to a few days either via dedicated coaching skills training programmes or, more usually, as a component of leadership development programmes. However, they're not feeling confident in their ability to train leaders in coaching skills or to conduct coaching themselves. Formal, accredited coach-training delivered by an approved, external provider enables HR professionals to increase in self-awareness and gain insight into the impact they have on others in their team and organisation. They build their personal and leadership capability so that they are able to handle situations differently when faced with tough decisions or team conflict. After receiving formal training as a coach, they realise that "there's this great big thing called coaching that we don't have anywhere in our organisation". Alternatively, they may have undertaken training delivered by an external company in the use and debrief of a 360-degree assessment instrument. However, unless this company's assessment programme is approved by an organisation such as the ICF, it will not comply with the definition of coaching according to international standards.

HR Develops In-House Coaching Skills Curriculum

When HR professionals attend external, accredited coach-training programmes, they may use this knowledge and their experience to design an internal coaching skills training programme either as a standalone training opportunity or as a component of the organisation's leadership development programme. The content is typically generic so that it can be implemented consistently across the organisation but also flexible so that it can be tailored to suit the needs of individual business units. Internally designed training or leadership programmes that "fit" culturally are more acceptable to staff and effective in terms of their outcomes. Employee representatives from different business units may be included in the design process to build the momentum for coaching within their business units. An internal design will position the programme as owned by the organisation rather that it being bought "off the shelf". External coach-training providers may be engaged to work with HR on the design of the in-house coaching skills training programme or leadership development programme.

Grow (Psychology): Cognitive Restructuring

In this first transition period, HR professionals experience being coached either during external, accredited coach-training that the organisation funds as part of their development plan or by attending an in-house coaching skills training programme which includes the experience of being coached. This experience typically opens them to new insights about themself and others. They gain greater self-awareness of who they are and their impact on others and use their learnings to make changes in their life and work almost immediately.

HR Professionals Experience Being Coached

Experiencing one-on-one coaching as part of an accredited coach-training programme gives HR professionals the insight they need to transition from a *transactional* approach to the work they do into a *transformational* appreciation of how effective coaching can be as a development tool. They develop their communication, relationship and leadership skills, and experience the transition from *transactional* manager to *transformational* leader of people. As a result of being coached, they come to understand and appreciate the benefits of coaching and how coaching can be used to enable and empower others on a broader scale, including all organisational leaders, to lead their teams more effectively towards behavioural change and performance improvement.

Lead (Management): Acquisition of Leader Competencies

In this first transition period, HR professionals want to transfer what they have learned and experienced about coaching into the development of all line managers so that they may become *leaders* (rather than *managers*) who enable and empower others through coaching. Because line managers are busy people concerned about their leadership, coaching is often woven into leadership development programmes. Leadership is something that line managers know about, relate to and are interested in. Hence, they will attend leadership development programmes but may not be enticed to attend coach-specific training programmes of which they know very little.

Coaching Is Positioned Within HR

In this first transition period, the responsibility for coaching transfers from line managers being responsible for arranging coaching to *remediate* a single direct report, to coaching residing within the HR function as a *development* tool to support employees perform better in their role. It is HR professionals who typically update their professional knowledge and skills to keep abreast of new ways to develop people. On completion of an accredited coach-training programme, HR professionals have much to share with willing participants in leadership programmes. They may also volunteer to coach line managers to practise their coaching skills before seeking credentialing from a professional association like the ICF. Professional associations have a requirement that certified members accrue a certain number of Continuing Coach Education (CCE) credits to maintain their credentialing. Hence, most HR professionals need to practise their coaching and log their coaching hours as they continue to learn and grow in their ability to provide first-class coaching services to their organisation. They want the organisation to be at the leading edge in terms of employee growth and development.

HR Develops the Infrastructure for Coaching

So that the in-house coaching skills training of line managers that is to be conducted in the next transition period will be successful, preparation must be made in this first transition period to support its introduction into the organisation and ongoing operation. HR professionals build the infrastructure to support coaching by reviewing and adjusting all HR systems, policies and procedures so they reflect and recognise a coaching approach to employee development. This includes revision of all recruitment and selection documentation, performance management systems, reward structures, talent management and succession processes. The first step is to include the requirement for leaders to coach in their job description as a KPI, identify the coaching skill set as a desirable selection criteria, and provide training in the probation period if the successful candidate doesn't have coaching skills. The next step is to develop a HR metrics system to record how coaching skills training is being delivered in the organisation and how coaching is conducted thereafter within each business unit. This information includes data such as attendance at in-house coaching skills training programmes – for example, names, numbers, positions and business units. Thereafter, the data metrics capture the number, frequency and quality of the coaching sessions that are being delivered by leaders in business units.

In addition, in this first transition period, HR professionals revise organisational structures to ensure that a leader's span of control allows them the time to coach as well as fulfil the requirements of their role. Leaders who have more than eight employees will find it difficult to coach individuals on a regular four to six weekly cycle. Job redesign processes can be utilised to make it possible for leaders to coach given the scope and complexity of the work they do as well as the number of their direct reports.

HR Establishes the Support for Coaching

As awareness of coaching spreads throughout the organisation, the HR function may be approached to respond to employee requests to be coached for *development* purposes. To manage such requests, HR establishes an intranet portal specifically for the purpose of providing information about coaching and its benefits. In addition, the portal may hold a downloadable form for employees to complete and email to HR to request that they be coached. Increasingly, these forms require the approval of the employee's line manager who attests to the coaching as a key component of their Development Plan. Having an approval process also ensures the commitment of the line manager to coaching. Employees are matched to a volunteer coach within the organisation or to an external coach, depending on the nature of their coaching request and needs.

Accredited Coach Network

HR professionals who are formally trained as coaches typically volunteer their services to coach others in the organisation via an *Accredited Coach Network* that they establish. Some CEOs, senior executives and organisational leaders who have been formally qualified as coaches may also volunteer their services. They are usually operational executives who understand how powerful coaching can be. They have high personal credibility and leadership qualities, are comfortable within themselves and, if not in the senior executive position, are able to coach upwards and relate well at that level. Volunteer coaches typically coach no more than two individuals at a time delivering say, 6–12 sessions over a period of 6–12 months to fit in with their operational duties. Caution must be exercised during the coaching sessions that the more senior and experienced coach doesn't slip into a mentoring role without first signalling a change of role and gaining permission from the coachee to switch intervention approaches.

Coaching Circles

To provide support for leaders to begin coaching their direct reports after attending the in-house coaching skills training programme, the HR function may establish Coaching Circles to fully embed the learnings from the training into daily operational practice. Coaching Circles may consist of attendees from a particular training programme but more often are mixed cohorts from different training programmes and business units. The conversations that occur on say, a bimonthly basis, are opportunities for leaders to seek advice and support on any situations they have found difficult to coach around because, even though the session follows the same coaching process, the outcomes from each session may be very different. The Circle encourages self-reflection as the Leaders-as-Coach ask themselves: "What's working for me?" "What's not working?" "Where are my weaknesses?" "How can I become better at coaching?" "Tried this – worked well – share it with the group". It is constant reflection and learning to improve coaching practice. Coaching Circles may last for say, 12 months post-training, but typically no longer unless they have ongoing support from HR to input additional training into the group.

Coaching Communities

To support organisational leaders who coach, Coaching Communities may be established to provide coaching supervision and maintain the quality and currency of internal coaching practice. The community may also explore and provide opportunities for Continuing Coach Education. HR professionals are usually injected into these communities to challenge current thinking and encourage the extension of the coaching skill set into other areas of leadership, training, and business transactions.

HR Establishes Coaching Panels

Because there will still be employees in the organisation who need expert coaching for other specialist purposes, HR may establish a coaching panel of external coaches who can deliver refereed and affordable coaching services to these individuals. It is the responsibility of HR to manage the coaching engagements with external coaches who may be called upon to support an individual for, say, performance improvement, role clarification, or when a manager is promoted to a more senior role. Individuals at middle management level and below are not usually coached by external coaches unless there is a particular need to do so - for example, talent management or a particularly sensitive issue. Rather, middle managers are coached by a volunteer coach in the Accredited Coaches Network.

To meet the particular coaching needs of senior executives, HR conducts a selection process to appoint a number of external executive coaches to a coaching panel. When a request for coaching is made, meetings are arranged between the executive and several executive coaches to access the "chemistry match" between them, which enables a trusting relationship to form and grow. Executives are often entitled to receive coaching when they enter the executive service either as a new external recruit or when transitioning from an internal manager to an executive position. An external executive coach may also be engaged when there is a performance or interpersonal issue with colleagues or staff, or when the coachee's focus is constrained by the complexity of their role and specific requirements of the job. The opportunity to be coached by an external coach opens up the possibility of "bigger picture" thinking about their situation, and challenges the coachee to think "outside the box" in terms of how they "show up" as a strategic leader in the organisation. Many senior executives use executive coaches to test out new ideas before they put them to the CEO, Board, or overseas parent company. They may use a coaching session to gain a different, neutral perspective on what they're proposing from a coach who will challenge them and maybe "push back" on their ideas, before they make a final presentation.

***

This chapter has outlined the strategies and mechanisms by which organisations transition from Stage 1, *Coaching-as-Intervention* to Stage 2, *Coaching-as-HR-Function.* The next chapter outlines the strategies and mechanisms by which organisations transition from Stage 2, *Coaching-as-HR-Function* to Stage 3, *Coaching-as-Leader-Capability.*

Chapter 10
Transition from Stage 2 to Stage 3

This chapter details the strategies by which HR professionals and organisational leaders assist the transition from Stage 2, *Coaching-as-HR-Function* to Stage 3, *Coaching-as-Leader-Capability*. It explains the educational processes by which line managers receive training to gain knowledge and skills relating to coaching (*Learn*) and the psychological mechanisms by which they experience a mindset shift from a *command-and-control* management style to a *coaching leadership style* (*Grow*). Thereafter, organisational leaders enact strategies from management research which assist them lead coaching practice within their business units, overcoming any barriers and enabling the transition from Stage 2 to Stage 3 (*Lead*). In this transition period, coaching becomes a leader capability required in the performance of their role and for career progression. The chapter also outlines the mechanisms that may hinder an organisation from progressing to the next stage.

The process model of coaching culture development (Fig. 3.1) identified four *barriers* which may hinder the organisation from progressing beyond the *Coaching-as-HR-Function* stage: stoic behaviours, role confusion, unproven benefits, and positional territorialism. The barrier of *stoic behaviours* arises when managers fail to appreciate coaching and the experience of being coached, continuing to maintain their traditional behavioural pattern of *command-and-control*. *Role confusion* may arise when managers cannot see how to fit coaching within their work role and lack the skills, motivation or experience to deliver coaching to their direct reports. A barrier may exist when managers question the positive outcomes reported from coaching and cannot see how coaching can be applied beyond the individual level. They consider the *benefits unproven*. *Positional territorialism* emerges when managers are able to exert power to protect coaching as an activity that belongs within their territory. It is these mental barriers and attitudes that HR professionals must first assist line managers overcome if they are to support the organisation progress to developing a coaching culture.

Two enabling strategies to progression help organisational leaders overcome these barriers: mental model shift, and agitator. The enabler of *mental mindset shift*

S. Knowles, *Coaching Culture*, https://doi.org/10.1007/978-3-031-09050-9_10

captures how the experience of being coached and growing their understanding of coaching can help line managers break their established patterns of thinking and start to believe in themselves as being capable of acquiring coaching skills and coaching their direct reports. The enabler of *agitators* involves one or more people within the organisation striving to shake up the status quo that positions coaching within HR. They have sufficient authority to influence coaching becoming the responsibility of business unit leaders. When these two enablers for progression (*mental model shifts, agitators*) are sufficiently powerful to outcome the four barriers (*stoic behaviours, role confusion, unproven benefits, positional territorialism*), Fig. 3.1 shows that the organisation moves to the third stage of developing a coaching culture: *Coaching-as-Leader-Capability*.

Let's look at how HR professionals train line managers in coaching skills as a core competency of their role within a leadership development framework and provide them with the experience of being coached. In this way, line managers become more confident in their ability to coach their direct reports and create a safe environment within their business unit for coaching to occur. They may also appoint internal coaches to support performance improvement and business progression and/or specialist coaches in discrete areas where they can prove optimally effective to achieve and exceed business targets. The strategies and mechanisms to bring about this *business transformation* are outlined in Table 8.1 and explained below.

Learn (Education): Malleable Perspective

In this second transition period, to facilitate the adoption of the two enablers (*mental model shifts, agitators*) and minimise the impact of the four barriers (*stoic behaviours, role confusion, unproven benefits, positional territorialism*), coaching becomes a valuable *development* tool that is included as a *core capability of leaders* within a leadership development framework and an essential skill for them to possess in order to progress in their career.

Coaching Is a Core Capability Within a Leadership Development Framework

In this second transition period, managers learn how to replace their immediate, task-oriented understanding of coaching with an appreciation of coaching as a short-term investment in developing their ability to *coach* and *lead* their people – to transition from *manager* into *leader* – someone who is capable of coaching their direct reports with confidence on a regular basis. As a designated core capability of leaders, *coaching* is embedded into either the organisation's capability framework, leadership development framework or career progression framework. For leaders to promote within the organisation, a coaching capability is required. Leader coaching capability enhances the organisation's human capital which contributes to its competitive advantage in the marketplace. Organisations become an *employer of choice* when they are renowned for their commitment to developing their people.

Managers Are Trained in Coaching Skills to Become Leaders

Line managers are trained in coaching skills not only to deliver coaching but also to become *leaders* of people. HR conducts *Leader-as-Coach* programmes for line managers and talented individuals as an investment in developing the leader capability of the organisation plus as a way to increase employee engagement and retention of valuable staff. Managers learn how to become leaders who coach their staff to achieve improved performance, behavioural change, and career progression. Talented individuals are retained within the organisation's succession plan. On completion of their training in coaching skills, some *managers* who have made the transition to *leader* may be offered the opportunity to become formally trained as a coach by an external coach-training provider.

Increasing the leader capability of line managers is particularly important in times of change such as when an organisation is restructured, acquired or merged. In such circumstances, it is the leader's role to make decisions about who should go and who should stay and to tell their staff, plus support both groups thereafter. Leaders need strength and resilience to cope with the changes themselves as well as lead their new team back to targeted performance levels which may have slipped due to what is often months of interruption.

Coaching Is Embedded into All Leadership and Executive Development Programmes

In this second transition period, organisations which are serious about reaping the benefits of coaching include a coaching skills component as an integral part of their leadership development programmes. These programmes support and align individual behaviours with the organisation's vision and values. Most organisations design their leadership development programmes so they are part generic, part flexible, and tailored to suit business needs and organisational culture. Executive coaches may be engaged to work with HR professionals and leaders to co-design the coaching component of the programme. The way that programmes are structured and delivered – the content, the language that is used, and the coaching model that is adopted – all reflect the purpose for which coaching is being introduced into the organisation and the desired outcomes. The programme is structured so that it is highly relevant to employees and consistent with the strategic goals and objectives of the organisation.

Grow (Psychology): Social Restructuring

In this second transition period, organisational leaders experience being coached. As a result of this experience, they come to view coaching not just as a way to change mindsets and behaviour but also as a valuable way to improve their leadership and the performance of individuals in their team. They adjust the way they relate to, and interact with, their team members and others in the organisation and create a more engaged workforce who feel individually and collectively supported and appreciated.

Leaders Experience Being Coached

When a coaching component is included in leadership development programmes, an individual coaching programme of, say, six sessions is usually attached to ensure that the learnings from the training are implemented back into the day-to-day working practice of each leader. This transfer of learning is essential if the organisation wishes to gain maximum traction from their investment in the training. External coaches may be engaged from a coaching panel, or qualified volunteer coaches may be sourced from the *Accredited Coaches Network*, to conduct the individual coaching sessions. Research shows that unless there is follow-up on the application of learning from training programmes, up to 80% of the learning may be lost. This is a huge, and unacceptable, bleed from an organisational investment to improve the leadership and capability of individuals and teams.

A Coaching Leadership Style Replaces Command-and-Control

A coaching culture can be described as one in which there is a commitment to coaching and development as opposed to *command-and-control*. In a coaching culture, the traditional management style of *command-and-control* is replaced by a *coaching leadership style* which enables the organisation to respond most effectively in a global, competitive market and retain talent. As expectations of the role change, many managers have to relinquish what they know and the behaviours they have been rewarded for in the past and replace this knowledge and behaviours with what is expected of them under a transformational cultural agenda.

A malleable mindset is required to shift from a *command-and-control* management mentality to one that is more supportive of individuals and their personal agendas for work and career. Leadership style change occurs when there is a will and the resources to utilise coaching as a vehicle to bring about a greater appreciation of the "people skills" that are required of today's leaders. Coaching is a powerful means of shifting management from the old school, archaic, *command-and-control* mindset to a *coaching leadership style* that organisational leaders need to possess in order to not only drive value for money but also engage a motivated and adaptable workforce. Coaching has been described as the "engine room" which unleashes discretionary effort and engagement, resulting in coaching relationships between people which are developmentally focused and positively intentioned.

Any Unwillingness of Leaders to Coach Is Addressed

Some line managers may welcome the opportunity to develop coaching skills, embracing the opportunity to learn something new as part of their growth and development as a *leader*. However, others may be sceptical that this is just the "next big thing" being expected of them. This scepticism may be because they don't understand what coaching is, have no desire to coach, and see no reason to change. Managers who are most sceptical about adopting a *coaching leadership style* are more frequently those with a *command-and-control* style of interacting with their staff. These managers may see coaching as a threat to their established way of interacting with employees. They may not see that coaching is part of their role in a transformational organisational culture. They may understand mentoring but not what it is to coach. However, in a coaching culture, the consequence for line managers who cannot change, or refuse to coach, may be termination.

One way to encourage line managers to change their *command-and-control* style is to use a 360-degree leadership or behavioural assessment instrument. The results deliver the evidence to support the need for a manager to make changes in their behaviour and/or way of interacting with staff. Feedback from the 360-degree instrument creates self-awareness of the impact a manager has on those in their team and others in their immediate environment. Debriefing the results of this instrument with the manager gives the coach an idea of how "coachable" the manager is likely to be. Some managers may be deluding themselves that they are good leaders. Hence, providing them with feedback from a commercially available assessment instrument may facilitate their insight into how to construct social interactions with others differently in the future to achieve better outcomes.

Lead (Management): Motivation and Performance Improvement

In this second transition period, the audience for coaching changes from an *individual* to a *group* focus on all managers in the organisation. The HR function now delivers training in coaching skills to all managers so that they acquire coaching and "people" skills and become *leaders* who coach. Leaders create a safe space for regular coaching sessions to occur, during which time they provide valuable feedback to team members on how they can improve. They use coaching as a way to incentivise employees to stay longer in the organisation and commit to a longer-term future supporting the organisation's vision and direction. When team members are more positive, greater opportunities exist for cooperation, collaboration and teamwork to occur.

Coaching Is Positioned Within Business Units

In this second transition period, as HR professionals deliver training in coaching skills to organisational leaders and greater recognition of the importance of coaching spreads beyond the HR function, leaders of business units start to realise how coaching can benefit their teams and team members. In consequence, the responsibility for rolling out coaching throughout the organisation transitions to business units. It is leaders of business units who must meet targets and budgets, and they start to see how they can use coaching as a way to improve individual and team performance. Those who coach their direct reports maximise the ability of staff to respond to emerging business needs and opportunities. Front-line staff, in particular, benefit from being coached to help them remove any barriers to their performance and assist them deliver on the expectations of their role.

HR professionals who have been formally trained as coaches are equipped to design and deliver the in-house coaching skills training programmes, possibly assisted by external coaches. From being externally coach-trained, they have a comprehensive understanding of what coaching is and have acquired the technical skills in how to conduct both *performance* and *pure coaching* conversations. To transition through this period, business unit leaders may need to fund the organisation's HR professionals to deliver in-house coaching skills training programmes to build a strong internal coaching capability within their business unit, but they only need to allocate funding for external coaches to be engaged when expert coaching is required. This business unit funding is a short- to medium-term investment in increasing leader capability within the business unit.

Leaders Coach Their Direct Reports and Others in the Organisation

In the first transition period, the requirement for leaders to coach their direct reports was written into their job description. This requirement is reinforced during this second transition period when training in coaching skills is conducted. After receiving the training, leaders are expected to deliver one-on-one coaching and feedback sessions to their direct reports on a regular basis. In addition, leaders are expected to use a coaching approach in all their interactions with staff to enable and empower them to improved performance. Leaders who coach encourage discovery and forward thinking. The coaching may also reveal previously unknown risks or threats to the business which can then be immediately addressed. Team coaching is conducted at any time the team meets but principally at the start of each week as the leader encourages all team members to generate new ideas and options to progress their current workload. A coaching feedback approach shifts the leader's language and the way they address daily problems. Conversations are more developmental, meaningful and constructive and serve to build up the individual and the team rather than take them down.

Leader delivery of coaching may prove to be a challenge in certain circumstances such as during an intense working schedule when time to coach is extremely limited, when team members are in different locations, or when the team is really a group of "stars" rather than people with a collective mentality. In this second transition period, leaders need to make the coaching of their direct reports a priority even when their weekly schedule is busy. They will reap the benefits when individuals know what to do and go do it without having to come back to them again and again. Initially, the leader's coaching efforts may appear to be "weak" but with practice and feedback on their coaching, their coaching ability will become stronger and they will gain in confidence.

In a coaching culture, leaders adopt a *coaching leadership style* first before they engage the organisation's performance management system. In doing so, they build relationships with their direct reports based on knowledge of them as people as well as team members. This understanding allows leaders to provide timely and considerate feedback to their direct reports on their performance which is often linked to the team member's Development Plan. These plans are individually tailored so that the team member knows exactly where their performance sits at any point in time from their leader's perspective. Leader-led coaching, when delivered as and when needed, is fast-paced and inspires far greater performance by virtue of the individual and team's engagement because they perceive themselves to be valuable contributors to the end result.

Leaders Create a Safe Environment in Which to Coach

When coaching is positioned within business units, leaders create a safe place for coaching to occur, for example, rooms can be booked to provide a quiet space for coaching. For a coaching culture to grow, employees need to feel safe in a space where there is no judgement. Leaders who role model coaching in a safe place demonstrate the importance they attribute to coaching and reinforce coaching as a process in which they and the employee can express anything and everything about what's working for them and what's not, in a respectful way. They encourage active dialogue to resolve issues in that private, confidential and secure space. Individuals become *coachable* when they feel it's safe to take a risk in order to be heard.

Regular Feedback Coaching Sessions Replace the Annual Performance Review

In a coaching culture, annual performance reviews become a thing of the past as the usual "tick-and-flick" system gives way to constructive feedback on a regular basis. Annual performance reviews typically focus on "what's gone wrong" with an employee rather than on what they have achieved during the year. In a coaching culture, the regular focus is on "What's going well?" and "How can you improve your performance, yourself, your career?" When leaders start their coaching conversations using these broad questions, it "dials down" the negative messages. Leaders can pre-empt their concern for an individual when a difficult conversation is about to occur by saying: "This is something that you might feel a little uncomfortable hearing, but I am approaching the discussion with positive intent because I have faith that this might be an issue, and I want you to know that there is general support from me". The emphasis changes from "box-ticking" to meet organisational requirements to "people-ticking" to equip individuals with the feedback and skills they need to perform better in their role. In a coaching culture with regular feedback coaching sessions, there are no surprises because it's constant feedback throughout the year. When leaders deal with failure from a coaching perspective as a learning opportunity, the organisation is beginning to change its culture.

Specialist Coaches Are Trained to Coach Within Business Units

In this second transition period, an important way that organisations are able to increase the productivity of their teams is by the appointment of internal full- or part-time specialist coaches positioned in revenue-generating business units. These specialist coaches typically have years of front-facing experience, understand customer needs and have identified the key triggers that make a sales pitch more likely to succeed. They coach front-line team members who interact directly with customers to generate sales. These specialist coaches may or may not be formally trained as coaches but they are trained in coaching skills. They understand people and how to interact with team leaders to achieve their best performance. The impartiality and independence of the specialist coach is an advantage in examining a possible contractual proposal or deal. The specialist coach has the authority to start interrogating organisational data and the ability to consider other ways of operating or areas of probability that the teams hadn't thought of before because they're "emotionally intent" on winning the deal. Coaching is a particularly useful tool to use with staff in a call centre environment to improve their customer interaction and increase sales.

Internal Coaches Are Appointed to Work Within Business Units

Large global organisations like technology and media companies, banks and superannuation organisations tend to be more "sophisticated and au fait" with coaching than most other organisations. These organisations have been around much longer than most and tend to be more developed in their coaching culture. They see coaching as important and have checks and balances to make sure that the coaching programmes they conduct deliver on what's required. In such organisations, a dedicated position of *Internal Coach* is often established as a full-time support to leaders in a particular business unit. The role of the internal coach is to challenge current thinking and guide employees into different ways of behaving and performing in their role to achieve better outcomes.

One of the selection criteria for appointment as an Internal Coach is that the preferred candidate has been formally trained as a coach to international standards with a proven number of logged coaching hours. From their formal coach-training, internal coaches have a deep understanding of what *pure coaching* is (as well as *performance coaching*) and what differentiates these forms of intervention from others such as mentoring, training, and supervision. Internal coaches need to maintain their coaching currency by being supervised and continuing to upgrade their professional skills. Leaders who have attended the *Leader-as-Coach* in-house coaching skills training are not eligible to apply for the designated position of Internal Coach unless they have a formal coaching qualification as well.

Internal coaches focus on the individual whom leaders believe, with encouragement and support, can maximise their potential. They work with "middle performers" or above to identify any behavioural or performance issues that are holding them back, as well as to identify opportunities that will unleash their potential. Appointing internal coaches is a clear sign that the organisation is investing in the potential of individuals "on the edge". It also means that, over time, leaders can spend more time with other team members whose performance they may have been neglecting. However, there are challenges to being an Internal Coach which relate to their ability to remain independent of the internal politics of the organisation and to coach upwards with executives where privacy and confidentiality are major concerns. In these instances, the services of an external executive coach may be required especially when credibility is important in terms of the coach's background and experience and their proven ability to deliver coaching results.

An Internal Coaching Team Is Established to Work Within Business Units

Organisations in advanced levels of developing a coaching culture establish not only a dedicated Internal Coach position but also an *Internal Coaching Team* of formally trained coaches to work within all business units to support teams and team members. The internal coaching team is separate from, and in addition to, organisational leaders who coach. The purpose of the team is to conduct *pure coaching* which leads to the elimination of limiting beliefs, creation of mindset shifts, and the provision of support for behavioural changes that underpin performance improvement. This allows leaders to focus on *performance coaching* of teams and team members to meet business unit targets and deliverables.

To begin the process of engaging an internal coaching team, organisations develop position descriptions not only for *Internal Coach* but also for *Senior Internal Coach* (in charge of the team) which specify the level of formal coach-training and experience required to be appointed to the coaching team. The position description, selection criteria, and interview formats can be used to recruit dedicated coaches and coaching teams into any business unit of the organisation. The position description also specifies the ongoing professional development required for the incumbent to continue in their role along a clearly mapped pathway of the learning, experience and competencies that an *Internal Coach* needs to acquire to progress into a *Senior Internal Coach* role.

Because the internal coaching team is costing the organisation money rather than making it money, the team is well-aware that they must assist the business unit increase its productivity to a level which will at least equal, if not exceed, the dollar value spent on their employment and overheads as a team. One of the keys to the sustainability of internal coaching teams is that they operate close to the business end of the organisation where they can have most impact. Hence, they can quickly evaluate the effect and the impact their coaching has on, for example, the sales results and service outcomes of the business unit in which they operate. The other important key to the success of internal coaching teams is that they can respond quickly to support the business unit leader in managing change events as they occur, as opposed to taking some time to respond, for example, if they were positioned within HR, and this gives the organisation a competitive advantage in the marketplace.

***

This chapter has outlined the strategies and mechanisms by which organisations transition from Stage 2, *Coaching-as-HR-Function* to Stage 3, *Coaching-as-Leader-Capability.* The next chapter outlines the strategies and mechanisms by which organisations transition from Stage 3, *Coaching-as-Leader-Capability* to Stage 4, *Coaching-as-Culture.*

Chapter 11
Transition from Stage 3 to Stage 4

This chapter details the strategies by which organisational leaders assist the transition from Stage 3, *Coaching-as-Leader-Capability* to Stage 4, *Coaching-as-Culture*. It explains the educational processes by which CEOs and senior leaders learn more about coaching and experience being coached (*Learn*) and the psychological mechanisms that support their mental transformation from thinking about ways to develop individual human capital into identifying strategies to unleash the potential of all employees (*Grow*). They enact findings from management research to lead the transition from Stage 3 to Stage 4 in the development of a coaching culture (*Lead*). To promote this transition, business unit leaders seek increased funding for coaching and coaching skills training of their staff as the demand for coaching grows. An internal, passionate advocate for coaching emerges at the senior executive level. This *coaching champion* makes a business case for the introduction of coaching into all business units. When funding is approved, they work with a dedicated team of coaching *advocates* to guide transformational cultural change across the entire organisation. The chapter also outlines the mechanisms that may hinder an organisation from progressing to the final stage in the development of a coaching culture.

The process model of coaching culture development (Fig. 3.1) identified three *barriers* which may hinder line managers' acceptance of coaching: failure to spread, financial conservatism, and risk aversion. *Failure to spread* arises when coaching stays within "pockets" in business units and remains disconnected from the wider organisation due to lack of information dissemination. *Financial conservatism* arises when organisational leaders impose tight control over the budget and resist spending funds on organisation-wide coaching programmes because they are difficult to quantify and justify using standard cost-benefit evaluations. *Risk aversion* occurs when organisational leaders are cautious and unwilling to invest in organisation-wide coaching skills training programmes because the likelihood of favourable economic outcomes is impossible to predict with certainty. It is these mental barriers and attitudes that CEOs and senior managers must first assist

S. Knowles, *Coaching Culture*, https://doi.org/10.1007/978-3-031-09050-9_11

business unit leaders overcome if they are to support organisational progress to develop a coaching culture. But first, they may need to know more about coaching and be coach-trained themselves.

Four enabling strategies to progression help the organisation overcome these barriers: organisational financial investment, structural support, shared norms, and champion. When business units engaged in coaching show a track record of generating positive economic returns, CEOs and senior executives develop the confidence needed to make a *financial investment* and commit resources to expanding coaching activities throughout the organisation. The work of developing *structural support* for coaching within HR policies and procedures such as the recruitment, selection and induction of leader candidates, and the redesigning of formal performance appraisal processes for staff, which began in the first transition period, is concluded in this third transition period. *Shared norms*, including a growth mindset and believing in the potential of all employees, are articulated by the CEO and senior executives as the predominant philosophy of how organisational members interact with each other and communicated via leadership development and all other training programmes. A *coaching champion* emerges when a senior executive is nominated to publically promote coaching and support business unit leaders who have had successful coaching experiences vigorously campaign in support of extending the organisation's investment in coaching. When these four enablers for progression (*organisational financial investment, structural support, shared norms, and champion*) are sufficiently powerful to outcome the three barriers (*failure to spread, financial conservatism, risk aversion*), the process model in Fig. 3.1 shows that the organisation moves to the final stage of developing a coaching culture: *Coaching-as-Culture*. When organisations are at the final stage of the model, employees don't *go* to be coached – they experience *being* coached in the course of their everyday interactions with their peers and leader. The strategies and mechanisms to bring about this *organisational transformation* are outlined in Table 8.1 and explained below.

Learn (Education): Learning, Growth and Development

In this third transition period, to facilitate the adoption of the four enablers (*organisational financial investment, structural support, shared norms, and champion*) and minimise the impact of the three barriers (*failure to spread, financial conservatism, risk aversion*), the CEO and senior executives are formally trained as coaches. They progress their understanding of coaching from a capability requirement for all leaders to a platform for organisation-wide, transformational cultural change. At this stage, the responsibility for coaching lies with the CEO and senior executives who determine that, as a strategic priority, coaching will be embedded into all business units, relationships and transactions so that it becomes part of the DNA and fabric of the organisation.

CEO and Senior Executives Are Formally Trained as Coaches

In many organisations which aim to develop a coaching culture, the CEO and senior executives have coaching capability. This capability may have been developed by attendance at in-house coaching skills training programmes or, increasingly, by completion of a formal coach-training qualification delivered by an external coach-training provider. In the former case, the CEO and senior executives may rely on internal coaching expertise such as within the HR function to assist them in driving the coaching agenda throughout the organisation. However, it is unlikely that a coaching culture will embed unless the executive team members have been formally trained as coaches so that they fully understand what *pure coaching* is (as opposed to *performance coaching*) and how it can benefit individuals, teams and the organisation.

CEO and Senior Executives Have Absolute Clarity About What Coaching Is and Is Not

For the coaching initiative to be successful, the CEO and senior executives need to have absolute clarity about what coaching is and what it is not and what the organisation is trying to achieve by developing a coaching culture. What is the purpose of introducing a coaching culture? What is the motivation behind building leader coaching capability? With this knowledge and understanding, they become fully engaged with how coaching can change an individual and team's work life and performance for the better. However, unless the CEO and senior executives are completely "on board" with coaching, it is unlikely that the coaching initiative will be successful.

CEO and Senior Executives Model Buy-In, Engagement and Sponsorship

Buy-in, engagement and sponsorship by the CEO and senior executives are absolutely critical to ensure that a coaching culture is developed and embedded within the organisation. If not the CEO or a senior executive, the initiative may start from somebody near the top level of the organisation who embraces coaching such as a business unit leader. Alternatively, it can start from someone at the core who is authorised and able to roll out a cultural change programme on behalf of the CEO and senior executives. Typically, the leader of the business unit would take on this responsibility. However, in large organisations in which senior executives and business unit leaders are extremely busy, and the HR professionals are transformational, it makes sense for a HR professional to manage the roll-out of the coaching initiative throughout the business unit and ultimately the organisation. The HR professional may need the support of the *coaching champion* to steward major decisions through the executive team.

During this final transition period, the CEO and senior executives role model the importance of coaching and signal coaching as a valid investment in an individual's growth and development. When the CEO and senior executives are committed to developing a coaching culture, they are seen "walking the talk" among employees at all levels of the organisation and messaging the importance of coaching and being coached. Opportunities to interact with senior executives are rare; however, such occasions can help employees, who may not have thought about coaching before, realise that they can develop the skills to be an inspiring leader who coaches. It's absolutely critical that leaders are role modelling the behavioural change they expect in their direct reports so that employees at lower levels of the organisation see the changes that are possible and the performance improvements that are being achieved when everybody is on the same coaching journey.

Grow (Psychology): Self-Regulation and Emotional Intelligence

In this third transition period, the CEO and senior executives commit to the experience of being coached. They adopt a *growth mindset*, believe in the potential of all employees, and identify opportunities to unleash that potential.

CEO and Senior Executives Experience Being Coached

The CEO and senior executives develop a better understanding of what coaching is and an appreciation of the benefits of coaching by having the experience of being coached themselves. Those who have experienced coaching are passionate and enthused about culture and capability as a whole and see the value of coaching in improving their professionalism and ability to manage difficult situations. However, it's only by having the experience of being coached that the CEO and senior executives really commit to developing a coaching culture with conviction. Individuals can know about and understand coaching from a cognitive perspective but it's only when they experience being coached that they "get it with their heart and their guts". They need to experience the difference between *command-and-control* (telling) and *curiosity and discovery* (asking). Once a CEO or senior executive has had that experience, they start to understand and explore: "What's in it for this organisation to adopt a coaching culture?" "What needs to change?" "Why does that need to change?" "How can coaching help my employees in their day-to-day job?" It's a coaching conversation that assists the CEO and senior executives make the decision to invest in developing a coaching culture.

Senior executives are typically coached by executive coaches rather than by internal coaches who are best suited to coach at the middle manager or team leader levels. This is because coaches at the executive level need currency across different organisations in order to bring rigour to the conversation. Executives need to be able to step out of their organisational thinking into a safe space for them to dialogue with an external coach about their issues, challenges and concerns and gain a deeper understanding of what they need to do differently. Executive coaches provide exceptional value because they have an external perspective and can genuinely coach with no agenda other than to support the executive in any way that's possible.

CEO and Senior Executives Adopt a **Growth Mindset**

During this third transition period, CEOs and senior executives adopt a *growth mindset* which means that they continually seek new horizons and ways to expand on the performance and productivity of their teams, recognising that such gains can only be achieved with and through their people. A *growth mindset* embraces new opportunities and challenges, facilitates the achievement of organisational deliverables, invests in learning and development opportunities specific to individuals and teams, connects individual aspirations with organisational vision, and harnesses the power of the team not only at the leader level but at all levels of the organisation.

To adopt a *growth mindset*, some managers may need to make a significant shift in how they think and behave especially if they rely on a positional power base where they are acknowledged for their authority as a manager, or have a technical power base where they are rewarded for their expertise. When a manager's authority is based on their title, they are inclined to be directive. Managers with technical expertise tend to have poor "people skills" and little patience, so they may rely on their expert knowledge to manage their staff. Managers whose personality type is introverted may not want to spend time with people and expect others to understand them intuitively. Hence, some managers may embrace coaching as an important way for them to grow and develop but others may see coaching as an imposition that they don't want. It may take longer for these managers to shift to a *growth mindset* – seeing people for all they are capable of becoming. Unfortunately for these managers in a coaching culture, the essential requirement of leaders who coach is to have a *growth mindset* which supports the view that employees want to be developed, want to have open and honest conversations with their leader, want to be able to put forth their views, and want to be empowered to make changes. Hence, in this third transition period, those *managers* who cannot make the transition to *leader* may not have their contracts renewed. Leaders with a *growth mindset* see the benefits of investing in employees who are able to "lay everything on the table", check their biases and assumptions at the door, and acknowledge their limitations in a safe space.

CEO and Senior Executives Believe in the Value and Potential of All Employees

In a coaching culture, all employees are supported to develop self-awareness and insight and unleash their potential. Leaders can assist in this process by "stepping back" at times to allow employees to gain in experience and then "hold the space" for them to lead. Self-development starts with self-awareness of one's own strengths, and self-management continues with recognising and supporting the development of others' strengths. As individuals start to "peel back the layers of self" to find out "Who am I and what makes me tick?", the focus of coaching becomes how to help individuals understand the behaviours that are holding them back and the ones that are propelling them forward.

Research has shown that individuals who are provided with developmental opportunities to expand their skills and experience remain longer in an organisation. Leaders who coach identify opportunities for employees to grow – whatever is needed for them to get from where they are now to where they want to be. Unleashing employees' potential allows them to grow personally and professionally whether that's at a skill or resource capability level. Coaching shifts employees' perception of how they are valued. Individuals who are coached feel acknowledged and appreciated because the organisation is investing in them and their potential.

One way to unleash employees' potential is to encourage them to apply to work in different parts of the business to obtain a broader perspective on organisational activities and reduce the "silo" effect. Another way is to provide them with the opportunity to "work up" in their area of expertise as people leave, go on holiday or accept promotions. A third way is to seek ideas for innovative projects from employees. After the ideas are scrutinised and a decision made to fund a particular project, the employee who put forward the idea is placed in charge of a project team to drive the idea through to completion. Organisations can also unleash potential by providing opportunities for employees to undertake additional skills training or enrol in external professional development programmes related to their career path.

Organisations which believe in the potential of all employees use coaching to attract and support new entrants to their leadership ranks and position them as future leaders responsible for managing change and implementing new initiatives. The aim is to identify potential in the early phases of an employee's career and then nurture that potential. Leaders are encouraged to recognise and utilise the diversity of their direct reports and use coaching to assist team members embrace that diversity too. Organisations recognise that the only way that they're going to keep growing and satisfying shareholders' terms and looking after their customers is if they promote skill development and performance improvement in all their people.

Lead (Management): Business and Relationship Improvements

In this third transition period, coaching is positioned as a strategic priority of the organisation. Goals and objectives for the coaching programme are defined and measured. A *coaching champion* is nominated to steward the coaching initiative across and down all levels of the organisation. As coaching practice progresses, every business transaction is analysed through a coaching lens and the two or three key business levers that can be enhanced though coaching are identified. Everybody is able to coach and be coached as scheduled or as the need arises, and coaching relationships are extended to all customers and suppliers.

Coaching Is Positioned at the Organisational Level as a Strategic Priority

Organisations that make a decision to develop a coaching culture make coaching a strategic priority – in which case "it will be done". Coaching becomes a key component of the organisation's cultural change strategy as it is cascaded down and across the levels to achieve its business targets. As a strategic priority, the coaching initiative is published in all corporate documents such as the strategic plan, and incorporated into all internal processes and documentation such as job descriptions, recruitment and selection, and performance management systems. Coaching is a particularly important tool to use when an organisation needs to reshape its organisational strategy in response to external opportunities or threats, for example, when transitioning from public to private sector ownership or downsizing as a result of loss of revenue, market share or changes in commodity pricing levels.

Organisations which have a transformational HR function use their coaching capability to drive cultural change throughout the organisation. Everyone new to the organisation is coached and develops coaching skills. Employees share a common coaching language and coaching becomes part of the way of "being and doing" things in the organisation which makes the business "unstoppable".

CEO and Senior Executives Align Coaching with Vision, Values and Behaviours

During this third transition period, before committing to the development of a coaching culture, the CEO and senior executives need to be very clear about their vision and values for the organisation, make explicit the kind of leadership they want in the organisation and define how coaching can contribute to the achievement of business outcomes. Do they know what their vision is? Do they know where they're heading? Do they know what they stand for? Do they know what their values are? Coaching is a developmental process that enables the answers to these questions to be considered and resolved.

Leaders who behave according to the organisational values are "living the values". The minute employees see someone behaving in an inappropriate way, who is not reprimanded for behaving in that way, they will say: "What's changed?" Therefore, everyone in the organisation has to live the values to develop the culture that the organisation desires, and coaching is an effective means of creating and sustaining the cultural change. When coaching becomes part of the organisation's value proposition as well as a powerful means of developing people, it contributes to organisational sustainability.

CEO and Senior Executives Define the Organisational and Business Goals from Coaching

Organisations need to be clear about what they are trying to achieve by introducing a coaching culture. There needs to be a well-defined goal and outcomes in terms of what the coaching can do for the organisation how coaching fits with the vision, goals and objectives of the organisation and what strategy to use to achieve them. The CEO and senior executives need to engage in discussion about: "What's going to change?" "What's that going to mean?" and "How does that connect with the broader values and goals of the organisation?" Ideally, this conversation happens at multiple levels across the organisation starting with the senior executive team.

One of the best ways to ensure that the desired outcomes from coaching are met is to devise a business case that defines the problem and opportunity, identifies the business gaps that coaching can contribute to, and predicts an investment result. The next step is to interrogate the organisation's development processes and people management systems to discover how coaching can be inculcated into these gaps to leverage individual, team and business opportunities.

A Recurrent Budget and Resources Are Allocated to Coaching

Organisations which accept the value and benefits of coaching have taken the first step towards developing a coaching culture. As a strategic priority, a considerable investment is made in skilling leaders in how to conduct coaching and feedback conversations. However, budgets and resources may be limited. Therefore, an organisation's investment in coaching must be both cost-effective and proportional but also a long-term commitment to building internal coaching capability. Even though coaching is becoming a more acceptable activity in organisations, actually putting the dollars behind it becomes a more difficult decision as budgets decline.

Consequently, some organisations are choosing to put resources into employees at the level one down from the top because that's where operational decisions are made, based on the assumption that the CEO and senior executives know all about coaching – which is not always the case.

The Return on Investment from Coaching Is Measured

The majority of organisations don't know how to measure the ROI from coaching because the outcomes are not always easy to quantify. They are often qualitative, not quantitative. Also, the ROI from coaching may take some time to become visible because one-on-one coaching relationships built on trust may become intense at times, especially if there are barriers to be broken down that have been formed over a period of years. Hence, it's harder to determine the ROI until the individual has completed an entire coaching programme and is applying the new learnings. However, there are some "hard" and "soft", "positive" and "negative" metrics that can be put in place to record the outcomes from a coaching programme.

Hard positive data may include financial indicators like sales figures and employee satisfaction ratings. *Soft positive data* may include self-report of improved leadership ability, other-report of improved personal relationships with team members, and observations of team morale. *Hard negative data* indicators may include reduction in staff complaints and turnover. *Soft negative data* indicators may include less observed conflict, and fewer communication issues within the team. A typical way to assess a coachee's progress in an individual coaching programme is to use a commercially available personality, performance or leadership assessment instrument pre- and post-coaching, which allows the coach to see shifts in the individual more obviously and understand how they are benefitting from the coaching.

Organisations are encouraged to take a customised approach to measuring the outcomes of coaching programmes based on acceptable outcomes which are negotiated upfront. Once these outcomes are determined, the coach and individual or team can be held accountable for getting the results. For example, a company may say that they want a 90 per cent success rate from a coaching programme as determined by specific metrics pre and post. However, when the coaching is of a generic nature - for example, learning how to "manage up" or learning to manage internationally, or not being so stressed in a management meeting under pressure - the ROI is more difficult to measure. In such instances, organisations can have the sponsor who has been appointed to monitor the coaching programme report from an observational perspective on whether they believe that the individual has changed - for example, is less stressed in meetings.

A Senior Executive Is Appointed as a Coaching Champion

During this third transition period, it's important that a *coaching champion* be appointed at the top level to steward through the coaching initiative. This person needs to be a strong advocate for coaching and the promotion of employee potential. They must be completely dedicated to transforming the organisational culture through coaching, be prepared to take the time to circulate through all levels of the organisation, and be approachable to address issues that employees raise to their attention. The coaching champion should already be formally coach-trained and have experienced being coached themself.

The impact of a coaching champion at the senior executive level, lauding the benefits of coaching, indicates the importance the organisation places on coaching. There is merit when the coaching champion publicly speaks from their own personal experience about the benefits of being coached. It can be inspiring and encourage others to do the same within their networks and business units. The coaching champion liaises with organisational leaders to identify the networks they can use to start spreading the news about the benefits of coaching. They are also responsible for measuring the success of the coaching programmes as they are cascaded down the organisation.

A Communication Strategy Is Developed to Introduce and Sustain Coaching Practice

When coaching has been declared a strategic priority to which people and resources have been allocated to implement coaching programmes, a communication strategy is devised to inform all employees of the value placed on coaching by the organisation and the intention for all leaders to coach their direct reports. For example, an information statement may announce that leaders will be trained in coaching skills as part of their leadership development programme. Attendance at these programmes by the CEO and senior executives, even for a short time, clearly demonstrates their support for coaching. Senior executives then share the message with their direct reports who cascade it down their business units.

It's important that every member of the senior executive team is "on board" with the coaching initiative; otherwise, the message is diluted. The message says something like: "Coaching is important to this organisation and to me, and I think that ultimately, it will be important to all of us, and here's why". Stating how coaching will be conducted and the benefits of coaching is important because there's not always clarity around what coaching is. Employees may think of coaching as another way of managing their performance, in which case they will anxiously believe that they are "on the edge" and ready to be "let go", whereas if the message is presented positively and in a way that demonstrates leadership commitment, any misconceptions will be quickly dispelled.

CEO and Senior Executives Analyse Every Aspect Through a Coaching Lens

When organisations embrace a coaching culture, coaching becomes the lens through which the organisation analyses everything that it does to identify areas where coaching can provide uplift. This process requires discipline and commitment to ascertain how coaching can be used to maximise the impact on the "bottom line" from all its activities. It may involve, for example, examining how training is conducted, how leaders are selected, scrutinising how deals are done and questioning the processes by which capability is transferred and applied to business situations. When coaching becomes the lens through which all business transactions are viewed and reviewed, leaders assess and analyse every aspect of their business systems and processes to incorporate coaching as appropriate, to increase productivity and achieve cultural change.

Organisational Levers to Maximise the Impact of Coaching Are Identified

When an organisation adopts a coaching culture, coaching is used to leverage the benefits of every business relationship and transaction into multiple areas of organisational activity. Business unit leaders examine every major focus area to identify the two or three levers where a coaching approach can be applied to increase productivity and competitive advantage. These levers may include, for example, incorporating coaching into the training of individuals in business acumen, including coaching as a selection criteria for leaders (also for a technical role), managing external stakeholders strategically, and increasing the organisation's ability to exert influence in the external marketplace. The reputational currency from externals who know that coaching is an integral component of all development activities and business transactions gives enormous credence to the organisation as a caring community which looks after the interests of its people, thereby attracting the best talent.

At the senior level, coaching can be used as a lever to bring about improved commercial outcomes through behavioural profiling and constructive feedback on executives' management and leadership style. When coaches work with executives, the quality of the conversation is raised to a higher purpose level, together with a higher consequence level about "getting it right, or getting it wrong". Businesses that conduct robust conversations at the executive level gain from the transparency that emerges which can be harnessed by all executives to improve the productivity of their teams and, in turn, cascade that learning down the organisation.

Coaching Is Applied More Broadly Across the Organisation

Coaching can have broader application than one-on-one formal coaching sessions and team coaching meetings. At any time, whilst performing any business activity, coaching can be used to challenge existing thinking, break free of limiting beliefs, unlock fixed mindsets, and neutralise the potential threat associated with discussion of politically sensitive issues. Although coaching can be utilised in any business function including corporate services, from a commercial standpoint coaching is highly applicable to revenue-generating, customer-facing areas of the business. This is because in these areas, the results of coaching are more quickly realised and visible in both "hard" and "soft" terms - for example, winning a sale or pacifying an angry customer. Coaching programmes can also be used to support the introduction of new initiatives into the organisation such as diversity programmes and how to work with millennials – helping leaders to understand the cultural gap in terms of managing expectations, utilising strengths, providing feedback, and exploring significant development opportunities.

A Coaching Framework Is Attached to All Training Activities

When an organisation is serious about having coaching as a strategic priority, coaching is applied to all training activities that are conducted and followed up with individual coaching sessions to transfer the learnings back into the workplace to sustain improved capability in the long term. For example, the coaching can be applied to training front-line staff in how to increase sales from individual customers and generate increased revenue from corporate customers. Hence, in a coaching culture, all training conducted within the organisation, no matter what the skill, is delivered with a coaching framework attached to it and supported thereafter by coaching conversations.

Coaching Is Conducted Throughout the Organisation

When a coaching culture is embedded in an organisation, coaching is conducted throughout the organisation across all levels starting at the CEO and senior executive level. However, unless there's investment from the top, a coaching culture will only be developed in "pockets", that is, in some business units whose executives believe in coaching, but not across the entire organisation. Starting at the top is definitely important because if the top level is not completely committed to coaching and actually displaying their commitment through delivering coaching to their direct reports and others in the organisation and being coached themselves, the chances of developing a coaching culture across the entire organisation are slim.

A coaching culture which promotes the development of all employees must be embedded in the organisation for it to survive when a supportive CEO leaves because a coaching culture is leader-centric and may only last as long as that leader is in place. For a coaching culture to be embedded, the executive team needs to own it, drive it and role model coaching. When key stakeholders including the CEO are committed to coaching, it becomes embedded in the organisation as a developmentally focused and supportive practice to grow all employees, which means that it will survive longer in the organisation even though a new CEO may not be fully supportive of coaching. Changing an organisation's culture takes time – maybe 5 years or more. Indeed, some organisations have been constantly "chipping away" at developing a coaching culture for 15 or 16 years as the organisation has restructured and made significant changes at the CEO and senior executive levels.

Peer Coaching Is Conducted Throughout the Organisation

In organisations with a coaching culture, it's everybody's role to coach and an expectation that everyone will receive the coaching they need either via dedicated coaching sessions, coaching conversations, or the demonstration of coach-like behaviours. When everyone in the organisation has been trained in coaching skills or in the conduct of coaching conversations, they are prepared to engage with others to support their development and growth. Coaching has then become an accepted practice to assist individuals do what they need to do to meet their development, performance, or career goals. Organisations may start establishing *peer coaching* relationships within a leadership development programme either by pairing participants within that programme or across other programme cohorts. Within a coaching culture, people habitually and automatically coach each other, that is, assume the role of peer coach. When peer coaching occurs throughout the organisation from the executive level to front-line leaders and their team members, that's a coaching culture in action. Peer coaching occurs at all levels of the organisation in different ways depending on the individual's level of responsibility, the issue to be resolved, and the goal to be achieved.

Coaching Relationships Are Extended to External Customers and Suppliers

In this third transition period, coaching relationships extend beyond organisational boundaries to include customers and suppliers. The interaction is both relational to cement long-term engagement and satisfaction, and business-oriented to achieve targeted results. When coaching is extended to improving relationships beyond the organisation, commercial outcomes are aligned with customer needs as well as with the organisation's strategic goals. All business transactions are underpinned by the commercial or strategic outcomes that the organisation is seeking.

Customers and suppliers may, at first, be unsure of the change in approach from organisational representatives. They may need to be assured that extending coaching into the external stakeholder environment is part of the cultural shift occurring within the organisation and be encouraged to come on board with the initiative. Within a political environment, coaching is an effective way to manage multiple agendas and navigate higher-order changes - for example, the legislative requirements of hiring and employing staff. In an industrial relations-driven environment, there's a whole raft of consultations that need to happen before cultural elements can be shifted, and coaching is the means to manage these consultations effectively.

In summary, in a rapidly changing global environment, organisational leaders must be adaptable to respond quickly to emerging needs, keep up with technology, grasp opportunities to maximise the productivity of the organisation, and consolidate social connections with external stakeholders. Coaching can be used to assist employees embrace change, promote innovation, and increase revenue. CEOs and senior executives know that their most valuable asset is their human resources who protect the organisation's intellectual property, safeguard its products and services, and maintain organisational culture. Employees do this by displaying the behaviours that uphold the organisation's values, being flexible and adaptable to change, and supporting the organisation's vision and direction. All of these activities are critical in helping the organisation achieve its mission. Unfortunately, the majority of leaders don't realise that they can use coaching skills more broadly than for individual and business performance to give them greater influence and leverage in the wider business community.

At this final *Coaching-as-Culture* stage, the organisation has an *organic conceptualisation* of coaching as "the way we do things around here" to enact the values. When coaching *is* culture, it occurs naturally and organically as an integral aspect of organisational routines. Coaching has a *transformational motivation* to drive cultural change as a long-term investment in creating competitive advantage. Coaching has committed CEOs and senior executives as *executive drivers* of cultural change, and coaching cascades down and across to all levels of managers, team leaders and front-line staff. Finally, coaching occurs through *integrated delivery* across the organisation as coach-like behaviour is woven into the daily activities of leaders, specialist and internal coaches, and it becomes everybody's role to coach direct reports and peers as a normal part of everyday work life. When organisations are at the final *Coaching-as-Culture* stage of the model at Fig. 3.1, employees don't *go* to be coached – they experience *being* coached in the course of their everyday interactions with their leader and peers.

***

This chapter has outlined the strategies and mechanisms by which organisations transition from Stage 3, *Coaching-as-Leader-Capability* to Stage 4, *Coaching-as-Culture*. The next chapter discusses the implications of implementing these strategies and mechanisms for CEOs and senior executives, organisational leaders and HR professionals.

Chapter 12
Conclusions

This chapter addresses the implications for CEOs, organisational leaders and HR professionals who wish to introduce a coaching culture into their organisation using the model of coaching culture development derived from my research findings (Fig. 3.1). The model contributes to the growing volume of academic research into how a coaching culture is developed and supports the theoretical base for coaching to emerge as a discipline in its own right. This final chapter summarises the strategies that CEOs and senior executives, organisational leaders and HR professionals need to take to progress the organisation's journey towards the development of a coaching culture. It also signals a number of areas that may present potential pitfalls that need to be overcome along the way.

Before embarking on a journey to develop a coaching culture, organisational leaders need to have a common conceptualisation of what *coaching* is and the purpose for which it is to be introduced into the organisation. They also need to state the monetary and "people" benefits they anticipate from what is a significant investment in: (1) funding the CEO and senior executives, selected organisational leaders and HR professionals to become fully qualified coaches; (2) developing and conducting coaching skills training programmes for managers through to team leaders across the entire organisation; (3) engaging external coaches to deliver coaching services to executives and others who need expert assistance; and (4) developing the infrastructure for coaching to be embedded within the organisation. Larger organisations generally have a better understanding of coaching than their smaller counterparts or newer organisations because they often have overseas affiliates which have been around and involved with coaching for a longer time, or they may be headquartered in the northern hemisphere where coaching is more well-known and accepted. Their conceptualisation of *coaching* is typically more mature; hence they may value *coaching* more highly and may employ dedicated coaches and coaching teams. The emphasis in many of these organisations, however, still tends to be on coaching for problem remediation and performance management rather than on investing in all employees to grow and develop their potential, which is the focus of organisations with a coaching culture.

S. Knowles, *Coaching Culture*, https://doi.org/10.1007/978-3-031-09050-9_12

A Blueprint for Cultural Change

A blueprint for transformational cultural change has been derived from the model of coaching culture development (Fig. 3.1) and is depicted in Fig. 12.1. It shows that the impetus for the development of a coaching culture can originate from any level of the organisation and, if not from the top, it most frequently emerges from within the middle management level. If it starts at this level, an *advocate* for coaching may develop a business case to convince the CEO and senior executives of the value of introducing coaching into the organisation. The business case outlines what coaching is and how it can be beneficial to the organisation both financially and from a human capital perspective. In addition, the *advocate* might offer recommendations regarding the ways that the benefits from coaching can be measured to evaluate the ROI from introducing a coaching initiative into the organisation.

To learn more about coaching, the senior executive team is encouraged to participate in a workshop to better understand what coaching is and what it is not and experience being coached themselves. Ideally, they become formally qualified as a coach by an external coach-training provider but if not, they receive in-house

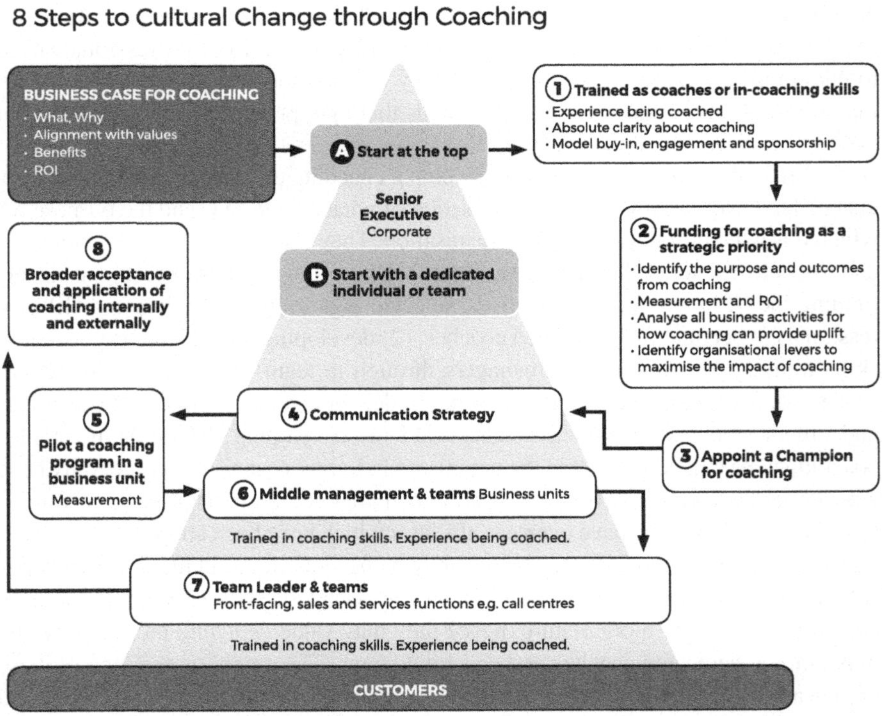

Fig. 12.1 Blueprint for transformational cultural change through coaching

training in coaching skills. If a decision is made to commence the coaching initiative, funding is allocated as a strategic priority and a senior executive appointed as a *coaching champion* to steward progress through the organisation. A business unit leader may volunteer to conduct a pilot programme in their area of responsibility to measure the success of the coaching initiative.

Before the pilot commences, it's beneficial for a communication strategy to be developed to inform employees in the business unit about the programme, as well as alert the wider organisational community to the coaching initiative. Coaching skills training programmes commence at the senior levels of the business unit and are cascaded down to all front-facing employees. A coaching approach is also encouraged in relation to interactions with customers and suppliers. Once each coaching programme is completed, the measures previously agreed to determine success are examined pre- and post-programme to ascertain the ROI from the coaching investment. With success, the coaching approach is progressively incorporated into all business unit relationships and transactions internal and external to the organisation. These steps are outlined in Fig. 12.1. Implications for the CEO and senior executives, organisational leaders and HR professionals, to implement this blueprint, are detailed in the sections that follow.

Implications for CEOs and Senior Executives

Successful organisational coaching initiatives have highlighted the criticality of the CEO understanding what coaching is and what it isn't and supporting the introduction of a coaching culture into the organisation. The CEO may have experienced being coached, in which case they really appreciate the benefits of coaching and the value it can add to individuals, teams and the organisation itself. If not, they and all senior executives are encouraged to experience being coached so that they can credibly role model the importance the organisation is placing on leaders coaching their direct reports and others, and promoting a coaching philosophy throughout the organisation.

For a coaching culture to permeate across all levels of the organisation, the CEO and senior executives need to have a *growth mindset* and an absolute belief in the value of providing developmental opportunities for all employees to reach their potential. They need to be absolutely committed to making coaching a strategic priority with an allocated budget and recurrent resources. It's important that they define the desired outcomes from investing in coaching and developing a coaching culture in measureable terms.

Even when a coaching culture is embedded in an organisation, the initiative may die very quickly if a new CEO is appointed who does not value coaching – unless there is a strong proponent of coaching who occupies a senior position within the organisation and who is tasked to continue with the initiative, that is, a senior *coaching champion* or another influential individual with a "seat at the table" such as a *transformational HR professional*. Organisations gain competitive "speed to respond" and "speed to market" advantage when internal coaches or internal coaching teams are positioned within business units and report directly to a senior executive *coaching champion* who can smooth their way if necessary.

As coaching cascades down and across the organisation "from the board chair to the gardener" and the benefits of coaching become more well-known, coaching is typically extended into all areas of the business including into interactions and relationships with customers and suppliers. However, the CEO and senior executives must be aware that cultural change takes time, often years, before it becomes embedded in the DNA and fabric of an organisation. Hence, organisations which decide to embark on developing a coaching culture need to be prepared to invest in the resources required to develop coaching skills in all existing and new leaders as these training programmes cascade through the organisation.

Implications for Organisational Leaders

In some organisations, there is still a *stigma* attached to coaching which may cause some external coaches or organisational leaders to refer to a coaching intervention by another name such as a "meeting" or "honest, open conversation". As leaders are increasingly expected to coach their direct reports and others in the organisation on a regular basis, they may find that the term *coaching* is more palatable for employees to understand and accept when it is incorporated within a leadership development framework as an essential leader capability. By providing timely feedback to employees, leaders are signalling the importance of supporting their growth, development and career aspirations. The focus of delivering coaching in a coaching culture is no longer on just the most talented of employees; the focus is on *all* employees. Under a *growth mindset*, every employee, given the encouragement, opportunity and support they need, can reach their potential.

Leaders who are trained in coaching skills display improved leadership capability which positions the organisation well during times of external change - for example, when commodity prices change, the stock market fluctuates, and environmental or regulatory changes are legislated. In addition, as organisations attempt to change their culture, their efforts may be significantly impacted by political or union influences and other external agendas that can get in the way of leaders taking the actions they want or need to take to change the culture. Navigating these particular environments calls for the use of coaching and negotiation skills to inform, influence and persuade, to achieve the organisation's agenda.

Leadership style, personality preferences, and cultural differences must be taken into account when attempting to develop a coaching culture. A *command-and-control* management style may become more malleable if managers are willing to be trained in coaching skills and be coached so that they can develop a *coaching leadership style*. The coaching initiative will then go ahead successfully. However, if managers' willingness occurs in only certain business units or "pockets" of the organisation, it is unlikely that a coaching culture will be fully developed and embedded into the entire organisation.

Implications for HR Professionals

When coaching is designated as a core competency of leaders, a *transformational HR professional* and HR function are required to take on the responsibility of developing programmes for all organisational leaders to receive training in coaching skills, deliver the coaching skills training, and develop the infrastructure for coaching to occur and be sustained throughout the organisation. HR professionals benefit personally and professionally by being formally trained as coaches so they feel more confident in passing on their knowledge and skills to leaders when delivering the in-house coaching skills training programmes. However, participating in formal coach-training delivered by an external coach-training provider takes time and requires a considerable investment of both personal and organisational resources. Hence, it is understandable that, unless the CEO and senior executives are completely committed to developing a coaching culture, such an investment may be an unsound business decision. As an alternative, some organisations decide to train their HR professionals in coaching skills rather than to become fully qualified coaches.

Training in Coaching Skills

Training in coaching skills may be conducted in-house as a standalone programme but increasingly is a component of leadership development programmes delivered to all functional leaders across the organisation. However, in-house coaching skills training programmes are typically only conducted over a few hours or days. This allocation of time is barely sufficient to train managers in the coaching skills and process and does not allow the opportunity for the extended practice that is needed for them to become confident in their coaching ability. In addition, they are typically unable to address any personal issues that may arise as they coach their direct reports, as this short-term training does not equip them to fully understand the power of coaching to resolve personal concerns that are interfering with what is typically the focus of such short training programmes – coachee performance.

Managers are frequently trained in the techniques of how to coach from a performance and feedback perspective (*performance coaching*) rather that from a *pure* coaching orientation (which focuses on the coachee's agenda rather than the organisation's agenda). Hence, it is questionable whether, during the short training, they have been able to develop an appreciation of individual differences, what motivates individuals, and how behaviours can be changed – unless the educational and psychological components of coaching were included in the training. Like an iceberg, these key underpinnings of how people learn and how change is enabled and enacted, sit below the surface of many short coaching skills training programmes and are not discussed unless time and expertise permits. Hence, managers who do not have any prior knowledge gain no deep understanding of coaching, the rationale for coaching, or of the need to park their own thoughts, judgements and preferred behaviours to embrace a new way of engaging with their team members. Being trained in coaching skills at the technical level is the first positive step towards developing a coaching culture but additional training is required to progress managers' understanding and experience of exactly how powerful coaching can be.

When organisations are committed to developing a coaching culture, in-house coaching skills training programmes are cascaded down and across the organisation to include all front-line staff. The *peer coaching* ability resulting from such training provides all employees with the opportunity to grow and develop as they learn from each other, improve their performance, and gain in career prospects. Training all employees to *peer coach* may initially be an expensive exercise – however with long-time benefits. As peers adopt coach-like behaviours, the culture changes and becomes more inclusive and accommodating of individual differences and accepting of the values and beliefs that build cooperation and teamwork. Managers step back to "hold the space" for others to lead. When a pilot coaching programme is conducted within a business unit to prove the benefits of coaching, peer coaching occurs on a needs basis, typically experienced as coaching conversations and coach-like behaviours which support colleagues in their performance and career progression.

Delivery

Generally, the CEO and senior executives are coached by external, executive coaches rather than by internal coaches who coach upwards. This is because executive coaches have a wealth of experience and expertise which gives them *business credibility* at that level (as opposed to other coaches, e.g. business or life coaches) and they are usually formally coach-trained (which gives them *professional credibility*). In addition, executive coaches have a wider perspective on the external marketplace and more experience gained from working across many organisations. Internal coaches who coach upwards in an organisation are not seen to have the same credibility or skills and may not be trusted with private and confidential information.

Once trained, the HR function provides follow-up support to leaders who coach in one of three ways. An *Accredited Coaches Network* of volunteer coaches is established to support formally trained coaches who, in addition to their "day job", deliver coaching on request to others in the organisation. Leaders at transition points may receive "role coaching" to settle them into their new role - for example, team member to team leader or technical specialist to team leader. Ideally, *Coaching Circles* are established to support leaders who have attended in-house coaching skills training programmes and subsequently deliver coaching to their direct reports, to maintain their coaching currency. In addition, *Coaching Communities* may be formed to supervise and verify the quality of the leader coaching practice that is delivered throughout the organisation and encourage the extension of coaching into all areas of the business. Unless follow-up mechanisms such as these are established to support leaders who coach, they may feel abandoned post-training and their efforts may falter.

Coaching Infrastructure

When coaching is designated as a strategic priority for the organisation, the ability to coach is written into all HR systems and processes including recruitment and selection, performance management, reward systems, talent management and succession planning. Coaching of direct reports is assessed against the leader's KPIs. Candidates for leadership positions who have coaching skills are highly regarded. A HR metrics system is developed to record the quantity and quality of the coaching being delivered within the organisation, and to evaluate its effectiveness by measuring both 'hard' and 'soft' results including the ROI from coaching.

Internal/Specialist Coaches

In organisations in the advanced stages of developing a coaching culture, a position of *Internal Coach* may be established and an *internal coaching team* formed of qualified coaches positioned within business units. The team reports directly to a senior executive *coaching champion* who can navigate current and emerging situations. Internal coaches are formally trained in *pure coaching* skills that meet international standards of coaching and ethical practice. Hence, they can provide not only motivational, behavioural, performance, and career coaching to employees and teams within business units but also personal coaching to individuals as needed. Specialist coaches may also be appointed within revenue-generating business units to *performance coach* front-line staff in how to identify which clients to approach to maximise the return on their time, effort and investment as well as how to build better business relationships with potential or existing external commercial partners.

***

In summary, developing a coaching culture in organisations takes time, dedication and a considerable financial investment. This book has presented a model of coaching culture development derived from research findings (Fig. 3.1) to guide CEOs and senior executives in its achievement. The barriers to progression have been identified as well as the strategies and mechanisms that enable successful transition through the four stages in the model. The model is dynamic, meaning that events may lead to regression at times. The process may start from a dedicated group of advocates at the middle management level before being elevated to the CEO and senior executive level. Thereafter, as a strategic priority, a *coaching champion* or *transformational HR professional* is nominated to steward the initiative throughout the organisation. They may form a Coaching Culture Development Team to facilitate the spread of coaching knowledge and practice and ensure that the entire blueprint for transformational, cultural change is enacted (Fig. 12.1). A coaching approach to cultural change is particularly effective at transition points - for example, when an organisation is in turnaround, to be restructured, or merged with another business entity.

Index

S. Knowles, *Coaching Culture*, https://doi.org/10.1007/978-3-031-09050-9

The manufacturer's authorised representative in the EU is Springer Nature Customer Service Centre GmbH, Europaplatz 3, 69115 Heidelberg, Germany. If you have any concerns regarding our products, please contact ProductSafety@springernature.com

Printed and bound by CPI Group (UK) Ltd, Croydon, CR0 4YY
30/09/2026
02225245-0001